Culture Wise
CANADA

The Essential Guide to Culture, Customs & Business Etiquette

Graeme Chesters

&

Sally Jennings

D1043037

SURVIVAL BOOKS • LONDON • ENGLAND

First published 2007

Copyright © Survival Books 2007
Cover photo © Ron Hilton
Maps and cartoons © Jim Watson
Other photographs – see page 238

Survival Books Limited
26 York Street, London W1U 6PZ, United Kingdom
☎ +44 (0)20-7788 7644, 🖷 +44 (0)870-762 3212
✉ info@survivalbooks.net
🖥 www.survivalbooks.net

British Library Cataloguing in Publication Data.
A CIP record for this book is available
from the British Library.
ISBN 10: 1-905303-21-1
ISBN 13: 978-1-905303-21-2

Printed and bound in India by Ajanta Offset

ACKNOWLEDGEMENTS

The authors would like to thank their many friends, family members and colleagues – unfortunately too many to mention – who provided information for this book. We would particularly like to thank Anna and Nicholas Clark for their invaluable opinions, David Hampshire and Joe Laredo for editing, Lilac Johnston for proof-reading, Grania Rogers for photo selection and editing, Di Tolland for DTP, and Jim Watson for the book and cover design, maps and cartoons. Finally a special thank you to all the photographers – the unsung heroes – who provided the superb photos, without which this book would be dull indeed.

THE AUTHORS

Graeme Chesters (g.chesters@virgin.net) is an experienced journalist, copywriter, non-fiction and travel writer. He has travelled and written extensively on regions as diverse as Europe, North America, the Middle and Far East, and Australasia, and is the editor of *Living and Working in Canada* and the author of a number of other travel guides. Graeme is also an enthusiastic wine drinker and writer, and the author of two wine books, including *Shopping for Wine in Spain* (Santana). He lives in south London (England) with his wife Louise.

Sally Jennings (ptp_edit@yahoo.com) is an enthusiastic writer, editor, teacher and urban planner. She has watched the world go by in Southeast Asia, the Antipodes, Europe and Canada. In her capacity as a writer, Sally has contributed to travel publications and guides worldwide. Her particular interests are history, architecture and archaeology, involving everything from ghost towns to Neolithic temples, and the behaviour that created them. Sally lives on Vancouver Island and highly recommends it. This is her first book.

'If you need to find out how France works then this book is indispensable. Native French people probably have a less thorough understanding of how their country functions.'

Living France

'It's everything you always wanted to ask but didn't for fear of the contemptuous put down. The best English-language guide. Its pages are stuffed with practical information on everyday subjects and are designed to compliment the traditional guidebook.'

Swiss News

'Rarely has a 'survival guide' contained such useful advice. This book dispels doubts for first-time travellers, yet is also useful for seasoned globetrotters. In a word, if you're planning to move to the US or go there for a long-term stay, then buy this book both for general reading and as a ready-reference.'

American Citizens Abroad

'Let's say it at once. David Hampshire's Living and Working in France is the best handbook ever produced for visitors and foreign residents in this country; indeed, my discussion with locals showed that it has much to teach even those born and bred in l'Hexagone. It is Hampshire's meticulous detail which lifts his work way beyond the range of other books with similar titles. Often you think of a supplementary question and search for the answer in vain. With Hampshire this is rarely the case. He writes with great clarity (and gives French equivalents of all key terms), a touch of humour and a ready eye for the odd (and often illuminating) fact. This book is absolutely indispensable.'

The Riviera Reporter

'A must for all future expats. I invested in several books but this is the only one you need. Every issue and concern is covered, every daft question you have but are frightened to ask is answered honestly without pulling any punches. Highly recommended.'

Reader

'In answer to the desert island question about the one how-to book on France, this book would be it.'

The Recorder

'The ultimate reference book. Every subject imaginable is exhaustively explained in simple terms. An excellent introduction to fully enjoy all that this fine country has to offer and save time and money in the process.'

American Club of Zurich

SAID ABOUT SURVIVAL BOOKS

'The amount of information covered is not short of incredible. I thought I knew enough about my birth country. This book has proved me wrong. Don't go to France without it. Big mistake if you do. Absolutely priceless!'

Reader

'When you buy a model plane for your child, a video recorder, or some new computer gizmo, you get with it a leaflet or booklet pleading 'Read Me First', or bearing large friendly letters or bold type saying 'IMPORTANT – follow the instructions carefully'. This book should be similarly supplied to all those entering France with anything more durable than a 5-day return ticket. It is worth reading even if you are just visiting briefly, or if you have lived here for years and feel totally knowledgeable and secure. But if you need to find out how France works then it is indispensable. Native French people probably have a less thorough understanding of how their country functions. Where it is most essential, the book is most up to the minute.

Living France

A comprehensive guide to all things French, written in a highly readable and amusing style, for anyone planning to live, work or retire in France.

The Times

Covers every conceivable question that might be asked concerning everyday life. I know of no other book that could take the place of this one.

France in Print

A concise, thorough account of the Do's and DONT's for a foreigner in Switzerland. Crammed with useful information and lightened with humorous quips which make the facts more readable.

American Citizens Abroad

'I found this a wonderful book crammed with facts and figures, with a straightforward approach to the problems and pitfalls you are likely to encounter. The whole laced with humour and a thorough understanding of what's involved. Gets my vote!'

Reader

'A vital tool in the war against real estate sharks; don't even think of buying without reading this book first!'

Everything Spain

'We would like to congratulate you on this work: it is really super! We hand it out to our expatriates and they read it with great interest and pleasure.'

ICI (Switzerland) AG

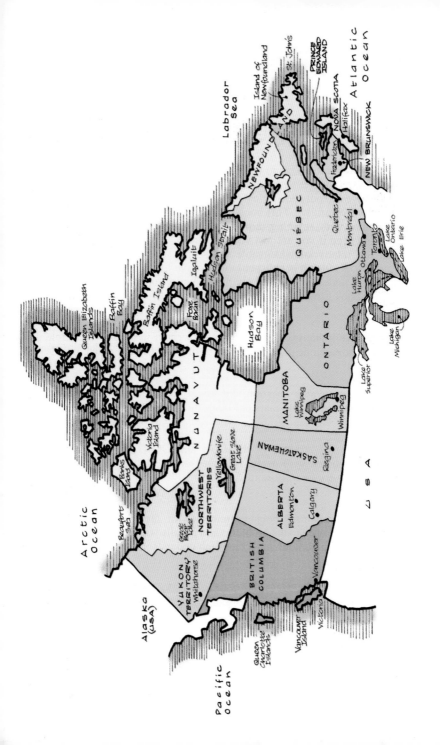

CONTENTS

INTRODUCTION

If you're planning a trip to Canada or just want to learn more about the country, you'll find the information contained in *Culture Wise Canada* invaluable. Whether you're travelling on business or pleasure, visiting for a few days or planning to stay for a lifetime, Culture Wise guides enable you to quickly find your feet by removing the anxiety factor when dealing with a foreign culture.

Culture Wise Canada is essential reading for anyone planning to visit Canada, including tourists (particularly travellers planning to stay for a number of weeks or months), business people, migrants, retirees, holiday homeowners and transferees. It's designed to help newcomers avoid cultural and social gaffes; make friends and influence people; improve communications (both verbal and non-verbal); and enhance their understanding of Canada and Canadians. It explains what to expect, how to behave in most situations, and how to get along with the locals and feel at home – rather than feeling like a fish out of water.

It isn't, however, simply a monologue of dry facts and figures, but a practical and entertaining look at life in Canada – as it really is – and not necessarily as the tourist brochures would have you believe.

Adjusting to a different environment and culture in any foreign country can be a traumatic and stressful experience, and Canada is no exception. You need to adapt to new customs and traditions, and discover the Canadian way of doing things; whether it's trying to avoid looking like a gorby on arrival, sharing a few forty pounders with your rigpig mates and not getting snocked, or learning to ski in a whiteout in your new dekey outfit without looking like a chucklehead. Eh? Canada is a land where many things are done differently: where riding a skidoo is as common as riding a bike, where a cross-country trip in winter can be a survival course, and where flying is as common as taking a bus in many other countries.

A period spent in Canada is a wonderful way to enrich your life, broaden your horizons, and hopefully expand your circle of friends. We trust this book will help you avoid the pitfalls of visiting or living in Canada and smooth your way to a happy and rewarding stay.

Good luck!   **Graeme Chesters & Sally Jennings**
July 2007

1.
ADAPTING TO A NEW CULTURE

With almost daily advances in technology, ever-cheaper flights, and knowledge about almost anywhere in the world at our fingertips, travelling, living, working and retiring abroad has never been more accessible, and current migration patterns suggest that it has never been more popular. But although globalisation means the world has in effect 'shrunk', every country is still a 'world' of its own with a unique culture.

Some people find it impossible to adapt to a new life in a different culture – for reasons which are many and varied. According to statistics, partner dissatisfaction is the most common cause, because non-working spouses frequently find themselves without a role in the new country, and sometimes with little to do other than think about what they would be doing if they were at home. Family concerns – which may include the children's education and worries about loved ones – can also deeply affect those living abroad.

> 'There are no foreign lands. It is the traveller only who is foreign.'
> Robert Louis Stevenson
> (Scottish writer)

Many factors contribute to how well you adapt to a new culture; for example, your personality, education, foreign language skills, mental health, maturity, socio-economic conditions, travel experience, and family and social support systems. How you handle the stress of change, and bring balance and meaning to your life, is the principal indicator of how well you'll adjust to a different country, culture and business environment.

CANADA IS A FOREIGN COUNTRY

Many people underestimate the cultural isolation that can be experienced in a foreign country, particularly one with a different language. Even in a country where you speak the language fluently, you'll find that many aspects of the culture are surprisingly foreign, despite the cosy familiarity engendered by cinema, television and books. Canada is perceived by many foreigners – particularly the British – as an easy option because of the English language (but don't forget that French is the main language in Quebec), its traditional links with Britain, multicultural society and well-established foreign communities in the major cities.

When you move to Canada,

you'll need to adapt to a totally new environment and new challenges, which may include a new job, a new home and a new physical environment. This can be overwhelming – and all this before you even encounter the local culture! In your home country, you may have left a job where you were the boss, extremely competent and knew everyone. In Canada, you may be virtually a trainee (especially if your English isn't fluent) and not know any of your colleagues. The sensation that you're starting from scratch can be demoralising.

Even if you move to a major city, many things that you're used to and take for granted in your home country may not be available in Canada, e.g. certain kinds of food, opportunities to practise your favourite hobby or sport, or books and television programmes in your language. The lack of home comforts can wear you down. You will also have to contend with an initial lack of a local support network. At home, you have a circle of friends, acquaintances, colleagues and possibly relatives

you could rely on for help and support. In Canada, there's no such network, which can leave you feeling lost for a while.

The degree of isolation you feel usually depends on how long you plan to spend in Canada and what you will be doing there. If you're simply going on a short holiday, you may be unaware of many of the cultural differences, although if you are, it will enhance your enjoyment and may save you from a few embarrassing or confusing moments. However, if you're planning a business trip, or intend to spend an extended period in Canada, perhaps working, studying or even living there permanently, **it's essential to understand the culture, customs and etiquette at the earliest opportunity.**

Canada has many extremes of climate and weather, and you mustn't underestimate the effect that this can have on you. Extreme cold can lead to a feeling of isolation and claustrophobia, due to spending most of your time indoors. In the winter in Canada, just about everywhere is centrally heated, and if you aren't used to this it can be draining and dehydrating

'If you reject the food, ignore the customs, fear the religion and avoid the people, you might better stay at home.'

James A. Michener (American writer)

CULTURE SHOCK

Culture shock is the term used to describe the psychological and physical state felt by people when arriving in a foreign country, or even moving to a new environment in their home country (where the culture, and in some cases language, may vary considerably by region and social class). Culture shock can be experienced when travelling, living, working or studying abroad. In addition to adapting to new social rules and values, you may need to adjust to a different climate, food and dress. It manifests itself in a lack of direction and the feeling of not knowing what to do or how to do things, not knowing what's appropriate or inappropriate. You literally feel like a 'fish out of water'.

> 'When you travel, remember that a foreign country is not designed to make you comfortable. It is designed to make its own people comfortable.'
>
> Clifton Fadiman (American writer)

Culture shock is precipitated by the anxiety that results from losing all familiar rules of behaviour and symbols of social intercourse. These rules and symbols are the thousand and one ways in which we orient ourselves to the situations of daily life: when to shake hands and what to say when we meet people; when and how to tip; how to buy goods and services; how to use a cash machine or the telephone; when to accept and refuse invitations; and when to take statements seriously, and when not to. These cues, which may be verbal, a gesture, or facial or hand expressions, are acquired over a lifetime, and are as much a part of our culture and customs as the language we speak or our beliefs. Our peace of mind and efficiency depend on hundreds of these cues, most of which are learned subconsciously.

The symptoms are essentially psychological, and are caused by the sense of alienation you feel when you're bombarded on a daily basis with cultural differences in an environment where there are few, if any, familiar references. However, there can also be physical symptoms, including an increased incidence of minor illnesses (e.g. colds and headaches) and more serious psychosomatic illnesses, brought on by depression. You shouldn't underestimate the consequences of culture shock, although the effects can be lessened if you accept the condition rather than deny it.

Stages of Culture Shock

Severe culture shock – often experienced when moving to a new country with a different language – usually follows a number of stages. The names of these may vary, as may the symptoms and effects, but a typical progression is as follows:

1. The first stage is known as the honeymoon stage, and usually lasts from a few days to a few weeks, although it can last longer, particularly if you're insulated from the usual pressures of life. This stage is essentially a positive (even euphoric) one, when a newcomer finds everything an exciting and interesting novelty. The feeling is similar to being on holiday or a short trip abroad, when you generally experience only the positive effects of culture shock (although this depends very much on where you're from and the country you're visiting – see 'Paris Syndrome' box).

2. The second (rejection or distress) stage is usually completely opposite to the first

and is essentially negative, and a period of crisis. As the initial excitement and holiday feeling wears off, you start to cope with the real conditions of daily life – except of course life is nothing like your previous experiences. This can happen after just a few weeks, and is characterised by a general feeling of disorientation, confusion and loneliness. Physical exhaustion brought on by jet lag, extremes of hot or cold, and the strain of having hundreds of settling-in tasks to accomplish, is an important symptom of this stage. You may also experience regression, where you spend much of your time speaking your own language, watching television, videos and reading newspapers from your home country, eating food from home, and socialising with expatriates who speak your language. You may also spend a lot of time complaining about the host country and its culture. Your home country suddenly assumes a tremendous

---

Paris Syndrome

A dozen or so Japanese tourists a year have to be repatriated from the French capital, after falling prey to what's become known as the 'Paris Syndrome'. This is what some polite Japanese tourists suffer when they discover that Parisians can be rude, or that the city doesn't meet their expectations. The experience can apparently be so stressful for some people that they suffer a nervous breakdown, and need to be hospitalised or repatriated under medical supervision.

importance, and is irrationally glorified. All difficulties and problems are forgotten, and only the good things back home are remembered.

3. The third stage is often known as the flight stage (because of the overwhelming desire to escape), and is usually the one that lasts the longest, and is the most difficult to cope with. During this period, you may feel depressed and angry, as well as resentful towards the new country and its people. It may include difficulties such as not being understood, and feelings of discontent, impatience, anger, sadness and incompetence. This is inevitable when you're trying to adapt to a new culture that's very different from your home country. Depression is exacerbated, because at this stage you can see nothing positive or good about the new country, and you focus exclusively on the negative aspects, refusing to acknowledge any positive points.

You may become hostile and develop an aggressive attitude

towards the country, which grows out of the genuine difficulty that you experience in the process of adjustment. If you're frustrated and have an aggressive attitude, people will sense this hostility, and in many cases respond in either a confrontational manner or try to avoid you. There may be problems with the language, your home, job or children's school, transportation... even simple tasks like shopping can be fraught with difficulties – and the fact that the local people are largely indifferent to all these problems only makes matter worse. They try to help but they just don't understand your concerns, and you conclude that they must be insensitive and unsympathetic to you and your problems.

4. The fourth (recovery or autonomy) stage is where you begin to integrate and adapt to the new culture, and accept the customs of the country as simply another way of living. **The environment doesn't change**

Transition between your old culture and customs and those of your new country is a difficult process and takes time, during which there can be strong feelings of dissatisfaction. The period of adjustment can last as long as a year, although there are expatriates who adjust earlier and (although rare) others who never get over the 'flight' stage and are forced to return home.

– **what changes is your attitude towards it.** You become more competent with the language and also feel more comfortable with the customs of the host country, and can move around without feeling anxiety. However, you still have problems with some of the social cues, and you won't understand everything people say (particularly colloquialisms, idioms and humour). Nevertheless, you have largely adjusted to the new culture, and start to feel more at home and familiar with the country and your place in it, and begin to realise that it has both good and bad points.

5. The fifth stage is termed reverse culture shock and occurs when you return to your home country. Depending on how long you've been away, you may find that many things have changed (you will also have changed) and that you feel like a foreigner in your homeland. If you've been away for a long time, and have become comfortable with the habits and customs of a new lifestyle, you may find that you no longer feel at ease in your own country. Reverse culture shock can be difficult to deal with, and some people find it impossible to re-adapt to their home country after living abroad for a number of years.

The above stages are present at different times, and everyone has their own way of reacting to them, with the result that some stages are longer and more difficult than others, while others are shorter and easier to cope with.

> 'The whole object of travel is not to set foot on foreign land; it is at last to set foot on one's own country as a foreign land.'
>
> G. K. Chesterton (English writer)

Reducing the Effects

Experts agree that almost everyone suffers from culture shock and there's no escaping the phenomenon; however, its negative effects can be reduced considerably, and there are a number of things you can do before leaving home:

● **Positive attitude.** The key to reducing the negative effects of culture shock is to have a positive attitude towards

> 'Travellers never think that THEY are the foreigners.
>
> Mason Cooley (American aphorist)

Canada (whether you're visiting or planning to live there). If you don't look forward to a trip or relocation, you should question why you're going! There's no greater guarantee for unhappiness in a foreign environment than taking your prejudices with you. It's important when trying to adapt to a new culture to be sensitive to the locals' feelings, and try to put yourself in their shoes wherever possible, which will help you understand why they react as they do. Bear in mind that they have a strong, in-bred cultural code, just as you do, and react in certain ways because they're culturally 'trained' to do so. If you find yourself frustrated by an aspect of the local culture or behaviour, the chances are that they will be equally puzzled by yours!

● **Research**. Discover as much as possible about Canada before you go, so that your arrival and settling-in period doesn't spring as many surprises as it might otherwise. Reading up on Canada and its culture before you leave home will help you familiarise yourself with the local customs, and make the country and its people seem less strange on arrival. You will be aware of many of the differences in Canada and be better prepared to deal with them. This will help you avoid being upset by real or imaginary cultural slights, and also reduce the chances of you offending the locals by cultural misunderstandings. Being prepared for a certain amount of disorientation and confusion (or worse) makes it easier to cope with it. There are literally hundreds of publications about Canada as well as dozens of websites for expatriates (see **Appendices B** and **C**). Many sites provide access to expatriates already living in Canada who can answer questions and provide useful advice. There are also notice boards on many websites where you can post messages or ask questions.

● **Visit Canada first.** If you're planning to live or work in Canada for a number of years or even permanently, it's important to visit the country to see whether you think you would enjoy living there, and would be able to cope with the culture

before making the leap. Before you go, try to find someone in your local area who has visited Canada, and talk to them about it. Some companies organise briefings for families before departure. Rent a property before buying a home, and don't burn your bridges until you're certain that you have made the correct decision.

- **Learn English (or French if you will be living in a French-speaking area). This isn't optional but is absolutely essential.** As well as a positive attitude, overcoming the language barrier will be the most decisive factor in combating culture shock and enjoying your time in Canada. The ability to speak English (or French) and understand the local vernacular (see **Chapter 5**) isn't just a practical and useful tool (the one that will allow you to buy what you need, find your way around, etc.), but is the key to understanding Canada and its culture. If you can speak English

(or French), even at a basic level, your scope for making friends is immediately widened. Obviously not everyone is a linguist, and learning English (or French) can take time and requires motivation. However, with sufficient perseverance, virtually anyone can learn enough English (or French) to participate in the local culture.

- **Make a conscious effort to get involved in Canada's culture; be proactive and go out of your way to make friends.** Join in the activities of the local people, which could be a carnival, a religious festival or a sporting activity. There are often plenty of local clubs where you can practise sport or keep fit, learn to paint, cook local dishes, taste wine, etc. Not only will this fill some of your spare time, giving you less time to miss home, but you'll also meet new people and make friends. If you feel you cannot join a local club, perhaps because your English (or French) isn't good enough, then you can always participate in activities for expatriates, of which there are many in the major cities. Look upon a period spent in Canada as an opportunity to redefine your life objectives, and learn and acquire new perspectives. Culture shock can help you develop a better understanding of yourself and stimulate your creativity.

- **Talk to other expatriates.** Although they may deny it,

many expatriates have been through exactly what you're experiencing, and faced the same feelings of disorientation. Even if they cannot give you any advice, it helps to know that you aren't alone, and that it gets better over time. However, don't make the mistake of mixing only with expatriates, as this will alienate you from the local culture and make it much harder to integrate. Don't rely on social contact with your compatriots to carry you through, because it won't.

● **Keep in touch with home.** Keeping in touch with your family and friends at home and around the world by telephone, email and letters will help reduce and overcome the effects of culture shock. If you're feeling homesick and it's feasible, make a trip back home.

● **Be happy!** Don't rely on others to make you happy, otherwise you won't find true and lasting happiness. If you need things to change, you must do it yourself. Every day we are surrounded by events over which we have little or no control, and to complain

about them only makes us unhappier. So be your own best friend and nurture your capacity for happiness.

FAMILIES IN CANADA

Family life may be completely different in Canada, and relationships can become strained under the stress of adapting to culture shock. Your family may find itself in a completely new and possibly alien environment, your new home may scarcely resemble your previous one (it may be much more luxurious or significantly smaller), and the climate may differ dramatically from that of your home country. If possible, you should prepare yourself for as many aspects of the new situation as you can, and explain to your children the differences they're likely to encounter, while at the same time dispelling their fears.

Culture shock is an unavoidable part of travelling, living and working abroad, but if you're aware of it and take steps to lessen its effects before you go, and while you're abroad, the period of adjustment will be shortened, and its negative and depressing consequences reduced

'And that's the wonderful thing about family travel: it provides you with experiences that will remain locked forever in the scar tissue of your mind.'

Dave Barry (American author & humorist)

should pay special attention to the needs and feelings of their non-working partners and children, because the success of a relocation depends on the ability of the whole family to adapt to the new culture.

Good communication between family members is vital, and you should make time to discuss your experiences and feelings, both as a couple and a family. Questions should always be raised and, if possible, answered, particularly when asked by children. However difficult the situation may appear in the beginning, it helps to bear in mind that it's by no means unique, and that most expatriate families experience exactly the same problems, and manage to triumph over them and thoroughly enjoy their stay abroad.

Culture shock can affect non-working spouses and children more than working spouses. The husband (it's usually the husband) has his work to occupy him. He's meeting new colleagues, going out to lunch, and his activities may not differ much from what he was accustomed to at home. The children may be at school all day, making new friends and keeping busy. The wife, however, has to operate in a totally new environment that differs considerably from what she's used to. She will find herself alone more often, a solitude intensified by the fact that there are no close relatives or friends on hand. However, if you're aware that this may arise beforehand, you can act on it and reduce its effects. Working spouses

MULTICULTURALISM

The good news for newcomers to Canada is that it's a tolerant, multicultural society (Canadians like to think of it as a multicultural mosaic rather than a melting pot), where people from numerous nationalities live, work and play together in harmony. This has not only greatly enriched the Canadian way of life and added to its diverse range of foods, religions, businesses and ideas, but makes it much easier for immigrants to integrate into society. Virtually all ethnic groups in Canada maintain active clubs and societies where newcomers are warmly welcomed.

Coined in Canada in the '70s, multiculturalism is an ideology advocating that immigrants can integrate into society, while at the same time retaining and valuing the most important elements of their own culture (including speaking their own language and teaching it to their children). In Canada, migrants are encouraged to maintain ties with their homeland along with its culture – rather than abandon them – while simultaneously being urged to embrace Canadian values. Consequently, Canada has one of the most ethnically diverse societies in the world, with a low level of inter-ethnic conflict and high levels of cooperation. Intermarriage between different ethnic groups is high.

A NEW LIFE

Although you may find some of the information in this chapter a bit daunting, don't be discouraged by the foregoing catalogue of depression and despair; the negative aspects of travelling and living in Canada have been emphasised only to help you prepare for a new culture. Although most people who travel and live in Canada experience occasional feelings of discomfort and disorientation, **the vast majority never suffer the most debilitating effects of culture shock.**

As with settling in and making friends anywhere, even in your home country, the most important thing is to be considerate, kind, open, humble and genuine – qualities that are valued the world over. Selfishness, brashness and arrogance will get you nowhere in Canada, or any other country. Treat Canada and

its people with respect and they will reciprocate.

The majority of foreigners living in Canada would agree that, all things considered, they love living there – and are in no hurry to return home. A period spent in Canada is a wonderful way to enrich your life, broaden your horizons, make new friends and maybe even please your bank manager. The authors trust this book will help you avoid some of the pitfalls of life in Canada, and smooth your way to a happy and rewarding future in your new home.

> 'Twenty years from now, you will be more disappointed by the things you didn't do than by the ones you did do. So throw off the bowlines. Sail away from the safe harbour. Catch the trade winds in your sails. Explore. Dream. Discover.'
>
> Mark Twain (American writer)

2.

WHO ARE THE CANADIANS?

Canada is renowned for its rugged natural beauty, outdoor lifestyle, unspoilt environment and friendly and unassuming people. Canadians are environmentally aware, fair, hard-working, honest, orderly and rugged outdoors people, and the country is one of the least corrupt, safest (deaths from hand guns number in single digits, while in the US they run into thousands) and most civilised in the world. It's a caring society, where the community comes before the individual, highlighted by the abundance of charitable and voluntary organisations in Canada that do invaluable work, both nationally and internationally.

> 'Canada is a nation of people who came from somewhere else.'
>
> Microsoft *Encarta*

Canadians are one of the most difficult peoples to categorise, and the country has been described as 'not so much a nation as a collection of different peoples on a continental scale'. For a nation that's made up almost entirely of immigrants, it's hardly surprising that many Canadians have an identity crisis and spend a lot of time pondering the eternal question: "What is a Canadian?". Apart from lifestyle, Canadians have little in common with Americans, and, indeed, are at pains to emphasise the differences between themselves and their neighbours. Canadians *don't like* being mistaken for Americans, who many see as arrogant, brash and vulgar.

Migrants have been drawn to Canada for hundreds of years, particularly from the UK and France. In recent decades, there has been an influx of migrants from all corners of the globe, particularly Asia, and the country is one of the most multicultural in the world. (Most immigrants and refugees would really like to go to the US, but are accepted by Canada instead, and eventually realise just how lucky they are.) The country's 30m inhabitants reflect a cultural, ethnic and linguistic diversity found almost nowhere else on earth, and today it still welcomes some 200,000 immigrants annually. These diverse peoples generally live, work and play together in harmony, alongside indigenous First Peoples and Inuit, and have enriched the country with their cultures and customs. Canada is recognised as one of the most harmonious societies, and Canadians the most tolerant of races.

While Canada certainly isn't a cultural desert, it has always been more about lifestyle than culture. It's rated as one of the top countries in the world for its quality of life (despite its harsh climate), notably by the United Nations, and Vancouver and Toronto are consistently rated among the best cities in the world in which to live. Canada is a country of great opportunity and choice – so much more than just a land of hockey, polar bears and snow.

To help you become more familiar with Canada and Canadians, this

chapter provides information about the country's history, people and icons.

> 'We peer so suspiciously at each other that we cannot see that we Canadians are standing on the mountaintop of human wealth, freedom and privilege.'
>
> Pierre Elliott Trudeau (Canadian Prime Minister)

TIMELINE

Although modern Canada is little more than 400 years old, it has a rich and chequered history, the main events of which are listed below.

Circa 32,000 BC – According to some archaeologists, the first settlers arrive on the North American continent, coming from north-east Asia over a land bridge that existed across what is now the Bering Strait. Objects found at sites in the Yukon have been dated to around 32,000 BC, although this is a controversial matter: some scientists think the objects are naturally occurring rather than man-made.

Demographics

Capital city: Ottawa

Area: 9,984,670km² (3,854,085 mi²)

Population: 33m

Population density: 3.2 people per km² (8.3 people per mi²)

Largest cities: Toronto (2.5m), Montreal (1.6m), Calgary (0.99m), Ottawa (0.81m), Edmonton (0.73m), Mississauga (0.67m), Winnipeg (0.64m), Vancouver (0.58m), Hamilton (0.5m), Quebec City (0.49m)

Race: Caucasian 83%, Asian 8%, indigenous 3.5%, others 5.5%

Languages: English 68%; French 23%, Chinese 2.7%, Vietnamese 2%, Italian 1.5%, German 1.3%, Indigenous languages 1%

Largest expatriate groups (overseas born): English (20.2 per cent), French (15.8 per cent), Scottish (14 per cent), Irish (12.9 per cent), German (9.3 per cent) and Chinese (3.7 per cent); around 16 per cent of the population was born overseas

Religion: Christian (77%), Muslim (1.9%), Jewish (1.1%); some 17 per cent of people claim no religion

C. 12,000 BC – Unequivocal evidence of prehistoric man in Canada.

C. 1,000 AD – Norsemen (Vikings) build a settlement at L'Anse-aux-Meadows on the northern tip of Newfoundland, thereby beating Christopher Columbus to the New World by nearly 500 years.

1497 – John Cabot claims Cape Breton Island (Newfoundland) for England.

1534 – Jacques Cartier explores the Gulf of St. Lawrence.

1583 – Sir Humphrey Gilbert claims St. John's for Britain.

1605 – The foundation of Port Royal, the first permanent French settlement in North America.

1608 – The city of Quebec is founded by Samuel de Champlain.

1621 – James I of England grants Acadia to Sir William Alexander, who renames it New Scotland (Nova Scotia).

1627 – The Company of One Hundred Associates is founded, to establish a French empire in North America.

1642 – The City of Montreal is founded.

1663 – Louis XIV assumes personal control of New France.

1667 – England gives Acadia to France as a result of the Breda Treaty.

1670 – The Hudson's Bay Company is formed.

1690s – Acadia passes back and forth between France and England as their conflict in North America ebbs and flows.

1713 – The Treaty of Utrecht cedes Acadia, Hudson Bay and

Chateau Frontenac, Quebec City

Newfoundland to France, while England gets the 'country of the Iroquois.'

1754 – The French and Indian War begins in North America, and becomes the Seven Years War when the fighting spreads to Europe.

1759 – The English defeat the French at Quebec and capture it.

1763 – The Treaty of Paris gives Canada (New France and Acadia) to England.

1774 – The Quebec Act guarantees religious freedom for Roman Catholic colonists.

1792 – Captain George Vancouver begins his explorations of the Pacific coast.

> **'After all, we fought the Yanks in 1812 and kicked them the hell out of our country.'**
>
> Farley Mowat (Canadian conservationist & writer)

Yaletown, Vancouver, BC

1818 – The 49th parallel becomes the British North America/US border from the Lake of the Woods to the Rocky Mountains.

1841 – The Act of Union unites Upper and Lower Canada.

1849 – The boundary of the 49th parallel is extended to the Pacific Ocean.

1857 – Queen Victoria names Ottawa as Canada's capital.

1867 – A Confederation of New Brunswick, Nova Scotia, Ontario and Quebec forms the Dominion of Canada.

1871 – British Columbia joins the Confederation.

1897 – The Klondike gold rush begins.

1899 – The Boer War begins and the first Canadian troops to serve abroad are sent to South Africa.

1900 – A federal immigration policy entices Eastern Europeans to settle in the Canadian West.

1905 – The provinces of Saskatchewan and Alberta are formed.

1914-18 – Canada participates in the First World War.

1931 – The Statute of Westminster grants Canada full autonomy from Britain.

1939-45 – Canada participates in the Second World War.

1949 – Newfoundland becomes Canada's tenth province.

1962 – The Trans-Canada Highway officially opens.

1969 – Canada's federal government becomes officially bilingual.

1976 – The *Parti Québécois* wins the Quebec provincial election on a separatist platform.

1980 – A majority of Québécois reject separation from Canada in a referendum vote.

1982 – A new Canadian Constitution is ratified by every province except Quebec.

1995 – In another Quebec referendum, the 'no' (to separation from Canada) side wins again, but by a narrow margin.

1999 – Nunavut is formed.

2000 – Jean Chrétien elected Prime Minister. His Liberal Party picks up votes in Quebec, weakening support for Quebec separatists.

2003 – **March:** Canada decides not to join the US-led coalition against Iraq; **August:** The biggest power cut in North American history hits Toronto, Ottawa and other parts of Ontario, as well as cities in the US; **December:** Chrétien retires after ten years in office. Former finance minister Paul Martin is sworn in as Prime Minister.

2004 – **June:** Paul Martin is returned to power in general elections, but his Liberal party is stripped of its majority.

2005 – July: Senate approves a bill to legalise same-sex marriages; **November:** Paul Martin's minority Liberal government is brought down in a vote of no confidence. **2006 – January:** Stephen Harper's Conservatives defeat Paul Martin in general elections, ending 12 years of Liberal government; **November:** Parliament agrees that the Québécois should be considered a 'nation' within Canada.

> 'A Canadian is someone who knows how to make love in a canoe.'
>
> Pierre Berton (journalist and writer)

THE PEOPLE

National & Regional Identity

Canada is an enormous, varied country, peopled by individuals from most corners of the world, as a result of which Canadians have struggled to develop a national identity and decide what it is exactly that makes them Canadian. A starting point is the common agreement that they are North Americans, but definitely not Americans. Indeed, the idea of not being something is an important part of the Canadian psyche, most notably with French-Canadians, who are keen not to be seen as English-speaking Canadians (or not Canadians at all but Québécois).

Geography has an important influence on how Canadians view each other: vast distances and long domestic flights mean that Canadians don't always get the chance to get to know one another. Parochialism has led to rampant regionalism, and many people have much stronger ties to their province or territory than to their

The Rant

Hey, I'm not a lumberjack, or a fur trader, I don't live in an igloo or eat blubber, or own a dogsled, and I don't know Jimmy, Sally or Suzy from Canada, although I'm certain they're really, really nice.

I have a Prime Minister, not a President. I speak English and French, not American. And I pronounce it 'about', not 'a boot'.

I can proudly sew my country's flag on my backpack. I believe in peace keeping, not policing, diversity, not assimilation, and that the beaver is a truly proud and noble animal. A toque is a hat, a chesterfield is a couch, and it is pronounced 'zed' not 'zee', 'zed'!

Canada is the second largest landmass! The first nation of hockey! and the best part of North America.

My name is Joe! And I am Canadian!

country as a whole; as a result of which the government has instituted programmes to encourage young Canadians to visit other parts of their enormous country.

Jeff Douglas 'starred' in a series of extremely popular TV 'I am a Canadian' ads for Molson breweries from 2000 to 2005, on the theme of Canadian patriotism, the most famous examples of which were *The Rant* (see box) and *The Anthem*. In the ads, Douglas's character, Joe, gives a speech about what it is and what it isn't to be a Canadian, making particular efforts to distinguish himself from both common Canadian stereotypes of Americans, and common American stereotypes of Canadians.

Mounties

The Mounties are thought to personify all that's best about the Canadian character: fairness, honesty, integrity, politeness and a great dress sense. Their proper name is the Royal Canadian Mounted Police (RCMP), and they have such renown in Canada that they've become a national icon, lauded in

song and legends. Indeed, their popularity, and the respect they generate, are thought to be part of the reason that Canada has a higher-than-average percentage of citizens who have confidence in the police force. In every province except Ontario and Quebec (which have their own provincial police forces), the RCMP enforce the law outside the municipalities. Within city boundaries, the local police enforce the law.

Multiculturalism

Canada was the first country in the world to adopt multiculturalism (see **Chapter 1**) as an official policy in 1971. In so doing, it affirmed the value and dignity of all Canadian citizens, irrespective of their racial or ethnic origins, their language, or their religious affiliation. The 1971 Multiculturalism Policy of Canada also confirmed the rights of Aboriginal peoples and the status of Canada's two official languages.

Canada is one of the most multicultural countries in the world (Toronto and Vancouver are among the world's most multicultural cities), and a nation of immigrants (apart from the First Nations and Inuit), but they often have little in common with one another. Canada isn't a universal melting pot but a union of minorities (there are so many that some are officially 'invisible'); it has been called a

> 'Canada has never been a melting-pot; more like a tossed salad.'
>
> Arnold Edinborough (author)

cultural mosaic, in which each person is proud of his or her origins, but prouder still to be a Canadian.

This approach is sometimes cited as an example of how multiculturalism can work, although the concept of multiculturalism has come under close scrutiny (and sometimes attack) recently, some people arguing that it cannot work. In fact, Canada has been described as a collection of different peoples on a continental scale, rather than a single nation. This may be why there's no such thing as a typical Canadian, and why many Canadians have an identity crisis.

That said, Canada generally manages to avoid racism and doesn't have the severe economic disparities that affect people from different cultures in some other developed countries. New immigrants are usually welcomed with an open mind and treated well, and this has helped Canada with its ongoing integration of First Nation peoples (although it's a fairly recent process, as they weren't allowed to vote until 1960).

Canada's cultural and ethnic diversity is apparent at all levels of society. Although recent immigrants from the developing world tend to be at the bottom of the economic scale, rapid economic progress is possible: Chinese and Japanese Canadians, for example, have done well over the past three or four decades, and some of them are now among Canada's wealthiest people (many were, admittedly, wealthy when they arrived).

On the other hand, many foreigners from the developing world struggle to fit in and be accepted, especially if they don't speak English or French. In some cities, including Toronto and Vancouver, new immigrants have clashed with the police. Social and economic deprivation among such newcomers has become a problem for Canada, and immigrants from Africa, the Caribbean and Central and South America don't fully integrate for a couple of generations after their arrival.

Canada is keen to attract clever, talented people from other countries – it needs to, to make up for the gifted people it has lost to the US over the years – but it's less keen to attract those who will struggle to contribute, or who don't try to assimilate. In recent years, there has been some resentment towards immigration, although it has mainly

> 'Canadians are generally indistinguishable from Americans, and the surest way of telling the two apart is to make this observation to a Canadian.'
>
> Richard Starnes (Canadian businessman)

preferring gradual rather than rapid change; they favour civilised evolution rather than disruptive revolution.

Canadians are fairly broad-minded and are generally tolerant of homosexuality. Many cities have Gay Pride days, when parades and other celebrations attract large crowds.

> 'Canada is a country so square that even the female impersonators are women.'
>
> Richard Benner (Canadian film director)

been low-key and is generally targeted at illegal immigrants.

Tolerance

Canadians have a reputation for tolerance, which probably stems from its 'pioneer' days. The early pioneers had a tough life, battling the country's extreme climate, sometimes-unfriendly natives and dangerous wildlife, and they had to rely on themselves and their neighbours. This experience taught them that people needed each other when the going got tough, and that if you treated people well, they would reciprocate. As a result, honesty, integrity and having a good reputation became highly valued, and still are. The pioneers learned to overlook people's differences, and this has promoted a spirit of tolerance towards others. Canadians don't overreact, but take a measured approach to life. Indeed, they have been described as 'gradualists',

Unpretentiousness

Canadians don't have the class distinctions common in other countries. They dress down as an indication of lack of pretentiousness – everyone can fit in and feel comfortable; it's the person who's important, not his clothes, accent or background. That said, Canada isn't a completely classless society, and status is as important here as it is elsewhere, although it's usually based on money and character rather than birthright. Canada lacks class or 'old school tie' barriers to success, and most people, however humble their origins, can fight their way to the top of the heap (although colour and gender barriers aren't always so easy to overcome).

Canadians are notably practical, down-to-earth, unstuffy and unpretentious. British Columbians are regarded as the (slight) exception which proves the rule: they're sometimes viewed as conceited about their climate (south-west British Columbia has the mildest weather in Canada, similar to that of north-west France).

Family & Community

Canadians are family-oriented, which is one of the most important foundations of their lives, although they're often willing to leave their family and move across the country to study or work. Canada is a caring society, where the community comes before the individual, which is illustrated by the abundance of charitable and voluntary organisations that do invaluable work (both nationally and internationally).

Outdoorsmen

If Canadians have an identity crisis, one thing that unites many of them is a love of the outdoor life. In winter, they play ice hockey, ski, hunt and ice-fish; in summer, they boat, camp, fish, hike, hunt and try to avoid becoming a bear's lunch. The outdoors is a major influence in the lives of many Canadians, despite the fact that most people live in cities. As an extension of this philosophy, many Canadians are keen conservationists, and numerous schemes exist to recycle waste and protect the environment.

> 'Canadians have been so busy explaining to the Americans that we aren't British, and to the British that we aren't Americans, that we haven't had time to become Canadians.'
>
> Helen Gordon McPherson

Politeness

Canadians are noted for their politeness. Like the English, they tend to apologise even when someone accidentally walks into them, and hold doors open for one another, not just for women. Canadians' politeness and regard for others deserts them notably in one area: when they don skates to play hockey. Neither does their politeness equate to formality. People invariably address each other informally, even in Quebec. The Canadian-French language is much less formal than in France, where it's wrong to use *tu* (the informal 'you', rather than the formal *vous*) with a stranger.

Sense of Humour

Humour is an integral part of the Canadian character, and its use will ease your way in social and business situations. The Canadian sense of humour resembles Canadians: understated, polite and unlikely to offend. British humour is sometimes spikier and more teasing than is the norm in Canada, and can be mistaken by Canadians as more spiteful than it's meant to be. American quick-fire 'gag' humour sometimes seems overstated, even pushy to Canadians; their approach is drier and more self-deprecating.

The fact that Canadians have a well-developed sense of humour is attested to by the number of successful comedians and comic actors who have emerged from the country (although many people assume they're American), including Dan Aykroyd, John Candy, Jim Carrey, Tom Green, Howie Mandel, Rick Moranis, Mike Myers and Leslie Nielsen. A TV programme that illustrates Canadian humour and satirises politicians and celebrities is *This Hour Has 22 Minutes*.

There are various traditions in Canadian humour, in both English and French. These include typical (sometimes stereotypical) family life, cultural and political satire, and absurdity. Satire is probably the

> In 1977, Calgary's Loose Moose Theatre Company invented a form of comedy which has become popular worldwide: improvisation – known as improv. Two teams of actors/comedians vie with each other to produce the funniest sketch, based on a set theme of which they have no prior knowledge. The audience then votes for the team they think is the funniest. Improv has become popular in comedy clubs in many countries, and is also popular on radio and television.

primary characteristic of Canadian humour. Canadians have a strong sense of regionalism, and so does their humour, with people from various regions mocked for their alleged characteristics and failings. A favourite butt of Canadian jokes is people from Newfoundland ('Newfies'), who are treated in the same way the British treat the Irish or Americans treat rednecks.

Canadian jokes also stereotype Toronto's inhabitants as arrogant, the people of Alberta as gun toting, and British Columbians as dope-smoking, body-pierced, vegetarian hippies. The US is another common target of Canadian humour, especially the general American lack of knowledge about Canada. American embarrassments and failures are lambasted remorselessly by Canadian comedians and joke-tellers.

Regional Differences

Canada is subject to rampant regionalism, and its provinces and territories have distinct characters, as do their inhabitants. There follows a

brief (and slightly tongue-in-cheek) character sketch of each province and territory.

By far the most dominant, heavily-populated areas of the country are the central provinces of Ontario and Quebec. The West begins west of Ontario and tends to feel ignored, as do the Atlantic provinces. Canada's provincial and territorial divides sometimes ignore important cultural and linguistic divisions. Quebec, for example, isn't home to all of Canada's French speakers, but sometimes acts as if it is and is treated as such. The First Nation peoples (who used to be known as Red Indians to differentiate them from Indians from India, now known as East Indians) are still trying to achieve self-government, although the Inuit (who used to be known as Eskimos) have fared better: in 1999, they were given self-governing power over their territory, the massive Nunavut, which is four times the size of France but has a population of a mere 30,000. This was a smooth, uncontroversial process, and most Canadians were happy to let them have what is generally regarded as a barren, frozen wasteland.

Alberta

Alberta is Canada's cowboy country, its equivalent of Texas, with cattle, money, oil, wheat and a fondness for cowboy boots, guns and hats. It's much more conservative than liberal British Columbia next door, and is protected from the BC hippies and dope by the Rocky Mountains. Ex-prime minister Jean Chrétien said he preferred not dealing with Albertans because 'they are a different type.' There was outrage at the remark.

Edmonton is known as Canada's Festival City and 'Gateway to the Canadian North', and its inhabitants as Edmontonians.

British Columbia

British Columbia is generally regarded as Canada's coolest province (but not weather-wise: its south-west corner has the country's mildest climate), known for artists, drinking coffee on patios, hippies, marijuana production, retirees, skiing, Vancouver, vegans and watersports. The climate is notably damp, meaning that British

'Despite what you may have heard about a fierce rivalry between Alberta's mighty cities, most Edmontonians, and I am one, bear no real animosity toward our bull-riding brothers and sisters in Calgary. Still, I couldn't help remarking that the TV program *Living in Calgary* is a contradiction in terms.'

Kevin Baker (journalist, National Post)

> The most interesting thing about Manitoba is that musical genius Neil Young hails from Winnipeg (although he sensibly now lives on a large ranch in California).

Columbians don't so much tan as rust. They're viewed as rather estranged from easterners (those from Ontario and Quebec), more unconventional, and having more in common with the inhabitants of nearby Seattle than faraway Toronto.

Manitoba

Manitoba was created in 1870, and was the first province officially recognised by the federal government created from the Northwest Territories. It's Canada's heartland, with lots of wheat, some fearfully low temperatures and inexpensive property. The capital and largest city is Winnipeg (pop. 700,000), which is home to half the province's population, called Manitobans. Manitoba has huge amounts of water, meaning that you can probably leave the car at home and canoe to work, which is nice.

New Brunswick

New Brunswick is small and unassuming, most notable for fishing, fog and high tides. It's Canada's only officially bilingual province, stuck between French separatists and Celtic fiddlers. There's a distinct cultural divide created by the two founding linguistic groups, and the English-speaking and Acadian French cultures rarely merge; an invisible line separates the two cultures, beginning on the eastern outskirts of Moncton and running diagonally across the province to Grand Falls.

Newfoundland/Labrador

Newfoundland is best known for its fog and fishermen, and for being England's first overseas colony. It's cold and wet, and the locals, Newfies, are the butt of Canadian jokes – picked on because of their accent, and supposed *penchant* for inbreeding. Newfoundland is Canada's newest province (1949), and has its own time zone, half an hour different from the zones on either side of it. This adds to the province's sense of being 'separate' and makes it appear that Newfies get their news half an hour after

> 'Down in Newfoundland, we can hardly sleep for wondering when St. Pierre and Miquelon are going to invade.'
>
> John Crosbie (on the state of Canada's military in 1983)

everybody else. Newfoundland's economy, such as it is (the province receives a lot of social assistance), is based on a declining fishing industry and burgeoning offshore oil. It's rumoured to be socially acceptable (normal even) to wear high waders on your wedding day and eat cods' tongues.

Northwest Territories

The Northwest Territories is an incredibly cold and isolated 1.17 million km² (451772mi²) of mountains, forests and tundra. Its rivers feed thousands of lakes, and the area is environmentally significant, home to bears, bison, caribou (reindeer), moose, whales and wolves. The locals (40,000 of them) speak up to eight languages – learning them provides something to do during the seemingly endless winters, brightened only by the spectacular Northern Lights (aurora borealis).

This is the legendary Land of the Midnight Sun, where, north of the Arctic Circle, the sun doesn't set below the horizon for the summer and doesn't rise above it in the winter, creating the effect of six months of darkness and six months of light. It's the home of the Midnight Classic Golf Tournament, the Canadian Championship Dog Derby – 150 miles across frozen Slave Lake on a dog sled – and the ubiquitous ice-sculpting contests.

Nova Scotia

Nova Scotia has a Celtic feel (possibly because most of its inhabitants play the fiddle), which is reinforced by the abundant rainfall. It's known for sailing, seafood and its inhabitants' strange accent. Halifax is one of Canada's most beautiful cities, but it pays to visit it with a peg on your nose to reduce the all-pervading odour of fish.

> 'Canada is like an old cow. The West feeds it. Ontario and Quebec milk it. And you can well imagine what it's doing in the Maritimes.'
>
> Tommy Douglas (Saskatchewan premier)

Nunavut

Nunavut (our land) was created from the Northwest Territories in 1999, and has a population of less than 30,000 in an area the size of Western Europe. It's the home of the Inuit and the unearthly Northern Lights, and is heavily subsidised by the federal government. Nunavut is colder than a husky's nostril, and prey to mosquitoes the size of bison during the several days of summer.

Ontario

Ontario is the home of Canada's business and political elite, and the site of Ottawa, the nation's capital; home to Toronto, the country's largest city, and to Niagara Falls (a large waterfall). The locals are regarded as arrogant by other Canadians, but they run the country and so think they're entitled to be; they're also regarded as more business-like and conservative than many other Canadians. As a payback, Toronto is the only Canadian city with anything like American crime levels.

Quebec

Quebec is part of Canada and yet very much French. It's famous for Céline Dion, the internationally-renowned Cirque du Soleil, hydro-electricity, maple syrup and its desire for independence. The people have a strong sense of cultural identity, are notably nationalistic, enjoy a drink and are 'cooler' than other Canadians, probably because of

> 'In any world menu, Canada must be considered the vichyssoise of nations; it's cold, half-French and difficult to stir.'
>
> Stuart Keate (Canadian journalist)

their French *savoir faire*. Quebec is one of the few places on the North American continent where **non**-smokers are the outcasts.

Quebec is Canada's largest province, and is often regarded as the country's black sheep – at home and abroad. Many of its people view themselves as so different from other Canadians that they would like to secede from Canada and become a separate country, but the separatists have never quite achieved a majority. Two referenda have been held on the question, in 1980 and 1995, when 40 per cent and 49 per cent of the vote was in favour of separation. Despite these failures by the separatists, many Québécois refer to the 'country of Quebec' or the 'two Canadas.' If a future

Montreal

> ### The Cremation of Sam McGee
> (Robert W. Service, Canadian poet & writer, 1874-1958)
>
> There are strange things done 'neath the midnight sun
> By the men who moil for gold.
> The Arctic trails have their secret tales
> That would make your blood run cold.
> The Northern Lights have seen queer sights,
> But the queerest they ever did see,
> Was that night on the marge of Lake Lebarge
> I cremated Sam McGee.

vote goes in favour of separation, the Supreme Court of Canada has indicated that the rest of the country won't oppose the secession (many would be glad to see the back of them).

Prince Edward Island

Small Prince Edward Island (often abbreviated to PEI) was named after Queen Victoria's father, and has two (very different) claims to fame: the novel *Anne of Green Gables* (which is set there) and potatoes. Japanese tourists are particularly fond of the book, and are drawn to the island accordingly. PEI doesn't share a border with the US, or anywhere for that matter, but has been less isolated since 1997, when the Confederation Bridge (13km/8mi) joined the island to the mainland.

Saskatchewan

Saskatchewan is known for being as flat as an iron and dull (hence the brevity of their entry) with lots of prairie, and producing good ice hockey players and enormous amounts of wheat. The province's flag sums it up well, with wheat in the south and forest up north. One of Saskatchewan's claims to fame is that it was the scene of Canada's first 'naval battle', fought in 1885, when a steamship engaged the native Métis at Batoche in the North-West Rebellion.

Yukon

The Yukon is old gold rush territory, up in the north-west of the country, next to Alaska. It provided the inspiration for Robert W. Service's poems *The Shooting of Dan McGrew* and the *Cremation of Sam McGee* (see box), written while he was living in Dawson City.

> 'For some reason, a glaze passes over people's faces when you say 'Canada.' Maybe we should invade South Dakota or something.'
>
> Sandra Gotlieb (wife of the Canadian ambassador to the US)

ATTITUDES TO FOREIGNERS

Canada has an official policy of multiculturalism, is pro-immigration, and its race relations are described as among the world's best. That doesn't mean that racism is unknown, however, and the indications in the early 21st century are that it's increasing, particularly against Arabs and Muslims, as a result of terrorism. Recent surveys (by Statistics Canada and the newspaper *Globe & Mail*) show that 36 per cent of 'visible' minorities feel that they've experienced discrimination because of their ethno-cultural characteristics. Nearly half of black people and Aboriginal people (living off-reserve) reported discrimination, but 'only' a third of Asians had experienced it.

Racism is most evident in the cities, where 95 per cent of visible minorities live. In Vancouver and Toronto, over a third of the population is a visible minority, projected to increase to half by 2016.

Inuit inukshuk

Canada's vastness affects how some Canadians view other countries. People who live on the west coast fail to take much interest in what happens on the (very) distant east coast (and vice versa), let alone in anything happening abroad, which might as well be on another planet. Events occurring even in Europe (the 'mother continent' for a lot of Canadians) are regarded as having little or no influence on life in Canada. Indeed, Canadians sometimes find it difficult to relate to events happening in small countries, i.e. most other countries, from a Canadian viewpoint. Compared to Americans, however, Canadians are extremely alert to international events, and their best newspapers are anything but parochial.

NATIVE CANADIANS

There are three distinct groups of Native Canadians: First Nation peoples (who are often referred to by specific tribal names and who used to be called Red Indians), Inuit and Métis, which are official classifications in Canada. The Inuit were formerly called Eskimos, but this term has fallen out of use, and is nowadays sometimes regarded as offensive. Métis (pronounced 'maytees') are people of mixed

> 'The great themes of Canadian history are as follows: keeping the Americans out, keeping the French in and trying to get the Natives to somehow disappear.'
>
> Will Ferguson (Canadian writer & novelist)

heritage, usually the descendants of marriages between indigenous women and the early French fur trappers.

Ancient History

Archaeologists disagree about the date of the first human occupation of Canada, but it's thought to be at least 30,000 years ago. The Yukon was probably the first area to be settled, being one of the few areas of Canada to escape glaciation. The first native Canadians are likely to have come from Siberia via a land bridge (which formed when sea levels were much lower than today) connecting it to what is now Alaska. Much of the rest of Canada wasn't populated until 10,000 BC, prior to which it was covered by a thick layer of ice and uninhabitable. The last areas to be inhabited, no more than around 4,000 years ago, were those in the far north now occupied by the Inuit (albeit only 30,000 of them).

First European Contacts

The first recorded contacts between Europeans and Native Canadians occurred when small groups of Norsemen (Vikings) landed sporadically around 1,000 AD, on Baffin Island and at various places along the Atlantic coast, either on voyages of discovery or as a result of being blown off course by storms. Practically nothing is known about these early encounters, because the Aboriginal peoples most likely to have had contact with the Norsemen – the Beothuk and Dorset – have since died out. According to archaeologists who have studied the

Inuit mask

site, the Norse settlement at L'Anse-aux-Meadows (Newfoundland) seems to have lasted for only 50 to 60 years.

Contact continued fitfully until the 16th century, when Europeans began to arrive in greater numbers to exploit the North Atlantic fisheries. To these 16th-century Europeans, Canada seemed to be a vast empty land, but it was far from being uninhabited. Native peoples – mistakenly called Indians by Europeans – lived throughout what is now Canada, and estimates of their total numbers range from 500,000 to 2m.

Lifestyle

In the 16th century, most of Canada's indigenous peoples practised a nomadic hunting and gathering lifestyle, which involved continuous movement in the never-ending search for new food sources. Of the two main regions where sedentary societies developed, the

Pacific coast had by far the largest population, thanks to its rich ocean and temperate rainforest resources. This allowed it to become one of the most densely populated areas of the world occupied by non-agricultural peoples, while in Ontario (the second-most populated region) the climate and fertile soil allowed farming.

Dealings with Europeans

The development of the fur trade in the 17th century led to much closer contact between Europeans and Native Canadians; Europeans relied upon the Natives, who received European material goods and technology in return for their local knowledge and services. The spread of the fur trade and the Europeans' rapid penetration of the interior wouldn't have been possible without the help of Aboriginal peoples. They also played an important role as guides and soldiers in the colonial wars between the British and the French, but the end of hostilities and the declining importance of the fur trade brought to a close the period of cooperation between Natives and Europeans. The flood of immigrants from Europe meant that by the early 19th century, Natives comprised just 10 per cent of the population of Upper Canada (equivalent to modern day Ontario).

Like the indigenous peoples of many countries 'discovered' by Europeans, Natives were treated with varying degrees of ignorance in Canada, coerced to give up their land and traditions and ultimately their lifestyle. In return, they received the 'benefits' of Christianity, European diseases such as measles, smallpox and tuberculosis (which killed them in droves), and addiction to alcohol, drugs and guns.

The mass slaughter of the buffalo herds by Europeans (mainly for their meat and hides, but also for 'sport') led to starvation for many Natives in the south and centre of Canada. At the same time, the over-fishing and hunting of whales and walruses seriously depleted the Inuit food supply. The discovery of gold from the mid-19th century in various regions created yet more problems for Aboriginal peoples, as their lands were invaded by waves

> 'In a world darkened by ethnic conflicts that tear nations apart, Canada stands as a model of how people of different cultures can live and work together in peace, prosperity and mutual respect.'
>
> Bill Clinton (US President)

of prospectors who paid little or no heed to the interests and rights of those who had been living there for thousands of years.

Suppression

The Indian Act of 1876 consolidated previous legislation regarding Natives, who had been 'herded' into reserves across the country. It was officially government policy to try to assimilate Native Canadians into the general population, and legislate against their traditional customs. Schooling was an important part of this crusade – as in Australia, with the Aboriginals, children were taken away from their parents to live in schools (often run by missionaries) to encourage the assimilation of 'white' culture – and, at the same time, reserve lands were gradually whittled away.

Self-determination

It wasn't until after the Second World War, when anti-colonial sentiment spread, that Canada developed a greater interest in, and sensitivity towards, the culture and heritage of its Aboriginal peoples. The 1951 revision of the Indian Act began the process of allowing Native peoples much more control over their affairs, involving a return to self-government, and elements

of their traditional life. In the '60s, they were allowed the federal vote without losing their status under the Indian Act, and the vexed question of land claims has begun to be addressed in recent years. The Canadian government took a huge stride in 1999 by granting the Inuit approximately 800,000mi2 (2,000,000km2) of the Northwest Territories as a separate and autonomous territory called Nunavut (which means 'our land').

The deal included the eviction of all non-Inuit-owned businesses, put federal agencies under Inuit control, and included payments totalling $500m, plus interest; however, it wasn't as generous as it seems. In return, the Inuit had to renounce claims to ownership of most of the territory, particularly the offshore gas and oil exploration areas – as John Paul Getty so succinctly put it, 'The meek shall inherit the earth, but not the mineral rights'.

> 'Canadians have an abiding interest in surprising those Americans who have historically made little effort to learn about their neighbour to the North.'
>
> Peter Jennings (Canadian-American journalist)

This agreement opened a can of worms, as other native groups are now pressing for similar deals, and what started as orderly protests, have become barricaded roads and armed confrontations in some areas. Support among the general population for Native causes seems to have peaked, and there's resistance to recognising further

indigenous claims to land and privileges.

ICONS

Every country has its icons – people, places, structures, food (and drink) and symbols – which are revered or unique to a country, and have special significance to its inhabitants and those around the world. The following is a list of some of Canada's icons that you can expect to see or hear reference to (with apologies to those Canadians who have been trying to live down their Canuck connections and won't appreciate being listed here).

Icons – People

Bryan Adams (b. 1959) – A Canadian rock singer, guitarist, songwriter and photographer, Adams' best-known albums include *Reckless*, *18 'til I Die* and *Waking Up the Neighbours*. He has been awarded the Order of Canada and the Order of British Columbia for his contribution to popular music and his philanthropic work, and was inducted into Canada's Walk of Fame in 1998.

Pamela Anderson (b. 1967) – Born in British Columbia (not on a California beach), Pamela Anderson is a sex symbol and actress (although many people would argue that her acting ability is negligible), best known for her large breast implants and raunchy private life, including failed marriages to two rock stars.

Margaret Atwood (b. 1939) – Arguably Canada's most famous living writer, Atwood is a poet, novelist, literary critic, feminist and political activist. Her novels include *The Edible Woman*, *The Handmaid's Tale* and *The Blind Assassin*.

Sir Frederick Grant Banting (1891-1941) – A medical scientist, doctor and the man who co-discovered insulin. Banting's groundbreaking research in the early '20s brought him worldwide acclaim, and earned him a knighthood from the British crown, and Canada's first Nobel Prize for Medicine.

James Eugene Carrey (b. 1962) – A Canadian-American rubber-faced film actor and comedian, best known for his manic, slapstick performances in comedy films such as *Ace Ventura*, *The Mask*, *Dumb & Dumber* and *Bruce Almighty*. Carrey has also achieved critical success in dramatic roles, and won Golden Globe Awards for *The Truman Show* and *Man in the Moon*.

Donald Stewart 'Grapes' Cherry (b. 1934) – Don was a hockey player and National Hockey League coach, but is famous as an outspoken, loud-mouthed, politically incorrect, hockey commentator for CBC Television, co-hosting the long-running sports programme *Hockey Night in Canada*. He's also an author and radio commentator for *The Fan Radio Network*.

Leonard Cohen (b. 1934) – A poet, novelist and singer-songwriter, whose work explores isolation, relationships, religion, sexuality and war. He has a reputation as something of a 'miserabilist' and of appealing to the confused, the depressed and the lovelorn.

Joseph Jacques Jean Chrétien (b. 1934) – Born in Quebec, Chrétien was the leader of the Liberal Party from 1990 to 2003, and the 20th Prime Minister of Canada, from 1993 to 2003. He's one of Canada's most experienced politicians, having served with six Prime Ministers, held 12 ministerial positions and served in Parliament for a total of 27 years.

Céline Dion (b. 1968) – Céline Dion came from humble beginnings (she was the youngest of 14 children in a poor family near Montreal) to become a worldwide musical phenomenon, selling over 150m albums, singing songs in two languages (French and English) and various styles, but most notably the 'power ballad'. Despite this huge success, she is a subject of some media ridicule, for her Quebecois accent, conservative nature and rather wooden stage presence.

Thomas Clement Douglas (1904-84) – A Scottish-born Baptist minister, Tommy Douglas became a prominent Social Democrat politician. For over 50 years, his staunch devotion to social causes (he was Canada's 'father of Medicare'), rousing powers of speech and pugnacious charm made him a popular political force.

Michael J. Fox (b 1961) – An award-winning, Canadian-born film and TV actor, Fox's best known roles include Marty McFly in the *Back to the Future* trilogy, Alex P. Keaton in *Family Ties* and Mike Flaherty in *Spin City*, for which he won many Emmy and Golden Globe Awards. Fox was diagnosed with Parkinson's disease in 1991and retired from full-time acting in 2000.

Terrance 'Terry' Stanley Fox (1958-81) – A Canadian humanitarian, athlete and cancer treatment activist, Fox became famous for the Marathon of Hope across Canada (5,376km/3,340mi) to raise money for cancer research, running with a prosthetic leg. He's considered one of Canada's greatest 20th-century heroes, and is commemorated each September by the Terry Fox Run in aid of cancer research.

Wayne Gretzky (b. 1961) – Widely regarded as the greatest hockey player of his era, perhaps of any era, Gretzky is nicknamed 'The Great One'. He broke 61 NHL records, racked up nearly 3,000 points and won four Stanley Cups. When he retired in 1999, his playing number (99) was officially 'retired' across the entire NHL – the only time a player has been given this honour. He played for the Edmonton Oilers from 1979 to 1988, and then moved to the Los Angeles Kings, ending his career at the New York Rangers. He now serves on countless charities and his foundation helps disadvantaged children participate in hockey.

Gordon Lightfoot (b. 1938) – Canadian folk singer, composer, lyricist and poet, Lightfoot began his career as a boy soprano, whose clear, high voice developed into a smoky baritone. He's a master songwriter and balladeer, many of whose songs have become standards worldwide.

Sir John Maxwell Alexander Macdonald (1815-91) – The first

> 'Canada is the essence of not being. Not English, not American, it is the mathematic of not being. And a subtle flavour – we're more like celery as a flavour.'
>
> Mike Myers (Canadian actor)

Prime Minister of Canada (born in Glasgow, Scotland), Macdonald is considered the founding father of Canada, who united the French and the English and facilitated the construction of the Canadian Pacific Railway.

Joni Mitchell (b. 1943) – A noted musician, songwriter and artist, Mitchell was one of the seminal figures of the '60s folk-rock scene, labelled the 'female Bob Dylan' (meant as a compliment but not appreciated by Mitchell), with a distinctive voice and lyrics. Among her most celebrated hits are *Both Sides Now*, *Chelsea Morning* and *Big Yellow Taxi*, which remain international favourites.

Anne Murray (b. 1945) – A Canadian singer known for her rich alto voice, who sings country, pop and 'adult contemporary' songs (whatever they are), and who has sold nearly 60m albums. She was the first Canadian female solo artist to reach number one on the US chart (for *Snowbird*, one of her signature songs), and is cited as the woman who paved the way for other Canadian female stars, including Céline Dion, Sarah McLachlan and Shania Twain.

Michael John Myers (b. 1963) – Mike Myers is an Emmy Award-

winning comic actor, screenwriter and film producer, best known for his comedy work in *Saturday Night Live*, and his starring roles in *Wayne's World*, the *Austin Powers* films and *Shrek*.

Martin Brian Mulroney (b. 1939) – The 18th Prime Minister of Canada, from 1984 to 1993, Mulroney was leader of the Progressive Conservative Party, and the first Conservative majority government in 26 years. A bilingual smooth-talker and a breath of fresh air, he won back-to-back elections, worked to get rid of apartheid, and with the Free Trade Agreement, and changed the economic landscape of Canada.

Lester 'Mike' Bowles Pearson (1897-1972) – Statesman, diplomat and politician, who was Prime Minister of Canada from 1963 to 1968, during which time he oversaw the introduction of the Canada Pension Plan, national Medicare, the Bilingualism and Biculturalism Commission, a national labour code and the Maple Leaf flag. He was awarded the Nobel Peace Prize in 1956 for his role in defusing the Suez Crisis through the United Nations.

Keanu Charles Reeves (b. 1964) – born in Beirut, Lebanon, Reeves is a Canadian actor raised in Toronto, Ontario. He's best known for playing

Neo in the action film trilogy *The Matrix*, but has starred in many other films, including *My Own Private Idaho* alongside River Phoenix.

David Takayoshi Suzuki (b. 1936) – A science broadcaster and environmental activist, Suzuki is best known for his TV and radio series and books (over 30) about nature and the environment. He's the host of the popular and long-running CBC TV science magazine, *The Nature of Things*, which has been sold to over 40 countries, and has been Canada's premier environmental guru for two generations of Canadians.

Pierre Elliott Trudeau (1919-2000) – The 15th Prime Minister of Canada, Pierre Trudeau was a charismatic, flamboyant figure who dominated the Canadian political scene from the late '60s to the mid-'80s. Trudeau's unique blend of charisma and fierce intelligence managed to keep him in power for nearly 16 years. During that time, he never wavered from his goal to create a unified and 'just' Canada. He worked to promote bilingualism,

> 'Canada is a country whose main exports are hockey players and cold fronts. Our main imports are baseball players and acid rain.'
>
> Pierre Trudeau (Canadian Prime Minister)

stamp out separatism and create a Canadian Constitution and Charter of Rights.

Shania Twain (b. 1965) – A successful country and western and pop/rock singer, and regularly voted as Canada's sexiest woman. Her third album, *Come on Over*, is the biggest-selling album of all time by a female artist, and the best-selling country music album ever made.

The Unknown Soldier – He died during one of the crucial battles of the First World War; in May 2000 his remains were retrieved from Vimy Ridge and reburied at the base of the National War Memorial in Ottawa. Though his history is 'unknown', his tomb ensures that the 116,000 Canadian soldiers who gave their lives for world peace and freedom will never be forgotten.

Neil Young (b. 1945) – A songwriter and musician since the '60s, Young has performed as a solo artist and in groups, including Buffalo Springfield, Crosby, Stills, Nash and Young (CSNY) and Crazy Horse. He's a master of many styles, including folk, country, rock and grunge – he's sometimes dubbed 'the father of grunge', influencing bands such as Nirvana and Pearl Jam. Young is one of rock music's most influential guitarists, and is arguably Canada's most important musician.

> 'A Canadian is merely an unarmed American with health care.'
>
> John Wing (Canadian comedian)

Icons – Symbols

The Bay – The Bay, or the Hudson's Bay Company (HBC) as it's officially called, is North America's oldest company, and at one time was the largest land owner in the world, controlling the fur trade throughout much of British-controlled North America for several centuries. With the decline of the fur trade, HBC evolved into a mercantile business, and today is best known for its department stores.

Beachcombers – A popular Canadian television series, broadcast on CBC between 1972 and 1990, making it the longest-running drama series on Canadian television (it ran to 387 episodes). It starred a Greek-Canadian log salvager in British Columbia, whose job was to track down logs that broke away from logging barges – the authors realise it sounds as if they made this up (they didn't).

Canadian Broadcasting Corporation (CBC or Radio-Canada) – The CBC (in French, *la Société Radio-Canada or SRC*) is Canada's national public radio and television broadcaster, and the oldest broadcasting service in the country, established in its present form in 1936. As a crown corporation, the CBC operates autonomously from the government in its day-to-day business, and its liberal stance is, not surprisingly, despised by Conservatives.

Bluenose Schooner – Built in Nova Scotia in the '20s, the Bluenose Schooner was a celebrated racing ship (and cod-fishing boat), which held the record as the fastest schooner for 23 years. 'Bluenose' used to be a nickname for Nova Scotians.

Calgary Stampede – The Calgary Stampede, which bills itself as 'The Greatest Outdoor Show on Earth', is a large, non-profit festival, exhibition and rodeo that has been held in Calgary for ten days each July since 1918. It's one of Canada's largest annual events and the world's largest outdoor rodeo.

Canadian Pacific Railway (CPR) – The CPR, built between eastern Canada and British Columbia between 1881 and 1885, was Canada's first transcontinental railway, now stretching from Vancouver to Montreal (it also serves a number of US cities). The CPR was instrumental in opening up western Canada to immigrants and settlers, although nowadays it's mostly used to carry freight (and tourists).

Canadian Hockey Joke

A man makes his way to his front-row seat for the Stanley Cup Final. Noticing that the seat next to him is empty, he asks his neighbour if someone will be sitting there.

"No," says the neighbour. "The seat is empty."

"This is incredible," said the man. "Who in their right mind would have a seat like this for Stanley Cup Final and not use it?"

The neighbour says "Well, actually, the seat belongs to me. I was supposed to come with my wife, but she passed away. This is the first Stanley Cup we haven't been to together since we got married in 1967."

"Oh ... I'm sorry to hear that. That's terrible. But couldn't you find someone else, a friend or relative, or even a neighbour to take the seat?"

The man shakes his head, "No. They're all at the funeral."

Dory – A small, shallow-draft boat of 5-7m (15-22ft) in length, seating two to four people, the dory (or doree/dorey) is a favourite 'mode of transport' in a country with vast amounts of water, being used as a working boat, tender and fishing platform.

Ice Hockey – Known to Canadians simply as 'hockey', ice hockey is by far the most popular sport in Canada – it's almost a religion – and playing and watching the game are an integral part of Canadian culture. The Championship trophy of the National Hockey League (NHL), and the oldest trophy (1892), competed for by professional athletes in North America, is the Stanley Cup (also known as simply 'The Cup' or 'The Holy Grail') – an icon in its own right.

Igloo – The igloo (*ighu* in Inuit) is a shelter constructed from blocks of snow, generally in the form of a dome. Although igloos are usually associated with all Inuit, they were predominantly constructed by the people of Canada's Central Arctic and Greenland Thule areas. Other Inuit people tended to use snow to insulate their houses, which were constructed of whalebone and hides.

Inuit Soapstone – Soapstone is a metamorphic rock with a talc base. The name comes from its soapy feel, and the Inuit sculpt animals from it.

Lacrosse – Lacrosse is North America's oldest team sport, played by Aboriginal people for hundreds of years before European settlement. It's now one of Canada's official sports, although of much less significance than the all-powerful hockey.

The Montreal Canadiens – The Canadiens are the most successful hockey sports team in North America, having won the Stanley Cup no fewer than 24 times – their nearest competitor is their mortal enemy, the Toronto Maple Leafs, with 13 wins. However, the last time the Canadiens or any Canadian team won the cup was in 1992-93.

Mounties – Canada's legendary Royal Canadian Mounted Police embody many Canadian virtues: fairness, honesty, integrity and politeness. The famous red uniforms are only ceremonial.

Parliament Building – Parliament Hill (or 'The Hill' to locals) is situated on the southern banks of the Ottawa river in central Ottawa, and is one of Canada's best-known symbols. It consists of three buildings: the Centre, East

'Until I came to Canada, I never knew snow was a four-letter word.'

Alberto Manguel (Argentinean writer)

and West Blocks; the main building is the Centre Block, which along with the distinctive Peace Tower houses the chambers of the House of Commons and the Senate. Built in a modern Gothic revival style, the current Centre Block was built between 1916 and 1927 to replace the original building destroyed in a spectacular fire in 1916.

Prairies – A vast area of flat sedimentary land stretching across western Canada between the Canadian Shield in the east and the Canadian Rockies. The Prairies cover much of the provinces of Manitoba, Saskatchewan and Alberta, known as the Prairie Provinces. The Canadian Prairies are one of the world's major farming areas (cattle, sheep and wheat) and the bread-basket of Canada and much of the world, wheat being the region's staple crop and the symbol of the Prairies.

Red Green Show – An iconic TV comedy aired by CBC from 1991 until 2006, the *Red Green* show is a cross between a sitcom and a comedy sketch series, and a parody of home improvement, DIY, fishing and other outdoors shows.

Rockies – The Canadian Rockies are part of the Rocky Mountain chain that stretches over 4,800km (3,000mi) from northern British Columbia to New Mexico in the US. They're home to Canada's premier winter ski resorts including Banff.

Snow – Canada receives enormous amounts of the cold, wet stuff and, rather than try to hide from their winters, many Canadians relish them and make the most of the many leisure possibilities that snow presents.

Tim Horton's – A coffee and doughnut fast food chain founded in Ontario in 1964, Horton's rapidly spread across the country to become its largest 'fast service' food chain, with over 2,700 outlets in Canada and 350 in the US. It has become entrenched in Canadian culture and is now seen as part of the country's identity.

Totem Pole – Totem poles are monumental sculptures carved from trees, typically giant western red cedars, by the Aboriginal peoples of the Pacific coast. The word 'totem' derives from the Ojobwe word *odoodem*, literally 'his totem, his kinship group'. Totem poles usually tell Native American legends, and contain family or clan symbols.

Ulu Knife – An Inuit woman's all-purpose knife, used for everything from skinning animals to cutting human hair, and shaping blocks of ice to build igloos, and hailed as a design classic. Ulu knives are traditionally made with a caribou

'The beaver, which has come to represent Canada as the eagle does the United States and the lion Britain, is a flat-tailed, slow-witted, toothy rodent, known to bite off its own testicles or to stand under falling trees.'

June Callwood (Canadian journalist & activist)

antler handle and a slate blade, although these days the blade is usually made of steel.

Icons – Flora & Fauna

Beaver – Canada's national animal is a quiet, industrious but stolid rodent that destroys ecosystems with its dam-building. The beaver was chosen because it was one of the main reasons that Canada was explored and settled (hunted for its pelts, which apparently make excellent waterproof felt for top hats). Sensitive though the matter is, it would be remiss not to point out that the word 'beaver' is commonly used as slang for a 'lady's bodily treasure'.

Canada Goose – An important game bird, the Canada goose is known for its almost incessant honking, and admired for its V-formation flying.

Canadian Horse – The Canadian horse is an official symbol of Canada, a breed developed in the country, and able to thrive in the harsh conditions. Although there have been several times when it almost became extinct, the Canadian horse has enthusiasts both within and outside Canada.

Caribou – There are a million caribou (known as reindeer in Europe) in Canada, and it also features on the 25-cent (quarter) coin.

Loon – The national bird of Canada is depicted on the Canadian one-dollar coin, which is known as a 'loonie'. The loon is an aquatic bird, the size of a large duck (or an undernourished goose), with black and white plumage and a spear-like beak.

Black & Sugar Maple Trees – The black maple (*Acer nigrum*) and sugar maple (*Acer saccharum*) trees are among the most important Canadian trees, being the major source of sap for making maple syrup. The sugar maple's sap is regarded as slightly superior.

Moose – Known as elk in Europe, the moose is the largest member of the deer family, and one of Canada's national animals. Collisions between moose (the plural of moose is moose) and cars are often fatal for both moose and motorist, due to the moose's particular body structure: a large, heavy body on spindly legs.

Polar Bear – The world's largest land predator, the semi-aquatic polar bear has no predators, but its existence is threatened by climate change, which is reducing the pack ice, thus limiting the polar bears' mobility and efficient hunting of seals.

Icons – Food & Drink

Beer – Beer is Canada's favourite tipple, accounting for 80 per cent of alcohol sales, and an integral part of Canadian life and Canadians' image of themselves. It's inextricably linked with hockey (see above): many Canadians men's ideal evening is watching hockey while guzzling beer. Canada's favourite beers include Coors, Labatt and Molson.

Doughnuts – Canada's favourite snack food, usually eaten in the morning with coffee (see **Tim Horton's** above). Canada has the most doughnut shops per capita in the world, and Canadians eat more of them than any other nation.

Ice-wine – Canada is the world's largest producer of ice-wine (due to its consistent freezes in winter), which is one of the world's most expensive wines. In November 2006, a bottle was sold for C$30,000 by Royal DeMaria, a small winery in Niagara-on-the-Lake.

Maple Syrup – A popular, sweet substance made from the sap of the maple tree. Canada produces most of the world's maple syrup, and Canadians like to pour it on a variety of foods, particularly pancakes.

Poutine – A love-it-or-hate-it culinary concoction, which hails from Quebec, *poutine* comprises French fries, cheese curds, gravy and, sometimes, the sauce of your choice (often tomato ketchup or barbecue sauce). It's the unofficial national dish of Canada.

3.
GETTING STARTED

One of the most difficult stages of adjustment to a new country is arrival and those first few days when you have a million and one things to do. This is stressful enough without adding the cultural differences in Canada. This chapter helps you prepare for some aspects of daily life, including bureaucracy, finding accommodation, renting or buying a car, obtaining healthcare, education, council services and utilities, the media, banking and taxation.

'Canada is all right really, though not for the whole weekend.'

Saki (British author)

ARRIVING BY AIR

Before your plane lands in Canada, the airline gives you a landing card (officially called a 'traveller declaration card') to complete. You must do so in pen in block capitals and in English or French. If you don't have an address in Canada, it's wise to enter the name of a hotel in an area or city where you're heading, or write 'touring', rather than leave it blank.

You're also given a Customs Declaration form by the airline, which must be completed and handed to the customs officer at your point of entry. The head of a family may make a joint declaration for all members residing in the same household and travelling together.

PERMITS & VISAS

Immigration

Canada doesn't have a culture of welcoming all and sundry into the country. It was described by the United Nations as 'the best country in the world in which to live' and wants to maintain this status. As a result, it restricts the entry of undesirables, misfits and anybody who's a threat to the health, security and welfare of Canada, by requiring applicants to undergo a medical, and produce a police certificate declaring that they don't have a criminal record.

The largest class of immigrants is described as 'skilled workers', decided by a points system that's heavily biased in favour of those with high-level qualifications, and work experience in jobs deemed to be in demand by the federal government. Total immigration is around 250,000 per year. Canada's birth rate is falling, and immigration is necessary to maintain the population at its current level, therefore immigration targets are rising rather than falling. Like most

developed countries, Canada has a problem with illegal immigrants.

Unlike the US, where possession of a visa isn't a guarantee of entry into the country, it's unusual for anyone with a visa or work permit (with the attached record of landing) to be refused entry to Canada, unless his circumstances have changed since it was issued. Only holders of permanent-resident or landed-immigrant visas and work permits may work in Canada. An immigrant visa gives you the right to live and work in Canada (and change jobs freely) on a permanent basis, and to apply for Canadian citizenship after three years' residence.

Work permits are issued for specific jobs and aren't transferable between jobs, but they can be extended in certain circumstances. The key to obtaining a work permit, apart from having a genuine job offer in writing, is for a prospective employer to prove that there are no unemployed Canadian nationals or immigrant-visa holders who can do the job.

Canada doesn't have an annual immigration quota, but sets annual targets that can be exceeded if there are many high-quality applicants; in years when there are fewer applicants, officials may be more lenient regarding marginal applications. As in many areas of life in Canada, the immigration rules for the province of Quebec are different from the rest of Canada.

> 'If there is anything a public servant hates to do, it's doing something for the public.'
>
> Kin Hubbard (American humourist)

BUREAUCRACY

Every country has a certain amount of 'red tape' and Canada is no exception (civil servants are a universal scourge). However, the country isn't one of the world's most bureaucratic and doesn't go out of its way to torment people with red tape; however, business people invariably complain that they have to deal with too much paperwork, especially if they are doing business in several provinces/territories, each with its own rules and regulations (see **Chapter 6** for further information). A notable exception to the absence of superfluous paperwork in Canada stems from the fact that the country is bilingual (English and French) and documentation often has to be produced in both languages.

Canada is also one of the world's least corrupt countries, at least at the official level, and Canadians rarely resort to bribery or use relatives or friends in high places to get things done (corruption certainly isn't a way of life in Canada).

ACCOMMODATION

In most areas of Canada, accommodation (the American English word accommodations is also used) isn't difficult to find. There are a few exceptions, notably in large cities (e.g. Montreal, Toronto, Vancouver and booming Calgary) and their suburbs, where good accommodation is in high demand and short supply. Three-quarters of Canadians live in urban areas, and two-thirds of families own their own homes, compared with 70 per cent in the UK, 55 per cent in France and 40 per cent in Germany. Canada has its own property terminology, which is shown below (note that igloo and teepee aren't included).

- **Condominium:** A flat (apartment), usually in a city or resort where building land is expensive.

- **Townhouse:** A terraced (row) house, with its own private ground-level entrance and attached to the next unit (some townhouse developments are classed as condominiums).

- **Duplex:** One building split into two separate homes with private entrances, either side-by-side or top and bottom, usually purpose-built. The term can be 'elasticated' to four-plex, i.e. one building split into four homes. Some are purpose-built condominiums, while others are large single family homes converted into two units.

- **Bungalow and bi-level:** Bungalows usually have only one floor, but can be bi-level or split-level with a basement, where the main floor has been raised so that the basement has windows above ground level.

- **One-and-a-half storey:** A two-storey house in which the upper floor rooms have a sharply pitched roof and gable ends, reducing useable floor space.

- **Standard two-storey:** A detached house on its own plot, usually with two or three bedrooms.

- **Executive home:** A detached house on its own large plot, with at least four bedrooms and two bathrooms.

- **Mobile home (trailer):** A mobile home (usually in a mobile home or trailer park in a rural area), on blocks, connected to utilities and mains sewerage. Trailers are a cheap option for buyers and renters.

Rental Property

Rental accommodation is freely available in most areas of Canada. Most property is rented unfurnished (although it usually contains at

least a stove and refrigerator) on a monthly or yearly basis. Rental costs vary enormously and are highest in metropolitan areas, notably Toronto and Vancouver. The laws concerning rental accommodation vary from province to province and even from city to city.

> 'Canada is like a loft apartment over a really great party. Like: "Keep it down, eh?"'
>
> Robin Williams (American comedian and actor)

Buying a Home

Nearly all Canadians buy and sell their homes through estate agents (realtors). The three types of estate agent are: vendor's agent (who works for the vendor), purchaser's agent (who works for the purchaser) and dual agent (who works for both). Estate agents' fees are negotiable in Canada, but are usually in the 3 to 7 per cent range. Canada has an online multiple listing system (MLS) that contains details of all properties for sale across the country, so you don't have to traipse around a number of agents.

As well as agents' fees, buying property in Canada involves the payment of property purchase tax or land transfer fees (0.5 to 2 per cent of the purchase price, excluding Alberta, rural Nova Scotia and Saskatchewan); goods and services tax and provincial sales tax in some provinces (it's normally included in the quoted price); survey fees; and legal and registration fees for the deed and mortgage (as well as other mortgage-related fees).

BUYING OR RENTING A CAR

Renting a Car

Car rental (Canadians don't use the term 'car hire') is popular in Canada, due to its vast size, and when travelling long distances most Canadians travel by air and rent a car on arrival (air travellers represent 80 per cent of car rental business). When renting a car, it's important to ensure that you have sufficient liability insurance. Insurance is usually included in the basic cost, although it may be restricted to the province where you rent a car, and there may be a high surcharge for inter-province travel.

You should check whether out-of-province insurance and collision (or loss) damage waiver (CDW/

> Winter driving can be dangerous in Canada. If you aren't experienced of driving on snow and ice, you're better off using public transport.

LDW) are included and, if not, how much they will cost. You should also ask whether cover includes personal accident insurance (PAI), supplementary liability or extended protection insurance (SL/EPI) and personal effects cover (PEC), which are automatically included in most private policies but may be excluded (or severely limited) from rental policies. CDW alone can cost as much as $20 per day.

Rental cars are graded into classes by body size, not engine capacity, e.g. sub-compact (the smallest), compact, mid-size and full size. Many companies also rent luxury models, convertibles (roadsters) and sports cars, four-wheel drive vehicles (SUVs), people carriers or mini-vans (with space for seven passengers) and mini-buses (which can carry up to 11 passengers). Apart from off-road vehicles, rental vehicles usually have automatic transmission.

Canadian rental companies won't rent to anyone under 21, and with some companies the age limit is 25. Those that do rent to people under 25 may levy a 'young driver' surcharge. If you have a foreign driving licence, you usually need an International Driver's Permit (IDP), which must be used in conjunction with your foreign licence and may not be accepted on its own. If a number of drivers are planning to drive a vehicle, they must all have an IDP.

Buying a Car

New Cars

Although it's difficult to make exact comparisons between new car prices in different countries (due to fluctuating exchange rates and the different levels of standard equipment), new cars are cheaper in Canada than in most other countries. The dealer mark-up is much lower, and most of his profit is made on options and selling finance and insurance.

The basic or sticker price (e.g. in an advertisement or showroom) may, however, provide little indication of the on-the-road price, which may be a lot more. Many options may already be fitted to a showroom model, and you have to pay for them whether you want them or not (or look elsewhere). Always check that any stated options are in fact present on a car by asking the salesperson to show or demonstrate them.

Almost 1.7 million new motor vehicles were sold in Canada in 2006 – the second-highest volume ever recorded.

List prices in Canada don't include GST or provincial sales tax and registration. Many dealers also include a charge, e.g. around $125, for the paperwork associated with buying a car; this is one of the many things you should haggle over. Canadian dealers expect you to haggle, so don't be afraid to walk away if the price isn't right. When sales are slow, dealers may offer incentives such as free Canadian Automobile Association membership, service discounts, options or special equipment, plus a free loan car for up to five days when a repair or service is required.

Used Cars

Used cars (also called second-hand, previously owned or pre-possessed) are also good value in Canada, particularly low-mileage cars less than a year old, where the saving on the new price can be as much as 25 per cent. When buying a second-hand car, you should check carefully for rust, as a huge amount of corrosive salt is used on Canadian roads in winter. Make sure that the vehicle you're buying has adequate cold-weather equipment (i.e. a good heater and an engine-block heater).

When buying a car privately, check that the seller owns it, via the Personal Property Registration Office in the provincial capital, and obtain a bill of sale, the proper registration and copies of all financial transactions. Check the registration month and year on the rear number plate, because if a vehicle is unregistered, you could be held responsible for the past year's registration fee. If a car is unregistered it's also uninsured, and needs temporary insurance before you can drive it on public roads. One of the best places to buy second-hand cars (and to compare prices) is local newspapers. When buying privately, used cars must be paid for in cash or with a certified cheque.

HEALTH SERVICES

Canadians are healthy people, outlived only by the Japanese and Icelanders. Perhaps the stereotypical picture of them is correct, and their good health is due to the outdoor activity they favour: sliding around on the ice and snow, hitting each other with hockey sticks and running away from bears.

State Healthcare

Each province or territory has its own compulsory healthcare

> 'Canadians don't deal with the same kind of health care problems and traumas we face. They have a health care system based on treating hockey injuries and curing sinus infections that come from trying to pronounce French vowels.'
>
> P. J. O'Rourke (American political satirist & writer)

system funded by taxes. As in many countries, harsh economic reality has recently led to cuts, but thanks to Medicare – Canada's government-sponsored cradle-to-grave health insurance – healthcare is of a very high standard, providing free basic treatment to Canadian citizens, permanent residents and refugees. In some provinces you must contribute, while in others it's 'free', i.e. paid for by general taxes rather than specific payments. Many Canadians also have private health insurance to pay for treatment that isn't covered by Medicare or to obtain faster or more specialised treatment.

Although it's generally referred to as Medicare, the name of the public health scheme varies from province to province. For example, in Alberta, it's the Alberta Health Care Insurance Plan (AHCIP), in British Columbia it's called Health Insurance BC, in Ontario it's the Ontario Health Insurance Plan (OHIP) and in Quebec it's known as the *Régie de l'Assurance-Maladie du Québec*.

If you qualify for free healthcare, you should register and apply for a health card as soon as possible after your arrival, by visiting the office of the provincial Ministry of Health in the city or town where you're living.

Doctors

The usual way to find a doctor is to ask your colleagues, friends, neighbours or acquaintances if they can recommend someone (but don't rely on their recommendations alone). The availability of medical services varies greatly with the area, and in remote areas, doctors and other medical practitioners may be scarce. All doctors operate on an appointment system, and you cannot just turn up during office hours and expect to be seen (unless you're going to a clinic where appointments are unnecessary). If you're an urgent case, your doctor will usually see you immediately, but you must still phone in advance.

Emergency Treatment

Canadian emergency medical services are among the best in the world. The action to take in an emergency depends on the degree of urgency. In a life-threatening emergency you should call 911. If necessary, an ambulance will be sent, usually staffed by paramedics and equipped with cardiac, oxygen and other emergency equipment. In Alberta and British Columbia, you must pay for an ambulance, while in other provinces they're free for emergencies. Alberta has a fleet of helicopter ambulances, the STARS air ambulance, used for emergencies in mountainous regions. Each region of Canada has a poison control number, listed at the front of phone books.

The life expectancy in Canada for both sexes combined surpassed 80 years for the first time in 2004, increasing from 79.9 years to 80.2.

Medicines

Medicines can be obtained from pharmacies, drugstores and supermarkets (many of which contain pharmacies), and may be cheaper than in other developed countries (although more expensive than in the US). A chain with branches throughout Canada is Shoppers Drug Mart. Pharmacies are packed with medicines for every ailment under the sun (hypochondriacs will think they've died and gone to heaven), and they may stock medicines that are available in other countries on prescription only.

However, there are strict controls on the sale of most medicines in Canada, where some medicines sold freely in other countries require a doctor's prescription. Some prescription drugs are covered by the provincial healthcare system and are therefore cheaper for residents. Many over the counter drugs, however, are more expensive than in the USA, although generic brands may not be. Many pharmacists keep a record of customers and the medicines dispensed to them, and you may be asked for personal details if you're a new customer.

At least one pharmacy is open in most towns during the evenings and on Sundays, for the emergency dispensing of medicines. A list is posted on the doors of pharmacies and published in local newspapers and guides. In most large cities, some pharmacies are open for 24 hours, seven days per week, and some provide a free delivery service in the local area.

Childbirth & Abortion

The traditional place to give birth in Canada is in the maternity ward

Abortion is legal in Canada when carried out by a qualified doctor, and over 100,000 are performed annually, although the government elected in early 2006 might review and tighten the abortion policy.

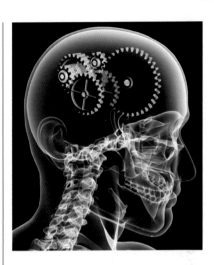

of a hospital, where a stay of three days is usual. If you wish to have your child at home, you must find a doctor and/or midwife who is willing to attend you. Some doctors are opposed to home births, particularly in cases where there could be complications, when specialists and special hospital facilities may be required.

For hospital births, you can usually decide (with the help of your doctor or midwife) the hospital where you wish to have your baby, but you should make sure that it has the facilities you require; for example, an epidural specialist. Your doctor may refer you to an obstetrician or you can find your own. In Canada, doctors are responsible for educating and supporting women during the childbearing period.

Hospitals

Canada has many excellent hospitals and clinics, including some 900 general public hospitals, 225 special public hospitals and 85 private hospitals (there are plans to build more of these). If you're a Medicare patient, you receive free accommodation, healthcare and meals, but must usually share a room with two or three other patients (if you want a private room you must

pay extra). You may need to wait for non-urgent treatment; waiting lists vary according to the budget available and political priorities. A general community hospital is adequate for most medical problems, and caters for surgery, internal medicine, obstetrics and paediatrics. For major surgery and serious illness, you're usually better off at a university or teaching hospital, where specialist skills are available (or in a hospital or clinic that specialises in your illness).

Block Parent

The Block Parent program of Canada is a unique volunteer organisation that operates throughout Canada. Their distinctive red and white 'Block Parent' window sign in the window of a home tells children, seniors and others that help is at hand if they are lost, frightened, or in distress (🖳 www.blockparent.ca).

Emergency Services

Canadian emergency wards aren't as overstretched as those in the US, partly because there are fewer shootings! A blip usually occurs on the first day of snowfall, when hundreds of 'fender-benders' occur on the roads, and the emergency services are stretched by whiplash injuries to motorists who delayed changing to winter tyres. The emergency services in the vicinity of popular skiing areas are trained to deal with sports injuries.

INSURANCE

Car Insurance

Car insurance is compulsory throughout Canada (a minimum of third party) and drivers must carry proof of insurance at all times. Car insurance is expensive and in some provinces must be purchased through the province's public insurance corporation. In others, you can split it between private corporations, independent insurance brokers and your bank's insurance division.

Many provinces have implemented 'no-fault' schemes, whereby accident victims, irrespective of fault, may claim compensation from their insurers for injuries. These schemes range from 'pure no-fault' (in Quebec and Manitoba), where there are no restrictions on claims, to 'threshold no-fault' (in Ontario and some other provinces), where certain limits are specified, above which lawsuits are permitted. Thresholds can be monetary (e.g. a certain value of medical expenses) or medical (i.e. a debilitating injury, or loss or impairment of bodily functions, etc.).

Newcomers to Canada may have difficulty obtaining car insurance at a reasonable cost, particularly if they come from the UK or another country where people drive on the 'wrong' side of the road. Insurers also require a complete record of your insurance history and no-claims discount, and may not accept evidence that's satisfactory in most other countries, e.g. renewal requests and certificates of insurance for a number of years (which they claim isn't proof that you kept the policies running throughout the year). The maximum no-claims discount for foreigners may be lower than for Canadians (e.g. 40 per cent), on the basis that they're unused to Canadian road rules and roads, and particularly to driving in severe winter weather.

Health Insurance

If you're living or working in Canada and aren't covered by Medicare or a company policy, it's extremely risky not to have private health insurance for your family, as you could be faced with some very high medical bills. When deciding on the kind and extent of health insurance, make sure that it covers all your family's present and possible future health needs before you receive a large bill. If you're in Canada for only a limited period, you may be covered by a travel policy or an international health policy.

As the cost of Medicare continues to rise, and federal and provincial governments reduce the cover, an increasing number of Canadians are turning to private insurance (called extended health cover) to cover them for non-insured hospital and medical expenses. Over a third of Canadians have extended health cover. Canadians spend several billion dollars per year on private health insurance, which typically covers the cost of private hospital rooms, special-duty nursing, paramedic services and eye treatment.

Social Insurance

Federal and provincial/territorial governments share the responsibility for social insurance (the name for social security in Canada), which includes benefits for the unemployed, the aged, the disabled and those with low incomes. Social insurance contributions are compulsory for most Canadian residents and are deducted from salaries by employers.

House Insurance

If you're buying a home in Canada with a mortgage, your lender will insist that it's covered by a homeowner's insurance policy. When the mortgage is paid off, it's wise to continue the insurance cover (and it's wise to have it even if you don't need a mortgage), as many people lose their homes each year as

a result of fires or natural disasters such as landslips, fires and floods. Many insurers insist that you insure your home for at least 80 per cent of the replacement cost. If you insure for less than 80 per cent, you receive a pro rata settlement of any claim, however small.

EDUCATION

Canada has no national education system: the ten provinces and three territories manage their own education. The 13 often disagree on the fundamentals of policy, e.g. at which grade pupils transfer from elementary to secondary school, how many years' schooling is compulsory and how schools should be funded. Relocating families are often distressed to discover that their children will have to repeat a grade, because the one they've just completed doesn't cover the syllabus to pass into the next grade in their new province or territory.

That said, full-time education is compulsory in all provinces and territories and this includes the children of foreign nationals, permanently or temporarily resident in Canada. However, admission to a public school for foreign children is dependent on the type and duration of the visa granted to their parents, and free schooling may not be available. Compulsory schooling in Canada usually begins at the age of 5, 6 or 7 and continues until between 16 and 18; the typical Canadian receives 12 or 13 years of education. The school year in Canada runs from the first week of September to the end of June (ten months) and is divided into terms or semesters.

Education in public (i.e. not private) primary and secondary schools is free, but parents must pay student fees of between $5 and $200 per year for extra-curricular classes such as art and music. Most students attend public schools and only 5 per cent of Canadian children are privately educated. Some public schools have special programmes for extremely bright children. There are no school uniforms in public schools.

School districts are usually run on geographic lines, but sometimes on linguistic or religious ones. Any religion with sufficient followers, for example, has the right to set up exclusive schools. Some English-speaking Canadians enrol their children in the French Immersion system, even in the west: all study and communication is in French, even during breaks. In some major cities, children are taught in a variety of foreign languages, e.g. in Vancouver, some schools teach in Cantonese, Japanese, Korean or Punjabi. Because of this flexibility, some places in Canada have a number of different school boards, run on various linguistic and religious lines. On Saturdays, many children attend a private local school, teaching in their native language.

The primary language of instruction in most Canadian schools is English, the exception being Quebec, where it's primarily French, although some communities have classes in both languages. In fact, most pupils in Canada receive lessons in both of the country's official languages. The closer you are to Quebec, the more important it is to learn French.

In most regions of Canada, it's necessary to send your child to the public school that serves the area where you live, and it's difficult to get your child accepted at a public school in another area. For this reason, homes within the catchment area of desirable schools are in demand and more expensive. Due to Canada's huge size, some children have to travel quite a distance to their nearest school; in rural areas, pupils ride to the nearest school in big yellow buses (children are picked up and dropped outside their homes), sometimes spending an hour on the bus each way. It's common for pupils to have time to do all their homework on the bus.

The internet has helped parents in Canada's far-flung corners (of which there are many) who want to teach their children at home. In recent years, government-sponsored distance-learning programmes have been improved, some aimed at First Nation peoples in the remoter northern regions of Canada.

Higher Education

Higher education in Canada is referred to as post-secondary (high school) education, and refers to study beyond secondary school level. It assumes that a student has undertaken 12 or 13 years of study and has a General Educational Diploma (GED). Students with inferior marks can take two years of university transfer courses at a college, before applying to university. Mature students aged over 25 are also admitted to these courses, whether or not they have a GED, though if they don't, they must take GED 'equivalency exams'.

Canada offers three levels of university education: undergraduate studies (bachelor's degree), graduate studies (master's degree) and postgraduate studies (doctorate). The country has 77 universities and 146 community colleges, with a wide

Around 75 per cent of Canadians proceed to some form of higher education after high school – one of the highest proportions in the world.

variety of admission requirements and programmes. The total annual university enrolment is some 600,000 full-time and 250,000 part-time students, over half of whom are female; 30,000 are overseas students.

The academic standards of colleges and universities vary greatly, and some institutions are better known for the quality of their social life or sports teams than for their academic achievements. Establishments range from vast educational 'plants', offering the most advanced training available, to small, intimate private academies emphasising personal instruction and a preference for the humanities.

UTILITIES

Electricity

Every householder, whether in an apartment or a house, has his own electricity meter. This is usually located in the basement of an apartment block or outside a house, where it can be read when a property is unoccupied. When you buy a new property, you pay a 'new meter charge' (connection fee) of around $10. In many areas, electricity is charged at peak and slack period (off-peak) rates according to the time of day and the season (usually summer and winter). Electricity costs vary with the area, e.g. from 5¢ to 8¢ per kilowatt-hour (KWH or KWHR). A small supply fee (service fee) must be paid every two months.

In Canadian homes, there are no switches on wall sockets, so electrical appliances should be fitted with their own on/off switches. Light switches are usually on when in the UP position (some switches operate from left to right), which may be indicated by a red spot. Standard and other lamps often have two- or three-way settings that provide levels of brightness (e.g. bright, medium and dim). Often, lamp switches (or knobs) must be turned or pushed/pulled rather than pressed.

Gas

Gas (usually natural) is available in most Canadian cities, when the same company may supply you with gas and electricity. You receive one bill for both, with gas and electricity costs itemised separately. Gas is available in all but the remotest areas of Canada, although most modern houses are all-electric and aren't connected to the gas supply. When you buy a new property there's a

In 2006, there were 18m mobile phones in Canada.

new meter charge (connection fee) of around $25. Outside cities, and in remote areas, gas may be supplied in bottles. Gas is usually billed by the gigajoule, which costs between around $5 and $7.

Telephone

Canadians are among the most habitual telephone users in the world, making more calls than people in almost any other country. Most Canadian households have at least one fixed-line phone, and 70 per cent also have a mobile or cell phone. Homes in Canada (new and old) are invariably wired for telephone services, and many homes have points (phone jacks) in almost every room.

To have a phone connected, contact a local phone company (their numbers are listed in telephone directories). You need to provide your name, current and previous address, social insurance number (if you have one; if not, your passport number), the type of monthly service you require, your choice of long-distance company, and how you'd like your directory listing to appear, or whether you'd like an ex-directory (unlisted) number.

Unless you're a previous customer, have a credit history with Visa or MasterCard or can prove that you own your home, you must pay a $200 deposit with your first bill. This is refunded, with interest, after

one year. Alternatively, you can find a co-signer, who has an account with the phone company, who will be responsible if you abscond without paying the bill. You're given a number when you apply.

Water

In many areas, you don't receive a water bill because the cost is included in local property taxes. In other areas, there's a charge; each building or apartment has its own water meter, and you're billed each month (or quarter) for the water you use. Bills may include a meter charge, e.g. $10 per month. Water rates are typically 30¢ to 60¢ per cubic metre, and water bills are $25 per month for a one-bedroom apartment, $70 for a 2,000ft2 (186m2) house and $200 or more for a four-bedroom, four-bathroom house.

Some provinces occasionally have restrictions on the use of water during the summer months, e.g.

for swimming pools, washing cars or watering gardens, when there may be bans between sunrise and sunset. Canadians usually drink water straight from their house supply, although some people find the taste of purifying chemicals (e.g. chlorine) unpleasant, and prefer to drink bottled water. Householders in many areas fit filters to cold-water taps to provide water for drinking or cooking. It's inadvisable to drink water from rivers, lakes, and streams in country areas because of the risk of beaver fever (giardiasis).

COUNCIL SERVICES

Rubbish Collection

Weekly household rubbish (garbage) collection services are made from most homes, except those in remote areas, where householders must take their waste to a tip (dump). Details of collection times and days are provided by local councils, and are usually made on the same day and time each week. Rubbish is normally collected from the kerb (curb) and must be put in mobile wheelie bins or bags. There might be a limit on the amount and/or weight of rubbish that will be collected each week, and there can be a charge for additional amounts, e.g. $2 per extra bag.

Councils also occasionally collect bulk household rubbish including scrap iron, metal, timber, white goods (including refrigerators), mattresses and old furniture. A schedule of collection dates may be sent to households and published at council offices, libraries and in local newspapers. Other waste must be taken to a local council rubbish dump, where you may have to pay if you cannot prove you're a local resident.

Councils also collect recyclable materials such as green waste (prunings, grass, leaves, etc. – used to make compost) and recyclable materials (paper, cardboard, glass, and plastic – see below).

Recycling

Over the past decade, concern about the environment has led to an increase in recycling in Canada. However, long before the growing levels of waste began to cause concern, recycling was a part of everyday life: since the '80s, most medium-size and large municipalities have had recycling schemes, whereby items such as paper, glass, aluminium, plastics, PVC (of various types) and steel cans can be separately disposed

An important part of Canada Post's job is dealing with over a million letters every year for Santa Claus. Santa tries to reply to them all, with Canada Post employees pitching in by volunteering to help.

of. There are various kerbside collection systems in different parts of Canada, using a variety of containers: blue boxes, green boxes, green bins, grey boxes and blue bags.

> 'Television is very educational. Every time it comes on I go into the other room and read a book.'
>
> Groucho Marx (American comedian)

CANADA POST

The Canadian postal service is reliable, but not especially cheap or fast. Postage in Canada is the same price, whether an item is going down the road or across the country – which in effect means that local post subsidises the cost of delivery to the (many) remote areas. In 2007, the standard letter rate was 52¢ within Canada, 93¢ to the US and $1.55 elsewhere.

STAYING INFORMED

Television

The average Canadian family watches over 20 hours of television (an essential part of Canadian life) a week; even the most modest motel or hotel boasts a colour TV in every room. Airports and bus stations have coin-operated televisions built into the arms of chairs, and bars, clubs and even launderettes have televisions. The pervasive influence of the US on Canadian television has led the Canadian government to mandate that all Canadian television stations must devote a certain percentage of time each day to Canadian-produced programmes.

Canada has four nationwide television networks: the Canadian Broadcasting Corporation (CBC), the Canadian Television Network (CTV), Global/Canwest and the Société de Radio-Télévision du Canada (SRC), the French-language division of CBC. There are also 40 regional networks.

Unfortunately, most Canadian-made programmes are every bit as mind-numbing as programmes made in the US, particularly those made by small stations with modest budgets. Even the programmes made by CBC can be pretty bad, particularly the poorly disguised clones of popular US programmes, such as *Street Legal* (*LA Law*), *North of 60* (*Northern Exposure*), *Degrassi* (*Saved by the Bell*) and *Side Effects* (*St Elsewhere*). However, not everything is rubbish, and Canadian television produces a big-business soap called *Traders*, and a crime series entitled *Forever Knight*, where the Toronto homicide cop hero is an 800-year-old vampire (a story of everyday life). CBC also shines with its wide range of documentaries and news coverage.

Swearing isn't permitted on tele-vision in Canada, and pornography

isn't available on terrestrial television. Another big difference between television in Canada and the US is the news. Canadian television shows international news, and doesn't descend into meaningless sensationalism (not much, anyway).

Radio

Radio is popular in Canada, and the average Canadian listens to around 14 hours a week. Canada has some 500 local radio stations, and in major cities you generally have a choice of 50 stations, although in remote areas you may be able to receive only a few. Canadian mainstream commercial radio (like commercial TV) is of little interest if you're looking for serious discussion or education, but excellent if you're into music, news or religion. Music stations can be highly specialised, offering easy listening, country and western or rock, although in recent years, many listeners have abandoned music stations for talk radio.

Poor sound quality is a problem on AM, therefore stations are turning to formats that don't require quality sound (three-quarters of Canadians have CD players in their homes or cars, which may have something to do with this). The situation may improve with digital technology, which provides better sound quality and is immune to interference from static or echoes.

> 'George is a radio announcer and when he walks under a bridge you can't hear him talk.'
>
> Steven Wright (American comedian)

If you're looking for serious radio, you need to tune to CBC (💻 www.radio.cbc.ca), government-subsidised at a cost to every Canadian of around 8¢ per day. CBC offers primarily news and public affairs programming (similar to BBC Radio) in English and French, plus a 24-hour cable news service in both languages. It has a Northern service in eight Aboriginal languages, and Radio Canada International (RCI), a short-wave radio service broadcasting around the world in seven languages. CBC started broadcasting in 1937, and has been called the 'ribbon of reason' that holds Canada together (just as the railway was once the 'ribbon of steel'). CBC has two radio channels: Radio One and Radio Two.

Other national radio networks include Radio Canada and the Société de Radio-Télévision du Canada (SRC), which are in French.

One of the most popular shows is the CBC's *This Morning*, which goes out between 9am and noon on weekdays; it's entertaining as well as educational, and provides a well rounded view of the nation's current opinions. *Ideas* is an excellent evening discussion programme, while *The Massey Lectures* are an annual series of lectures spread over a week, given by a leading academic.

The Press

Canada doesn't have much of a national press and most newspapers are regional (covering a province) or local (city or town). Apart from the *National Post*, the closest that Canada has to a national newspaper is the influential and respected *Globe & Mail*, a Toronto newspaper established in 1844, which contains articles and news of interest to Canadians from coast to coast; although it does have a habit of printing condescending statements such as 'out in Vancouver…'. Both are printed regionally – headlines

might be the same but advertising and editorial are regional. This, of course, reinforces regionalism, which Canada has enough of already.

Quality regional newspapers include the *Edmonton Journal*, the *Ottawa Citizen*, the *Toronto Star* and the *Vancouver Sun*. Quebec's newspapers are printed in French, and some other newspapers are printed in both English and French editions.

Over 100 daily newspapers are produced in Canada, many owned by just a few conglomerates. As in many countries, the serious newspapers are usually broadsheets, while the tabloids are more interested in scandal, sex and sport. A third of Canadians (i.e. those living in the major cities) have newspapers delivered to their homes. Newspapers are sold in towns from honour vending machines, where you insert the exact money in a slot and pull down the handle to open the door; you're trusted to take one copy only, hence 'honour'.

Weekly news magazines such as *Maclean's* (known as Maclone's by those who think it's a copy of *Time*) are popular, and a good way to catch up on the most important Canadian and international news. Other popular Canadian magazines include *Canadian Geographic*, *Today's Parent*, *Country Life*, *Now* and *Chatelaine*.

The Internet

Canadians enjoy some of the cheapest internet access in the world (from around $20 per month),

You can find an internet service provider (ISP) in Canada via Canadian ISP (🖳 www.canadianisp.com), which allows you to compare ISPs and their services throughout the country.

and Canada is one of the most 'connected' countries in the world, with two-thirds of adults connected to the internet at home. The highest concentration of internet use is in Alberta and Ontario, and the lowest in Quebec. Internet use from home is more common in households with young people. As in most other countries, a bewildering, ever-changing range of internet packages is available.

However, if you live in a remote area, you should note that Bell Canada hasn't yet upgraded the lines for high speed (broadband) internet, and only a dial-up service is available. Therefore the only way to receive high speed internet may be via a satellite dish, which costs around $70 per month, plus several hundred dollars for equipment and installation.

BANKING

Canada's banking system is dominated by the 'big five' chartered banks (Canadian Imperial Bank of Commerce, BMO Bank of Montreal, Scotiabank, Royal Bank of Canada and TD/Canada Trust), which between them control 80 per cent of all banking assets. The big five have a network of several thousand branches, and offer telephone and internet banking. Many smaller

domestic banks include credit unions (which are increasingly popular because of their range of services, lower charges and friendly service), and, in Quebec, *caisses populaires*, plus over 40 foreign banks.

Accounts

The three types of bank account are: current or cheque (chequing) accounts, savings (deposit) accounts and a combination of the two, known as 'cheque-savings' accounts. Most Canadians have at least one bank account, and most have a number.

Cash

The unit of currency is the Canadian dollar, which is divided into 100 cents (¢). Canadian coins are minted in values of 1¢ (penny), 5¢ (nickel), 10¢ (dime), 25¢ (quarter) and 50¢ (half-dollar, which is rarely seen nowadays), one dollar and two dollars. The penny is copper, the 5, 10, 25 and 50 cent coins are silver-coloured (an amalgam of silver and copper), the $1 coin is 11-sided and gold-coloured, and the $2 has a nickel outer rim and an aluminium-bronze centre. Silver 'dollars' and a

Canadian Banknotes	
Denomination	Illustration (person/building)
$5	Sir Wilfred Laurier (Canada's second Prime Minister)/West Block of Parliament
$10	Sir John A. Macdonald (Canada's father of confederation and first Prime Minister)/Library of Parliament
$20	Queen Elizabeth II/Centre Block of Parliament
$50	William Lyon Mackenzie King, Canada's third Prime Minister/Peace Tower
$100	Sir Robert Borden, Canada's eighth 8th Prime Minister/East Block of Parliament

'$1' pure gold coin, the Maple Leaf, are minted, the price (and value) of which fluctuate with the price of gold and silver.

All coins have an image of Queen Elizabeth II on one side. The $1 coin has a bird (the loon) on the reverse and is called a 'loonie', while the two-dollar coin (which has a polar bear on the reverse) is called a 'twoonie'. Quarters and loonies are the most useful coins, and you should carry some with you for parking meters, bus and underground fares, road tolls, payphones, baggage lockers, vending machines, etc.

Banknotes (bills) are printed in denominations of $5 (blue), $10 (purple), $20 (green), $50 (red), $100 (brown) and $1,000 (purple). Canada no longer has a $1 bill; the $2 bill (red), although still legal tender, is no longer printed and has virtually disappeared. Canadian banknotes are mostly illustrated (on the obverse or front) with politicians (see box) and Parliament buildings (no prize for guessing who had a hand in their design – it was nice of them to include HM Queen Elizabeth II).

Charges

Cheque accounts incur flat fees of between around $4 and $25 per month, depending on your balance and the services offered. All cheque accounts include an internet service as well as phone and branch services, monthly statements, a bill-paying facility, standing orders/direct debits (pre-authorised payments), transfers between accounts and cheque books. Standard, basic cheques are provided free.

Opening Hours

Usual banking hours are from 9am to 5pm, Mondays to Fridays, and from 10am to 3pm on Saturdays, although opening times of individual branches vary. All banks are closed on federal and provincial holidays.

As Canadians effectively work for the government until June every year, 'reducing one's tax burden' is a national sport and an obsession.

CREDIT & CHARGE CARDS

Over 600 institutions in Canada issue credit and charge cards, including American Express (Amex), Diners Club, Discover, MasterCard and Visa. There are over 50m cards in circulation with a combined debt of well over $20bn. Before issuing a credit card, companies require an assurance that you won't disappear owing them a fortune, and will check your bank, employer and credit rating to ensure that you're credit worthy.

It's difficult for newcomers to obtain credit cards, even when they have excellent references, or have previously held credit cards in another country. New arrivals should present a letter of introduction from their bank manager in their home country, regarding their banking status. A credit card company may offer you only a pre-paid card, whereby you deposit money with the credit card company and use the card to spend it! Even with a pre-paid card, you may have a paltry 'credit' limit. It may also be possible to obtain a card from an offshore bank that can be paid in Canadian dollars (or retain your credit cards from your home country until you can obtain one in Canada).

When using a credit card in Canada, you may be subject to a more rigorous check than in other countries. For example, you may be asked for further identification (e.g. a driving licence). On the other hand, many businesses are extremely lax about checking signatures, which makes it easy for crooks to use stolen cards.

TAXES

Income Tax

If you're resident in Canada, you must pay federal and provincial income tax. The calculation of an individual's tax is a two-step process. First, your income liable to federal income tax is calculated, from which you can deduct your personal tax credits and a tax credit for dividend income. The result is your 'basic federal tax payable'. Provincial income tax (except for Quebec) is then calculated by applying the appropriate provincial rate to the 'basic federal tax payable' for the tax year.

Your employer usually deducts income tax from your salary in Canada, while those with business or property income usually pay their income taxes by instalments throughout the year. The Canadian tax system is based on self-assessment, which requires less bureaucracy than in many other countries, but puts the onus on individuals to declare their income correctly. A wealth of tax books and magazines, plus free advice in financial magazines and newspapers, is published, particularly in the few months leading up to 30th April (tax filing day).

Individuals resident in Canada (unless exempt) must file a tax return for the previous tax year (1st January to 31st December) by 30th April, when main post offices remain open until midnight to date stamp tax returns (if you owe tax and are a day late filing, you're charged interest). Individuals aren't permitted to establish a different tax year-end, although corporations are. Corporations must file annual tax returns, although individuals need to file only if they owe taxes or if they're eligible to claim tax credits, such as the child tax credit or a sales tax credit. There are no joint tax returns for married couples and families.

Property Tax

Property tax is levied annually on property owners in all provinces to help pay for local services such as healthcare, primary and secondary education, police and fire services, libraries, public transport, waste disposal, highways and road safety, maintaining trading standards and social services. Tax rates are fixed by communities and are expressed as an amount per $100 or $1,000 (the 'mill' rate) of the assessed value of a property. For example, if your home is valued at $100,000 and your local tax rate is 15 mill (1.5 per cent), your annual property tax bill will be $1,500.

The rating method varies considerably, depending on the province, county and municipality, and different rates occur within a single province (e.g. British Columbia has 1,400 tax rates in its 70 jurisdictions). Property taxes on a house of average value vary from zero, in areas where houses valued below a certain amount are exempt, to over $5,000 per year in high-value communities. In a recent survey, taxes were highest in Winnipeg, Regina and Montreal, averaging

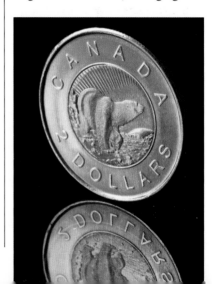

over 2 per cent of a home's market value, and lowest in Saint John (New Brunswick) and Vancouver at less than 1 per cent.

COST OF LIVING

It's difficult to calculate an average cost of living in Canada, as much depends on where you live, your accommodation costs, your family's circumstances and your lifestyle. The cost of living varies from province to province, but is generally similar to the US, and usually lower than Europe, especially the UK. Vancouver, Toronto and Montreal are the most expensive areas to live, while Charlottetown, Winnipeg and Edmonton are much cheaper. A large proportion of your cost of living will be accommodation, unless you're fortunate enough to be able to buy a home outright. Property prices are much higher in British Columbia than elsewhere, and property is also relatively expensive

Cost of Living

In a cost of living survey of 144 cities across six continents, conducted by Mercer Resource Consulting in 2006, Toronto was rated Canada's most expensive city, and was placed 47th out of the most expensive cities in the world (no other Canadian city featured in the top 50). Ottawa was Canada's cheapest city, coming 90th.

in the Northwest Territories and Alberta; the lowest are in Prince Edward Island, New Brunswick and Saskatchewan.

The cost of living in rural areas is, not surprisingly, lower than in the major cities (particularly housing). Even in the most expensive cities, however, the cost of living needn't be astronomical. If you shop wisely, compare prices and services before buying, and don't live too extravagantly, you'll be pleasantly surprised at how little you can live on.

4.

BREAKING THE ICE

One of the best ways to overcome culture shock and feel more at home in Canada is to meet and get acquainted with Canadians. Making new and lasting friends anywhere is never easy, but it's easier in Canada than in many countries – though, of course, there are certain social niceties to be observed. This chapter provides information and advice about important aspects of Canadian society such as sexual attitudes, how to behave in social situations and topics to avoid in conversation.

'I do not believe that friends are necessarily the people you like best, they are merely the people who got there first.'

Peter Ustinov (British actor & writer)

NEIGHBOURS

Canadians don't have as many problems with their neighbours as in some countries because they don't live on top of one another. Canada is a huge country with a relatively tiny population, and there's such a lot of space that cities have usually spread horizontally rather than vertically. This means that a high percentage of Canadians live in detached properties: 68 per cent (compared with, for example, only 25 per cent in the UK), with the lowest percentages in Quebec (46 per cent), British Columbia (55 per cent) and Ontario (58 per cent), the highest in Saskatchewan (76 per cent), Newfoundland and Labrador (75 per cent) and New Brunswick (73 per cent). This means that far fewer Canadians than average live in properties which share walls and/or common areas with neighbours, leading to fewer problems – noise is the main cause of disputes between neighbours. Canada's climate also means that people use their gardens for less of the year than in many countries, which further reduces the noise that people inflict on their neighbours, via children, barbecues, lawnmowers, etc.

Community Life

As soon as you move to a new home, you should try to become part of your local community. Introduce yourself to your immediate neighbours and greet others with a cheery good morning when you meet in the lift or in the entrance. If possible, shop in local stores and get involved in the local community. This gives you the chance to practise your English (if it isn't your mother tongue) and for others to get to know you – receiving a greeting from neighbours and local business people will also help you feel more at home. Although the onus is on you to take the initiative, most Canadians are friendly and polite, and won't be shy about striking up a conversation with you.

It isn't uncommon for neighbours to invite newcomers around for a cup of coffee, although in cities (where people living alongside each other often remain strangers) you may have to go out of your way to meet your neighbours. If you're invited to a barbecue, it's usual to take a bottle of wine, a salad or a six-pack of beer and you may also be asked to bring your own meat or whatever else you wish to eat. Some invitations ask guests to bring along a dish from which everyone can help themselves. Block parties are a feature of Canadian life, when Canadians invite their neighbours for a party to celebrate Canada Day or another national holiday.

SEXUAL ATTITUDES

Canadian moral attitudes vary with the gender, age and background; for example, the older generation, those from rural areas and some immigrant communities are much more conservative than most of the younger generation in the major cities. Canada has a much more liberal attitude to teenage sex than some other countries. The age of

consent in Canada is generally 14, but increases to 18 where one partner is in a 'position of trust or authority'. The current Conservative government may raise the age of consent to 16, while retaining a 'close in age' exception, allowing 14- and 15-year-olds to have sexual relationships with individuals less than five years older than themselves.

Canada's attitude to prostitution is unclear and confusing: while prostitution is theoretically legal, practising it isn't. The trend in many developed countries has been to decriminalise or turn a blind eye to prostitution, but this has been slow to take root in Canada. That said, some Canadian police forces operate a policy of prosecuting soliciting on the street but ignoring it if it happens behind closed doors.

Canada isn't overly liberal about public nudity either (probably because there's little opportunity for it in such northern climes). Under Canadian law it's illegal to be naked in a public place or in a

> 'I believe that sex is the most beautiful, natural and wholesome thing that money can buy.'
>
> Steve Martin (American actor)

private place where you might be exposed to public view (such as a back garden). Canada has a number of beaches where nude sunbathing and swimming are accepted (notably in Halifax in Nova Scotia and Vancouver in British Columbia), although there are only a couple of 'clothing-optional' beaches.

Pornography can legally be sold in Canada to those aged 18 and over and no specific law controls its distribution, although most pornography is sold in 'adult stores' or via websites. Child pornography is illegal and the government is introducing what it maintains are the most stringent laws in the world against internet-accessed child pornography.

While young Canadians enjoy normal, healthy sex, Canada's baby-boomers (those aged between 40 and 64) apparently devote an average of over 30 hours a week to watching television and using the internet, but only a fraction of that to being romantic or having sex (although most people would consider 30 hours a week a bit excessive). Many older Canadians blame stress, fatigue and work as major obstacles to a better sex life.

> 'If a man speaks in a forest and there's no woman around to hear him, is he still wrong?'
>
> Rich Makin

Men

Many Canadian men view themselves as traditional men and love hockey, barbecuing large hunks of meat, all kinds of machinery – lawnmowers, powerboats, chain saws, snowmobiles, quad bikes and SUVs (sports utility vehicles, i.e. urban jeeps), etc. – and outdoor pursuits such as camping, fishing, hunting and skiing. Despite being well educated, Canadian men try to avoid being seen as too intellectual, which wouldn't go down well with the guys when watching hockey in the bar. Women are regarded as partners who provide food and run the home and Canadian men have a pragmatic relationship with their wives and girlfriends; they don't expect doe-eyed romance and think of themselves and their wives as a team.

Some Canadian men, however, don't conform to the above stereotype. So-called SNAGS (sensitive new age guys) are a reaction against the traditional Canadian male. They enjoy shopping and housework, ride bicycles rather than drive gas-guzzling SUVs, drink fair-trade coffee and are sensitive souls who know about art, French

cinema and interior design. The average SNAG is married to a creative, fey, hemp-wearing woman and the couple usually haven't decided whether to have children. SNAGS are an urban rather than rural phenomenon and are most common in liberal, environmentalist Vancouver and its surrounds.

Women

Canada's pioneering history has contributed to its women being practical, no-nonsense people. However, despite their integral part in the 'taming' of Canada, women didn't achieve 'equality' until 1929, after which they could vote, own land and make decisions concerning their children. The Second World War reinforced women's emancipation, as they successfully took on many traditionally male roles while their men-folk were away in Europe or elsewhere.

Canadian women don't allow themselves to be dominated by men and are well aware that Canada is a country where everybody is equal and free. Neither do they pander to male ideas of beauty and they aren't usually clothes horses, forever fiddling with their hair and make-up; comfort and practicality are their main sartorial considerations. Jeans and tracksuits are much preferred to *haute couture* – unkind souls have suggested that a Canadian woman's idea of femininity is donning a pink tracksuit.

Despite their refusal to play the 'little woman' and the fact that half of them work full time, Canadian women do much more than their fair share of the housework and child-rearing. Women remain under-represented in the top tiers of business and in politics, although this is changing. In 1970, women comprised just 2 per cent of Canada's politicians, which had risen to 11.5 per cent by 1988 and to 23 per cent by 2001.

Canada's various ethnic minorities have different attitudes to the 'correct' role of women, which has led to conflict in some communities between parents with traditional views and daughters who have been born and bred in liberal, gender-equal Canada. In some Asian communities, for example, parents find it difficult to accept that their daughters expect to be treated in the same way as their sons, with equal levels of independence and opportunity. In Quebec women have taken

'The trouble with women is that they never put the toilet seat back up.'

Simon Nye (English comedian)

longer to gain equality with men than in Canada's other 'European' communities, which stems from the province's conservative, rural make-up and the influence of the Catholic Church. However, the last 30 years has seen a huge decline in the influence of the Church and the importance of agriculture, leading to more equality for women.

Homosexuals

Canada has more rights for LGBT (lesbian, gay, bisexual and transgender) people than most other nations, including the US and UK, and is arguably the most gay-friendly nation in the world. Homosexuality was decriminalised in Canada in 1967 by the then Justice Minister and Attorney General (later Prime Minister) Pierre Trudeau, who famously commented, 'There's no place for the state in the bedrooms of the nation.'

In 1977, Quebec became the first jurisdiction (larger than a city or county) in the world to prohibit discrimination based on sexual orientation and in 1978, the Canada Immigration Act was amended, removing a ban on homosexuals as immigrants. Same-sex marriage was legalised across Canada by the Civil Marriage Act enacted on July 20th 2005. Since 2003, court decisions have legalised same-sex marriages in eight out of the ten provinces and in one of the three territories (covering 90 per cent of Canada's population). Most of the legal benefits associated with marriage had been extended to cohabiting same-sex couples by 1999.

However, tolerance of homo-sexuality and equal rights for gay people isn't universal in Canada. At the end of 2006, the Conservative government brought in a motion asking whether the question of same-sex marriage should be reopened to support the traditional definition of marriage. The motion was defeated (by 175 to 123) and the most recent opinion poll on the subject of same-sex marriage (in mid-2006) showed that Canadians accept gay marriage by a 59-33 majority (with the balance undecided). Nevertheless, the numbers against legal recognition of gay rights is probably

'I don't know if my first experience was heterosexual or homosexual because I was too polite to ask.'

Gore Vidal (American author)

lower in Canada than almost any other country.

Some of Canada's cities are noted for the size and vibrancy of their gay communities and gay 'scene'. Vancouver has a substantial gay community, while Ottawa's has a smaller but lively gay scene. Montreal is reputed to have the largest 'Gay Village' in North America, while Toronto is the home of Woody's (on Church Street), the world's most popular gay bar.

MEETING PEOPLE

Meeting people in Canada isn't a problem, as most people are friendly and Canadians are happy to socialise with their colleagues and business associates (unlike people in some countries), although they tend to go home early. Among the many 'facilities' for meeting people and making friends in Canada are:

- **Work:** Meeting people isn't a problem if you're an employee, although you may have to take the initiative and ask others to join you for lunch or coffee, or a drink or meal after work. Office parties occur at Christmas, birthdays and on special occasions such as farewell get-togethers for employees leaving their jobs.

- **Babysitting co-ops:** Groups of local women with young children sometimes organise a rota for babysitting each other's children, which is a good way to meet people of your own age who are similarly surviving on two hours' sleep a night and covered in baby food. It's also a good way for your children to make friends so that they'll have someone other than you to torment.

- **Expatriate networks:** Expatriates from many countries run a variety of associations, clubs and organisations in cities (ask at embassies and consulates for information).

- **Local clubs:** If you want to integrate into your local community, one of the best ways is to join a local club. Clubs organise a wide range of social activities including art and music classes, bridge and chess evenings, local history tours, food and wine classes and evenings, sports activities, and theatre and cinema outings. You can find out about local clubs and societies from town halls, libraries and local newspapers. You should also consider joining a local sports club – Canadians are keen sports people and sports clubs are ideal for meeting people and keeping fit at the same time.

- **Newcomers' groups:** These hold monthly lunches and/or meetings in members' homes and are a good way to meet other newcomers to your area.

- **Schools:** School playgrounds provide a ready-made opportunity for contact with other parents. Check school notice boards for news about forthcoming events and meetings. Most schools have parents' associations, which are worth joining and welcome offers of help. Many associations organise social events for parents as well as fund-raising activities and other ways of improving school facilities.

If you're retired, you may find that your local council publishes a programme of recreational activities for the retirees in your area. Most councils publish a calendar of local sports and social events, and libraries provide information about local associations, clubs, groups and organisations.

Singles Scene

There's a vibrant singles scene in Canadian cities, where it's easy for young people to meet. However, it isn't so easy for middle-aged or mature people and, as in other developed countries, a wealth of dating agencies and organisations arrange social events for more mature singles. Note that singles' clubs in cities and large towns tend to be dominated by women. Internet dating has also become popular with single Canadians.

Paying

Canadians don't automatically pay the bill when they invite someone to lunch or dinner, and unless they offer to pay (either before or at the end of the meal) you should expect to pay your share. Canadians usually assume they will go 'Dutch' (i.e. each person pays for what he has had) when making casual arrangements to go out. On more informal occasions, those present invariably buy their own drinks and Canadians rarely buy rounds.

INVITATIONS

Receiving Invitations

Invitations to private homes are rare in Canada but are more common in the western provinces than elsewhere. Lunch invitations usually mean you should arrive

around 11.30am or noon and lunch is usually served between midday and 1pm. Dinner is served any time between 6 and 8pm and you're normally asked to arrive half an hour earlier for drinks. You should never arrive earlier than suggested, but arriving very late is also considered bad manners (when it's often better never to arrive at all). Invitations usually extend to your partner or spouse, but if your host isn't aware that you have a partner, it's acceptable to ask for him or her to be included. If you have children, you shouldn't take them with you unless your host specifically invites them.

Dress Code

Canadians are casual dressers and you can generally wear anything in most public places (bearing in mind, of course, the need to protect yourself against the elements, especially during winter). However, some restaurants and private clubs have dress rules which may exclude jeans, T-shirts, trainers and shorts, requiring instead 'smart casual' dress, i.e. long trousers (slacks) and a short- or long-sleeved shirt (with a collar) for men and a dress or skirt and blouse for women. If you're expected to wear anything more formal – such as a suit or a tie – it will be indicated in the invitation or you will be told. For casual social events during the day, such as a barbecue, shorts are usual, with flip flops, sandals or trainers, and a T-shirt. Canadians dress up for formal occasions such as weddings and celebrations, but these are exceptions.

Gifts

You may wish to present your hosts with a gift as thanks for their hospitality. Usual gifts include a bottle of good wine or a box of chocolates. A bouquet of flowers is suitable for special occasions such as a birthday or anniversary and is always gratefully received by ladies. It's common to ask whether you can provide a salad or dessert. Sometimes an invitation will ask you to 'bring a plate', which means a plate of food; this is common for barbecues (barbies) and informal lunches, where food is pooled and everybody helps themselves.

The Meal

Some Canadians serve one or two courses plus dessert at lunch and dinner, although many people have one or two rather than three courses. Portions for guests are invariably generous and the host may insist on serving you extra – it's rude to decline as it looks as if you don't like the food. Bread and water may be provided, although they aren't customary among Canadians and you may have to ask for them (don't expect fresh bread to be served at meals).

You should keep your hands above the table at all times and, in common with most western countries, cutlery is used from the outside inwards, e.g. the cutlery on the extreme left and right is for the first course. Canadians tend to use a knife and fork in the British fashion, holding the fork upside down in their left hand and the knife in their right, although some eat in the American fashion and cut up their food first and eat it with a fork in the right hand.

Drinks are usually offered on arrival and may consist of cocktails, beer or wine, which may be accompanied by appetizers. Beer or wine may be served with the meal, although wine is more common, especially in Quebec. The host may serve coffee after the meal. You should remain seated while the meal is served, although it's considered polite to offer to clear up.

CONVERSATION

Common Topics

In common with many people who have British antecedents, Canadians talk about the weather a lot. They often do so in the form of a question, e.g. 'Cold enough for you today?'– delivered casually as frozen birds drop from the trees. Canadians particularly like to talk about winter weather. Even though many of them try to avoid all but minimal contact with it, they like to exaggerate the temperatures they've experienced

and endured. In the average Canadian weather conversation, it doesn't get really cold until it's -40C and you're outside wearing nothing but a stupid grin and a paper hat. The exception to this rule is the inhabitants of southern British Columbia, who are much more likely to drone on about how balmy their weather is – positively Hawaiian in fact. You can, however, puncture their boasting by pointing

> 'Don't knock the weather; nine-tenths of the people couldn't start a conversation if it didn't change once in a while.'
>
> Kin Hubbard (cartoonist and humourist)

out that British Columbia is also as wet as a haddock's bathing costume.

Another favourite conversational gambit is complaining, generally about Americans, the government and, of course, the weather. The recurring Canadian complaint about Americans is that they invariably seem indifferent to Canada and know little about it. Safe topics of conversation usually include hockey, American football and other topical sports, films (movies), gun control in the US (always a hit topic), Toronto's overbearing influence (unless, of course, you're in Toronto), the Canadian healthcare system and the failings of politicians.

Faux Pas

Canada's national animal is the beaver and Canadians are proud of the beast. So it's best not to ask them why they didn't choose something more impressive, like the eagle – there are more of them in British Columbia alone than in the whole of the US and yet the eagle is the Americans' national animal. Other suitable alternatives might

have been the bear, bison, musk ox or wolf, rather than a large, buck-toothed water rat that slaps its tail on the water to warn of danger. It's also best to avoid asking why, despite it being the national animal, some provinces (e.g. Manitoba) spend hundreds of thousands of dollars every year bulldozing and dynamiting beaver dams to stop them flooding arable land, roads and train lines.

More seriously, the following topics are best avoided: Quebec separation, Anglophone-Francophone relations, the value of the Canadian dollar (usually falling), politics in Asia or Europe (which many Canadians have little knowledge of or interest in), aboriginal land rights, the immigration policy and the brain drain to the US. Controversial remarks about religion are best avoided in the Prairie Provinces, Canada's so-called 'Bible Belt'. Although Canadians joke about the amount of tundra their country has and the harshness of Canadian winters, it's unwise to overplay the 'frozen north' humour.

Don't expect an English-speaking Canadian to know French well, or vice versa, although it's more common for Francophone Canadians to be bilingual than Anglophone

Montreal is home to the bilingual (English and French) 'Just for Laughs' festival, one of the largest in the world. A television programme of the same name features highlights from the festival.

Canadians. When beginning a conversation, it's polite to use the native language of the person you're talking to. If you don't speak that language, it's good manners to tell the other person and to ask if they speak your language.

SOCIAL TABOOS

Canadians are generally quite relaxed and there isn't a long list of social do's and don'ts to acquaint yourself with. Punctuality is valued, but Canadians aren't obsessive about it – especially in French areas, where people are often a little late. People are more uptight about smoking and it isn't done to light a cigarette (or anything else) in the home of a non-smoker. The exception to this is (as ever) Quebec, which has a continental European devil-may-care attitude to smoking, which remains popular.

Failing to thank and compliment a host or hostess is regarded as rude, as is telephoning or visiting people uninvited late at night. Avoid asking people their age or weight, unless they're under 30 or obviously fit. Not looking somebody directly in the eye when speaking can be seen as evasive, especially when emphasising a point. Unless the host says otherwise, it's usual to remove your shoes when entering a home, although this may only apply in winter.

Canadian men tend to avoid intimate contact with other men beyond a handshake, a slap on the back or (with younger men) roughhousing. French-Canadians are an exception, likely to hug and kiss each other.

DEALING WITH ABORIGINAL PEOPLES

Canadian culture and etiquette demands respect for the lifestyles of First Nations peoples. When they speak, it's unacceptable to interrupt or to speak until they say or indicate that they are finished. Interruptions are regarded as particularly offensive among most First Nation cultures and particular care must be taken when conversing with elders and community leaders.

It isn't advisable to confuse different aboriginal peoples. There are three distinct groups in Canada: First Nation peoples (who are often referred to by their tribal names, not as Indians or Red Indians), Inuit and Métis, which are official classifications in Canada.

The Inuit are the peoples of the Arctic coasts of Canada (and Alaska, Greenland and Siberia). They used to be grouped together with other indigenous peoples, but are now thought to have arrived on

- **Pacific coast tribes:** Major groups include the Athapaskan, Haida, Kwakiutl, Nootka, Salish (coastal and interior), Tlingit and Tsimshian. These tribes traditionally relied on fishing – mainly salmon and eulachon (a small ocean fish) – and exploited the coast's abundant forests to make dug-out canoes and totem poles and build wooden houses.

- **Plains tribes:** Major groups include the Anishinaabe, Blackfoot, Dene, Nakoka, Okanagan, Plains-Cree, Tastline and Tsuu T'ina. These tribes traditionally lived in teepees (sometimes spelled tepees or tipis), conical tents made from animal skins or birch bark. Their lifestyle was based around the bison, which provided food and skins for clothing and shelter. Plains tribes were noted for the elaborate feather headdresses of some of their leaders.

- **Western sub-Arctic tribes:** Major groups include the Cree, Dene, Dunneza, Gwich'in, Han, Kaska, Tagish, Inland Tlingit and Tutchone. They traditionally lived in the boreal forest of Canada's western areas, including the Yukon and Northwest Territories, and their

the continent separately from other native groups and much later (well after the Beringia land bridge had disappeared beneath the ocean). Their traditional way of life involved fishing and hunting Arctic animal life, primarily caribou, musk oxen, polar bears, seals, walruses and whales.

Métis (pronounced 'maytees') are people of mixed heritage, usually the descendants of marriages between aboriginal women and early French fur trappers.

First Nations people include the following tribes:

> 'The white man knows how to make everything, but he does not know how to distribute it.'
>
> Sitting Bull (American Indian Warrior & Chief of the Dakota Sioux)

lifestyle was based on caribou, moose and the fur trade.

- **Eastern sub-Arctic tribes:** Major groups include the Anishinaabe, Cree, Innu and Ojibwa, who lived in a similar fashion to the western sub-Arctic tribes.

- **St. Lawrence River Valley tribes:** The major group is the Iroquois Confederacy, which was originally five tribes – the Cayuga, Mohawk, Oneida, Onondaga and Seneca – later joined by the Tuscarora. Their lifestyle was traditionally based on horticulture, hunting and gathering. The term 'Iroquois' is regarded as derogatory by some members of the group.

DEALING WITH OFFICIALS

Bureaucracy isn't usually oppressive in Canada (there are many worse places), but you'll inevitably have encounters with officials, e.g. civil servants, the police, parking wardens and public transport staff, some of whom may be deliberately obstructive. To ease your path, there are certain codes of behaviour that you should follow when dealing with officials:

- Be polite and maintain a sense of humour, which can often break the ice.

- Stay calm and patient, and never lose your temper.

- Dress smartly when visiting an office, which may earn you more respect and achieve better results.

- Don't expect officials to be sympathetic – many have an innate ability to remain aloof in any situation.

Police

Canadian police officers are generally civil and polite, and they're much more likely to remain so if you're courteous and helpful. If you're stopped by a police officer, either in a car or when walking, don't make any sudden movements and keep your hands where they can be seen. Some police officers may interpret any movement as an attempt to reach a concealed weapon. All police are armed and in crime-prone inner-city areas they carry pepper spray (they also use rubber bullets in riot situations).

Civil Servants

Civil servants 'control' many aspects of life in Canada, such as your visa and residence permit, social security entitlements and driving licence, and encounters with them are likely to be frequent. In dealings with civil servants you should be polite and patient and always thank them for their help (even if they

haven't been helpful – the sarcasm will usually be lost on them). Few civil servants speak any language other than English or French, therefore if you don't speak English or French fluently you should take an interpreter with you (some departments provide interpreter services).

If you have an issue or problem that concerns another country, don't expect Canadian civil servants to know the details of social security or tax agreements between your previous country of residence and Canada. Check all information with the relevant department in your previous country and compare it with what you've been told in Canada. Many countries have reciprocal arrangements with Canada which are so complicated that the rules often differ for individual cases.

> Those who can, do, those who can't teach; and those who can do neither, administer.
>
> Calvin Calverley

Teachers

One of the unique aspects of the Canadian public school system is decentralisation and the degree to which schools are run by local school authorities. Each province is divided at the local level into school districts governed by a superintendent and a locally elected school board (or board of education) that decide instructional policies,

hire teachers, buy equipment and generally oversee the day-to-day running of schools. As a result, teacher qualifications and standards vary from area to area, as does the level of parent-teacher interaction. Some schools have regular parent-teacher evenings, where your child's progress is discussed, while others don't, and you must make an appointment to see a teacher, usually during school hours.

As a general rule, however, parents in Canada are encouraged to participate in their child's education and schools are constantly seeking volunteer 'teacher's assistants' to help with reading, art and special projects. If you don't speak fluent English (or French in Quebec) you should take an interpreter if you have an appointment with a teacher or school official.

5.
THE LANGUAGE BARRIER

English and French are Canada's official languages and the country is bilingual, with all government documents published in both languages. English dominates in the majority of the country, although French is very much the first language of Quebec (under law 101 – The Charter of the French Language – French is, in fact, the only official language of Quebec), and there are a significant number of French speakers in some of the surrounding provinces. However, even if English or French is your mother tongue, you shouldn't expect to understand everything Canadians say. Many use words and expressions that may be unfamiliar to other English and French speakers, and especially to those for whom English or French is a second language.

> 'Not only does the English language borrow words from other languages, it sometimes chases them down dark alleys, hits them over the head and goes through their pockets.'
>
> Eddy Peters (writer)

LEARNING ENGLISH

A good knowledge of English is a prerequisite for living and working (or even holidaying) in Canada. If you cannot speak and write English well, you'll find it difficult to secure a job: English is the major language of business and spoken by nearly everyone. Canadians rarely have the need to learn foreign languages, and most English-speaking Canadians aren't even willing to learn more than a smattering of French, their country's other official language.

CANADIAN ENGLISH

To the uninitiated, Canadians sound like Americans, but there are subtle differences between Canadian and American accents (see **Pronunciation** below). Canadian spelling usually follows British rather than American norms (see below) and grammar also follows British English, but also has its own quirks. For example, Canadians use 'as' to mean 'because' or 'since', e.g. 'I came home early, as I was bored', and begin sentences with 'as well,' meaning 'in addition'.

> The term 'eh?' – pronounced like a long A – is affixed to every sentence some people utter, from the sublime (I love you, eh?) to the ridiculous (Let's get married, eh?) and everything in between (Gimme a pack of Export, eh?).

Canadian English has been influenced by Quebec French and indigenous languages, and has developed its own unique words, but generally it's a blend of British and American English. For example, Canadians use the British terms cheque, jam, porridge and tap, and pronounce the last letter of the alphabet 'zed' rather than 'zee', but use the American terms gas, potato chips and truck. The adoption of American terms and spelling is increasing among young people due to the influence of television and films, and the American English used in computer games and software.

A quirk of Canadian speech is the colloquial use of 'eh' to indicate a degree of uncertainty, an unwillingness to lay down the law, and a tendency to avoid directly answering questions and expressing opinions. It's the equivalent of 'right?', a form of friendly nudge in the ribs – and it's used in Canada's two national languages, a rare example of English-French Canadian unity.

History

The term 'Canadian English' was first mentioned in a speech by Reverend A. Constable Geikie to the Canadian Institute in 1857. Geikie was a Scottish-born Canadian who had the Anglocentric views that would prevail in Canada for the next century, and called Canadian English a 'corrupt dialect' to distinguish it from what he regarded as the correct English spoken by immigrants from the UK.

Canadian English has developed during four waves of immigration over two centuries. The first wave (and linguistically the most important) was of British Loyalists fleeing the American Revolution, chiefly from the Middle Atlantic States of the US. The second wave was of British and Irish settlers, encouraged to settle in Canada after the War of 1812 by the governors of Canada, who were worried about anti-English sentiment among its citizens. Two further waves of immigration from various parts of the world (peaking in 1910 and 1960) were less influential

> 'A synonym is a word you use when you can't spell the word you first thought of.'
>
> Burt Bacharach (American pianist & composer)

linguistically, but transformed Canada into a multicultural country that was prepared to accept linguistic influences from all parts of the globe.

Throughout its history, the languages of Aboriginal peoples and Canadian French have also influenced Canadian English.

Spelling

Canadian spelling falls between two stools: older people favour English spelling, while younger people tend to use American spelling. Differences of opinion and regional variations exist which, at first sight, appear irritating, but actually mean you've less chance of being wrong! For example, Canadians commonly keep the 'u' in words such as behaviour, colour and harbour, but interestingly, they 'lost' the 'u' at one point and then voted it back in.

To try to find a consensus, in the '80s the Freelance Editors' Association of Canada (now called the Editors' Association of Canada) surveyed academics, editors, publishers and writers about their choice of spelling, to discover their preferences. With words like colour/color, three-quarters of those surveyed preferred the British -our

ending. With centre/center and theatre/theater, 89 per cent preferred the British -re ending. A similar proportion preferred cauldron to caldron and the British long forms of axe, catalogue, cigarette, moustache and omelette, but the American program beat the British programme.

Around 80 per cent chose the British -ce ending over the US -se in nouns such as defence, practice and pretence, but amended the ending to -se when such words were used as verbs, e.g. to practise the piano. The British -ise ending was rejected in favour of the American -ize on words such as organize. The double ll was favoured by 90 per cent of respondents on words such as enroll, fulfill, install, marvellous, signalled, traveller and woollen. If the survey was done today, however, the results might be slightly different.

Canadians generally opt for advisor rather than adviser, co-ordinate rather than coordinate (although hyphenation is gradually disappearing), grey not gray, sceptical rather than skeptical (although some newspapers use the k) and sulphur rather than sulfur. They favour the American tire and curb over the British tyre and kerb.

Some Canadian spelling rules stem from Canada's trade history. For example, Canada's use of the British cheque (rather than check)

> 'Where Canadians got the monotone that you're listening to now I don't know – probably from the Canada goose.'
>
> Northrop Frye (Canadian literary critic)

is probably the result of Canada's once-important ties to British financial institutions. Canada's automobile industry, on the other hand, has always been dominated by American companies, thereby accounting for Canada's use of the American spelling tire.

RUE SAINT·PAUL
OUEST

Pronunciation

Canadian pronunciation is similar to American pronunciation, especially in Ontario, which resulted from the influx of United Empire Loyalists who resettled in what was then British North America, after the British defeat in the American Revolutionary War. Droves of Scottish schoolteachers were encouraged to come to what is now Canada to reinforce Britishness, and this resulted in the most notable difference between Canadian and American pronunciation: the sound of words such as house and out, which to American ears sound like 'hoose' and 'oot' (although some people think they sound like 'hoase' and 'oat'). Many Canadians (except in the Atlantic provinces) exhibit the so-called Canadian Shift, and pronounce cot in the same way as caught and collar in the same way as caller. This is generally absent in most of the US, although California has a similar vowel shift. Canadians have a tendency to turn 't' sounds into 'd' sounds, so 'gold is a metal' becomes 'gold is a meddle', the capital city is pronounced 'Oddawa' and 'waddle and daub' once appeared in a national newspaper instead of wattle and daub.

There are, of course, regional differences in pronunciation within Canada. Montreal and Toronto developed their own intonations, which were influenced by Italian and Jewish newcomers. More recently, Vancouverians have begun to pick up Chinese influences on their speech. The island of Newfoundland has a distinctive dialect known (imaginatively) as Newfoundland English (see below); many people in the Maritime provinces (New Brunswick, Nova Scotia and Prince Edward Island) have an accent more reminiscent of Scottish English (and in some places, Irish English) than Canadian.

> 'Canadians are the people who learned to live without the bold accents of the natural ego-trippers of other lands.'
>
> Marshall McLuhan (Canadian philosopher & scholar)

There's a French influence in the pronunciation of some English-speaking Canadians, notably those who live around and/or work with French-Canadians. In Quebec, English pronunciation is an interesting blend of French and Jewish influences (see below for more about Quebec English). In the Ottawa Valley, pronunciation is heavily influenced by the Irish who settled there, and the accent is the most closed-mouthed in Canada.

Vocabulary

Canadian English shares vocabulary with American English and British English (see above), and in some cases American and British terms coexist; for example the word holiday, which is used interchangeably with vacation (although holiday tends to mean a national or provincial (public) holiday, while a vacation is what you go on when you take a break from work). As a member of the British Commonwealth, Canada shares many institutional words with the British, for example, constable

for a junior police officer (although they pronounce it 'konstable' rather than 'kunstable') and chartered accountant. Canadian English also features words that are seldom (if ever) used elsewhere in the world (see **Appendix D**).

Home

Canadians tend to follow British usage when it comes to items in the home, although this is changing. For example, a tap rather than a faucet. Similarly, older Canadians tend to say tin rather than can, although can is more common.

Measurement

Canada is further along the road in the adoption of metric units than the US, because of a government push during the Trudeau era. Official measurements are metric, including road speeds and distances (the term 'klicks' is sometimes used for kilometres), fuel volumes and consumption, and weather statistics. But Canadians also use imperial measures, such as pounds, feet, inches and miles. In supermarkets, produce is marked in pounds and kilos – one area in which Canadians are fully bilingual.

Transport

Canadians use the both the British 'railway' and the American 'railroad', although railway is more usual, e.g. Canadian National Railway and Canadian Pacific Railway. Apart from this, however, most railway terminology in Canada follows the American rather than the British usage, e.g. cars and ties rather than wagons and sleepers. American English triumphs over British English on the roads too. Canadians use the terms highway, expressway and freeway (all of which the people of Quebec might call an autoroute). The British term motorway isn't used in Canada, although car and automobile are interchangeable.

School

Canadian students refer to their level of education using the American term grade, but with the number after it, e.g. grade ten, rather than following the American English practice of using an adjective, i.e. tenth grade. Most Canadian students use the British word marks to refer to their results, rather than the American grades, but oddly, they write exams rather than taking or sitting them. Canadian universities publish calendars or schedules, not catalogs as in the US. The American terms sophomore, junior and senior aren't widely used in Canada, although first-year university students are sometimes called freshmen. In Canada, a university student is somebody studying for a bachelor's degree, while a college student is someone studying for a post-secondary technical or vocational qualification, e.g. a business diploma.

Law

Those in the legal profession in Canada are usually referred to as lawyers, although the terms barrister and solicitor are also understood (except in Quebec, which has its own civil law system). The word counsel is also used. In Quebec, the terms advocate and notary (two distinct professions in Quebec civil law) refer to the province's equivalents of barrister and solicitor, respectively. In Canada's other provinces and territories, the term notary means a notary public.

In Canada, attorney generally refers to somebody who has been granted power of attorney, a lawyer who prosecutes criminal cases on behalf of the government (i.e. a Crown attorney); an American lawyer with whom a Canadian lawyer is dealing, or an American lawyer who works in Canada and advises Canadians on American law.

Politics

The term Tory is used much as in the UK, to mean a political conservative, i.e. a supporter of the federal Conservative Party of Canada, the historic Progressive Conservative Party of Canada, or a provincial Progressive Conservative party. A 'Red Tory' is somebody who supports the community-related

> 'Dialect words are those terrible marks of the beast to the truly genteel.'
>
> Thomas Hardy (English writer)

aspects of the conservative tradition, and the welfare state (a 'Tory wet' in British terminology). A 'Blue Tory' is a conservative who supports free enterprise, low taxes and the devolution of power to the provinces (a 'traditional Tory' in British parlance). 'Grits' are supporters of the Liberal Party of Canada.

'Frenglish'

There are a number of French influences on Canadian English that aren't restricted to Quebec (see below). They've led to what is sometimes called 'Frenglish' or 'Franglais', the result of mixing the languages or their forms (and some mistranslation). One example is the use of French collocations, e.g. 'close the TV' (turn/shut off the TV), 'close the door' (lock the door), 'open the light' (turn on the lights), and 'put your coat' (put your coat on).

There's also a tendency to use French grammar forms. Many of the resultant constructions are grammatically correct but only out of context. Examples are the overuse of the definite article to mean 'in general', as in 'I like the fish and the white wine', meaning 'I like fish and white wine'; and the 'translation' of *vouloir*, as in 'Do you want to wash the dishes?', meaning 'Will/would you wash the dishes?'.

The use of false cognates (*faux-amis*) is quite common, and these French words are pronounced using English sounds. Examples include perfect, meaning fine (from *parfait*); 'subvention', meaning a (government) grant; and acetate, meaning a transparency.

Regional Variations

There are a number of regional variations of Canadian English, the most significant of which are outlined below.

Newfoundland

The dialect spoken in the province of Newfoundland and Labrador is often regarded as Canada's most distinctive, though 'dialects' would be more accurate, because the way people speak can vary widely from community to community – reflecting the fact that, until recently, many communities were isolated. Some Newfoundland dialects are similar to the speech and accent of south-east Ireland, others borrow from the West Country of England, while some are a combination of the two.

Vancouver

An interesting feature of Newfoundland English is its affirmative 'yeah', made with an inhalation rather than an exhalation, which according to linguistics experts is a rare 'pulmonic ingressive phone'. Newfoundland dialects are losing their distinctiveness because of the mass media, and an educational system that aims to teach 'proper' English; surviving Newfoundland expressions include 'Whadd'ya at?', which means 'How's it going?' or 'What are you doing?'; 'Where ya to?', meaning 'Where are you going?'; 'Flat on the back for that!', an expression of approval used by female speakers; and 'Get on the go', which means 'Let's go' or 'Let's party'.

British Columbia

Chinook Jargon is a trade language (or pidgin), which was spoken on the west coast of North America from Oregon to Alaska. It was used widely by all ethnic groups throughout the Pacific north-west well into the middle of the 20th century, and British Columbian English still uses a number of words taken from Chinook Jargon, including:

chuck and **saltchuck** – a body of water and a body of salty water

masi – an adaptation of the French *merci*

muckamuck – a big feed or important banquet

potlatch – originally a ceremony involving food and the exchange of gifts, nowadays a potluck dinner or, sometimes, the donation of possessions to friends

quiggly – down or underneath

skookum – able, big, genuine, reliable or strong; one of the most commonly used Chinook Jargon words, e.g. 'a skookum guy' and 'That's skookum', meaning 'That's fine'.

tyee – boss or leader

Quebec

First, some Quebec terminology: an 'Anglophone' is a person whose mother tongue is English and who still speaks it as a first language; 'Francophone' is the corresponding term for a French speaker; and 'Allophone' is the term for somebody who's neither Anglophone or Francophone. These terms are also used in New Brunswick, which is an officially bilingual province (as is the federal district of Ottawa).

Quebec English is the term for the English spoken in the province of Quebec, but more particularly for that spoken in the Greater Montreal Area (where 90 per cent of Quebec-born, first-language, English-speakers live). It has no unifying and unique characteristic that would qualify it as a dialect, but a number of unusual and interesting features. One is its use of French official names of institutions and organisations that have no English names, which tend to be pronounced as in French, especially in the broadcast media. However, acronyms are sometimes used for these institutions and organisations, and the pronunciation of these is English.

As might be expected, Quebec English uses a (small) number of Quebec French terms for items with English equivalents. Their pronunciation is sometimes English and the terms may be abbreviated; for example, 'dep' instead of corner or convenience store (from the French *dépanneur*) or 'cinq à sept' for a cocktail party or happy hour in a bar (roughly 5 to 7 pm).

> 'Quebecers must realize that Bill 101 was passed in a kind of euphoric state of mind where we believed ourselves to be in a francophone country. The Supreme Court is simply there to remind us that, for as long as we are a province, we are but a minority in an English country.'
>
> Guy Bertrand (Canadian lawyer)

Toronto

The English spoken in Toronto resembles that spoken in the northern US, and includes many American English slang terms. Toronto English has also borrowed slang terms from its many immigrant communities, most of which speak English as a second or even third language. The people of Toronto have a number of slang terms for their city. Some call it 'Hogtown', which comes from west Toronto's history as a major meatpacking centre (particularly pork); some call their home city 'T.O.', which stands for Toronto, Ontario; others call it 'Tdot'. Those who call Toronto by its usual name, however, pronounce it in their own particular way (in what is referred to by linguistics experts as an elided form), T'rana or T'ronno; Edmonton is likewise Emmonton.

Aboriginal Contributions to English

A number of Canadian contributions to the English language come from Aboriginal culture, which was established well before Europeans arrived. Words like igloo, parka and mukluk (leather or sealskin moccasins) come from Inuit, while the Plains Tribes gave the

Toronto

language 'chinook' (a warm winter wind), teepee and wigwam, and the Algonquins contributed moccasin and toboggan.

Colloquialisms, Slang & Swear Words

As mentioned earlier, the word 'eh' has become ingrained in working class Canadian speech, and is used to check the level of comprehension and interest of the listener. It's argued that it's also used as a way of not offending people, because the eh distances the speaker from the comment, and consequently from anything that might be offensive.

The word rubber is Canadian (and American) slang for a condom, but in Canada it's also sometimes an alternative to eraser (as in British

English). In the plural, Canadians use it as slang for overshoes or galoshes. The term bum is used in both the British and the American senses, to mean either the human posterior or a homeless person, respectively. It's used by Canadians as a politer form of the ruder butt, ass or arse (the last is commonly used in Atlantic Canada, and by older people in Ontario).

Although swearing isn't permitted on television in Canada, it isn't viewed quite as negatively as it is in the (rather prissy) US, and the situation is even more relaxed in Quebec. Some Canadians swear quite regularly in informal settings, as using swear words is sometimes considered a sign of familiarity and inclusiveness. Be careful, however, because many older Canadians find swearing unacceptable, so it's best not to do it in front of people you don't know well.

The French-speaking approach to swearing is interesting: the folk of Quebec sometimes use religious rather than sexual or scatological terms to express their anger and frustration. Therefore, somebody might say 'Oh, tabernacle' (or baptism, chalice or host), but such terms wouldn't be printed in the local press, because they're deemed too profane. On the other hand, words that are shocking in English – including slang terms for sexual acts – are mild in Quebec French, gentle enough to appear in the media.

French visitors find this use of religious words dumbfounding, because they escaped church domination many years ago; whereas

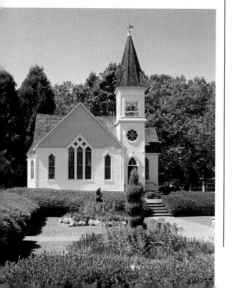

Quebec only began to shake off religion around 40 years ago, during the so-called 'Quiet Revolution' of the '60s, when people rebelled and stopped going to church.

CANADIAN FRENCH

French is a minority language in Canada (although French-speakers are accused by English-speakers of behaving as if it's the majority tongue), so it has been necessary to take steps to ensure that it isn't overwhelmed by English. A language regulation – Bill 101 – made it illegal for businesses in Quebec to display signs outdoors in any language other than French. Indeed, the Canadian French are more zealous about their language than the French themselves (which is saying something). While the latter are happy to say *le hot dog*, in Quebec it's more likely to be *le chien chaud*.

In fact, the French spoken in some parts of Quebec is arguably more 'French' than that spoken by the folk in France: even the French admit it, and French linguists come to study the language spoken in northern Quebec, as it's the closest to the French that was spoken in medieval France. (This is because French settlers arrived in Canada before the French revolution, and continued to speak the language of that period, whereas the language has evolved in France.) On the other hand, the patois of parts of Quebec, *Joual* (see below), is so different from French that some people regard it as a separate language.

The most pure French is spoken in Quebec City, while informal Canadian French tends to include a lot of Anglicisations foreign even to the French, e.g. *downtown*, *faker* (to pretend), and *le computer* rather than *l'ordinateur*. For this reason, Québécois films shown in France require subtitles, and, when French people visit Quebec, they often find it easier to communicate in English!

> 'The die is cast in Canada: there are two ethnic and linguistic groups; each is too strong and too deeply rooted in the past, too firmly bound to the mother culture, to be able to swamp the other.'
>
> Pierre Trudeau (Canadian politician)

Joual

Of the French dialects spoken in various parts of Quebec, *Joual* is the best known. *Joual* is a Canadian take on the French language, which is completely unknown to the French and has been described as Québécois cockney – a working-class French dialect that began as Montreal street slang. The word *Joual* is a transliteration of how the French word *cheval* (horse) is pronounced by those who speak *Joual*. Common *Joual* terms include the following:

toé – toi (you)
moé – moi (me)
chu – je suis (I am)
té – tu es (you are)
ché – je suis (I am)
pantoute – pas du tout (not at all)
pis – puis (then)
y – il (he)
a – elle (she)
ouais/ouin – oui (yes)
icitte – ici (here)
ben – bien (well)
frette – froid (cold)

The term *Joual* was originally an insult and it still has a hint of that, so be careful how you use it. In order to avoid causing offence, some people prefer to say Quebecois or Montrealais.

> 'If you want to live in the same room with Canadians, you must talk about two things: the weather and hockey.'
>
> Martin O'Malley (politician)

ABORIGINAL LANGUAGES

Around 50 Aboriginal languages survive in Canada, although a dozen are on the brink of extinction and, over the last century, ten once flourishing languages have disappeared. Of the 50, only three (Cree, Inuktitut and Ojibwe) have

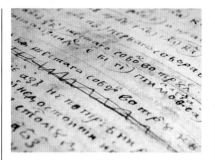

large enough numbers of speakers to be regarded as safe from the threat of disappearance in the long term. This is partly because only a small number of Native Canadians speak an aboriginal language fluently and no more than around 25 per cent (around 225,000 people) consider one to be their mother tongue; even fewer speak one at home. The fact that most aboriginal languages are mainly oral has added to their fragility. When such languages disappear, so does their unique way of looking at and explaining the world; in fact, aboriginal languages are one of the most obvious symbols of Native Canadian identity – a link connecting people with their past, and reinforcing their social and spiritual life.

Of the three most common aboriginal languages, Cree is spoken mainly in the centre and east of Canada, from Alberta to Labrador. Like many Native Canadian tongues, it's highly complex. A Cree word can be very long, and express something that takes a series of words in English. Ojibwe is spoken in a similar part of the country, and is likewise 'polysynthetic'.

Inuktitut is the collective name

for the various Inuit languages that are spoken north of Canada's treeline, especially in Nunavut and the Northwest Territories. Like Cree and Ojibwe, Inuktitut is richly morphological (morphology is the field within linguistics that studies the internal structure of words), adding prefixes and suffixes to root words to indicate, what in English, would take several words to express.

FOREIGN LANGUAGES

English-speaking Canadians often follow the general English-speakers' 'tradition' of not bothering to learn other languages, although some at least make the effort to learn French (few speak it well). However, thanks to Canada's policy of multiculturalism, many foreign languages are spoken by the country's immigrant communities. There are a significant number of speakers of East Asian languages, notably Cantonese and Mandarin, and increasing numbers of speakers of the various Indian and Pakistani languages. There are also many recent Canadian immigrants who speak a range of other languages, including Arabic, Italian, Polish and Spanish. A recent poll in a Calgary high school of 2,200 pupils revealed that they came from 87 different 'language backgrounds'.

> 'Eloquence is the ability to describe Pamela Anderson without using one's hands.'
>
> Mike Harkness (Canadian businessman)

BODY & SIGN LANGUAGE

Canadians tend to be quite relaxed in their body language, often touching a friend on the arm during conversation as a friendly gesture. Meeting and greeting among friends often involves hugs (Canadian bumper stickers advocate 12 hugs a day for psychological health!). French-Canadians are generally more animated and expressive in their body language than other Canadians, but some gestures have different meanings in Quebec. For example, the 'thumbs down' sign is thought to be offensive, as is slapping an open palm over a closed fist. The 'thumbs up' sign is fine throughout Canada, meaning 'okay'; but the American 'okay' sign making the letter 'o' (for 'okay') with the index finger and the thumb means 'zero' in Quebec. The 'V' for 'victory' sign is an insult throughout Canada if your palm is facing yourself. If you must use this sign, face your palm outward.

Try to sneeze as quietly as possible and, if you're coughing, leave the

OK or zero?

room. In Quebec, sit with your knees together or with your legs crossed at the knee; don't sit with your legs apart or with your feet on chairs or tables.

Personal Space

Canada is enormous and thinly populated, and people have become used to having plenty of space. Even Canadian cities haven't had to grow vertically until recently, but have sprawled horizontally and cover large tracts of land. Most urban houses have a lawn or lawns, many of them large enough to accommodate a number of trees. Because of this abundance of room, Canadians also value their personal space, and don't stand close to one another; about three feet apart is the normal distance. As ever, French-Canadians are different, and don't have this strict concept of personal space.

FORMS OF ADDRESS

Canadians are slightly more formal than Americans with names and titles. In business and formal situations, you should use last names and appropriate titles, until invited by your Canadian hosts or colleagues to use their first names. In relaxed, social situations (especially with younger people), Canadians use first names immediately upon meeting someone. Western Canadians tend to use first names more quickly and more often than eastern Canadians. This might seem impolite or presumptuous, but is actually friendly and welcoming. Honorifics such as Mr and Mrs are still sometimes used, certainly in a work environment, and with somebody who's significantly older than the other people in a group.

In Francophone circles, Madam and Mrs, and Monsieur and Mr are interchangeable. In Quebec, colleagues of similar status generally use first names in private, but surnames in public. The formal you (*vous*) is appropriate in a business setting, even after long acquaintance. French-Canadians regard academic titles and degrees as important, so you should make the effort to get to know and use them properly.

In the UK, a dentist or surgeon is Mr, but in Canada he's Doctor. Few children address their parents or grandparents by their first names, even when the children themselves are adults. Children usually call their parents 'mom' and 'dad', while cultural heritage is sometimes revealed in the familiar names given to grandparents, e.g. *oma* and

> 'Everyone has the right to pronounce foreign names as he chooses.'
> Winston Churchill (British Prime Minister)

opa (German) and *baba* and *dido* (Ukrainian).

GREETINGS

Canadians are generally more reserved than Americans, and take meeting and greeting etiquette a little more seriously. Men should shake hands firmly – you should remove your gloves if wearing them – when meeting Canadian men for the first time, while maintaining eye contact. Men usually also offer their hands to women when being formally introduced. When a woman enters or leaves a room, it's considered polite by older people for men to rise.

Most Canadians aren't demonstrative with people they don't know well, so it's best to avoid a Mediterranean excess of hugging and kissing when meeting or leaving people. The exception, of course, is French-Canadians, who hug and kiss freely in public, but most Canadians reserve this greeting for family.

In Quebec, kissing on the cheeks in the French manner is quite usual, especially with family and friends. An older French-Canadian man may kiss the hand of a woman (this should be accepted graciously), but a foreign man shouldn't kiss the hand of a French-Canadian woman, who would be shocked. Most French-Canadians speak and understand English, but prefer to use French, and it's appreciated if you at least try to greet them in their preferred language. The Québécois in particular appreciate it if people make the effort to speak to them in French.

As elsewhere, when you meet somebody, it's considered good manners to take off your hat or sunglasses, and to keep them off while you're speaking to them. It's considered to be impolite in Quebec to talk with your hands in your pockets.

Standard greetings such as 'Good morning/afternoon/evening', 'Hi' and 'Hello' are commonly used, and Canadians also favour the greeting 'How are you?' This question doesn't require a detailed, literal answer; the standard response is 'Fine, thank you'. When parting, common expressions include 'Goodbye', 'Have a nice day', 'Good night' and 'See you later'. People will often say 'Have a safe trip' if the other person is about to undertake a journey.

When somebody says 'Thank you', expected responses are 'You're welcome', 'No problem' or 'Happy to help'.

Parliament building, Ottawa

6.

THE CANADIANS AT WORK

One of the most common mistakes foreigners make when coming to Canada to work or start a business, is to assume that they can continue working in the same way as they did in their home country, particularly if they had a successful business. Many expatriates underestimate the differences in culture between the Canadian way of working and that in other countries, although if you're coming to Canada from the UK, Ireland or the US, things will be fairly familiar. For other newcomers, working in Canada may involve a radical learning experience – professionally, linguistically (if your mother tongue isn't English, or French if you're in Quebec) and culturally.

Canada is one of the most multicultural countries in the world, so don't assume that everyone will be familiar with American/British ways of doing business.

Foreigners still sometimes think of Canada as little more than a provider of raw materials, but it's actually a global player in many industries. The country boasts one of the world's top ten economies and one of the highest standards of living. The Canadian labour market is kept fresh by the annual addition of some 250,000 new immigrants, and many provinces and territories offer support programmes and incentives to companies that are willing to hire and train immigrants.

This chapter contains information about the cultural differences you can expect to experience when working for or with Canadians, setting up a business in Canada, and business etiquette.

WORK ETHIC

Like the beaver, Canada's national animal, Canadians are hard working. Many of the oldest families are descended from the pioneers who left their home countries for a distant, unknown wilderness, and retain their 'survivalist' attitude and 'Protestant' work ethic. Although the work ethic isn't as pervasive as in the US, Japan and other parts of East Asia, it's at least as strong as in most other industrialised nations. Work is regarded as an important part of life – but not the only thing.

Canadians have a liking for physical work (a legacy of the pioneer days and Canada's reliance on primary resources), as shown by the large numbers of people who work in the mining, oil, steel and timber industries; over 100,000 Canadians are directly or indirectly employed in the forestry industry

alone, while jobs in the oil fields in the far north are a huge draw, due to the high salaries on offer. Many urban Canadians have done outdoor work in their time, and students often pay their tuition fees by working during the summer as tree planters. Many Canadians go to university in another province in order to gain experience of living away from home, as a result of which they tend to be more flexible regarding where they will work.

With the exception of immigrant groups and French-Canadians, Canadian business hasn't always been international, although this is changing. British Columbia and Alberta see themselves as part of the Pacific Rim and have strong business connections with Asia. Vancouver, for example, has one of the largest Asian populations outside Asia, although most of Canada's trade is with the US.

Canadians admire the entrepreneurial, risk-taking nature of US business, but they're don't slavishly follow US customs and lifestyle choices, and are quick to point out the failings of the US vis-a-vis the way things are done in Canada, e.g. gun control and general lawlessness. Many Canadians relish non-business-related events that cast the US in a poor light, e.g. the Clinton-Lewinski affair, and the failings of the US electoral system during the 2000 presidential election debacle (see **Business Relations with the US** below).

Canada's entrepreneurial ethos is concentrated in the newer immigrant communities, where immigrants run many of the small corner shops, launderettes and restaurants. Canadians like franchises and most city main streets and shopping malls have plenty of franchise operations, including clothing outlets, hotels, car rental companies, restaurants, video/DVD hire shops and much else. Franchises are attractive businesses because they offer extensive market research, good product selection, regional and national advertising, and turnkey operations, which makes them less risky than independent businesses, although they have less growth potential.

Canadians are also noted for being easy going and pleasant to do business with. Most Canadians are laid-back, open and highly trustworthy, with a high level of responsibility to clients, and respect for contracts and the law.

Standards

Canadian business values high standards. Federal and provincial/territorial governments closely monitor health and safety standards,

Canada and the US do more trade than any other two countries in the world, and, somewhat surprisingly, Canada invests as much in the US as the US does in Canada.

while workplace standards are vigorously enforced by unions and support groups, and proper procedures and safety equipment are required. Canadian products must not only meet stringent health and safety standards, but are also subject to extensive government testing and vetting by consumer organisations.

Business Relations with the US

Business relations between Canada and the US are somewhat overshadowed by Canadian annoyance at American ignorance of how important a trading partner Canada is to the US, which is part of the general American ignorance about all things Canadian. Many Americans associate Canada with little more than cold weather and ice hockey players, while, in complete contrast, Canadians avidly follow US culture, current affairs and sports. Indeed, it's difficult to think of another international trading relationship that has such an imbalance of shared interest and knowledge. Canada is attractive to US companies, however, being close, easy to access, largely English-speaking and culturally similar. When American firms want to venture into Canada, they often make a trial run in Calgary, the most American of Canada's cities.

In order to achieve the economies of scale required to compete with US businesses, some Canadian businesses have grown to a size where they're virtual monopolies, e.g. Air Canada (the dominant airline), Chapters/Indigo (the ubiquitous book seller) and Tim Horton's (which dominates the café market).

The North American Free Trade Agreement (NAFTA) between Canada, the US and Mexico, will eliminate most trade barriers between the countries by 2008.

Caution

The Canadian business environment tends to be cautious, and prefers to stick to what it knows and what has worked before. This probably stems from the long-standing importance of the resources industry, which is a 'straightforward' business sector. Canadian banks, despite being highly profitable and having vast funds at their disposal, are often reluctant to invest in new business

sectors without giving them long, deliberate consideration. There has been a tendency in Canada to be suspicious of, and sometimes to mock, risk-takers, although this is changing – in large part due to the entrepreneurial spirit of some of the new immigrant communities, particularly Asians.

Environmental Concerns

Canada is an energetic participant in the global environmental movement and was the home base of Greenpeace during its early years. British Columbia, in particular, has a strong environmentalist philosophy. As a result, Canadian businesses must be aware of and respond to environmental concerns. The major polluting industries – power stations, pulp and paper, and smelters, among others – must invest heavily to comply with environmental standards, and environmental assessments have become an important part of new industrial and resource operations. At the individual level, Canadians are militant about environmental matters, and communities frequently protest against proposed industrial developments.

UNEMPLOYMENT

Canada's official unemployment rate in mid-2007 was 6 per cent, which was a 33-year low. Whereas the country's manufacturing sector has been struggling, natural resource industries and the service sector have been creating jobs, and the success of women and workers aged over 55 has contributed to Canada's relatively low unemployment rate. However, as with most aspects of life in Canada, there are regional variations in the number of unemployed, which varies from a low of around 3.5 per cent in Alberta to a high of 13 per cent in Newfoundland.

BUREAUCRACY

Canada's system of government can create confusion for people starting businesses, particularly foreigners. National matters are dealt with by the federal government and local matters at provincial/territorial level, which creates a lot more regulations for those doing business in Canada. Environmental regulations vary from province to province, as can tax rates, regulations and much else besides. Most businesses work more closely with provincial/territorial governments than with the federal government, while staying within the framework established at the national level.

Canada's provinces and territories compete with each other for business and investment, and foreigners wishing to establish a business in Canada might find that several provinces will compete for their business with incentives and subsidies. This inter-province/territory rivalry means that Canada presents a blurred, inconsistent face to the rest of the world, and some investors have become adept at playing the provinces off against each other in order to increase the inducements.

> Women are well-represented in business in Canada, where a businesswoman can invite a businessman to lunch or dinner with no problem of status or sexuality arising.

DISCRIMINATION

Women

Although Canada isn't as advanced as some countries in accommodating working women, it's better than many countries. For many years, discrimination in Canada prevented women from competing equally with men and entering male-dominated professions. In the last few decades, however, women have succeeded in breaking down the barriers and now officially compete on equal terms with men. Many Canadian companies have rules to ease women's professional progress, e.g. generous maternity leave and day care facilities.

There's increasing economic pressure on women to seek employment to supplement the family income, and they now constitute 45 per cent of the labour force. Some 60 per cent of women work full or part, time and they make up 65 per cent of part-time workers (although many would prefer full-time work).

Women are prominent and successful in the Canadian business world, but there are still many more male senior executives than women. However, an increasing number of women are going into business, even in fields traditionally dominated by men, e.g. accountancy, engineering and law. Around 40 per cent of corporate managers are women, most of those in high positions being employed in the federal and provincial governments, although many are also self-employed or work in the health sciences. The number of women entrepreneurs is also increasing, and women now occupy top positions in all walks of life in Canada.

Women still encounter prejudice, however, and resistance and inequalities exist, not least in salaries. Despite laws prohibiting job discrimination on the basis of gender and requiring equal pay for equal work, women's pay remains between 70 and 85 per cent of men's for many full-time jobs.

Professional women are common in Canada and have more equality than their counterparts in many other countries, although some find it difficult (or impossible) to reach the top ranks of their profession. The main discrimination against professional women isn't salary, but promotion prospects, as many companies and organisations are reluctant to elevate women to important positions – a phenomenon known as the glass ceiling. Generally, the closer women get to the top, the more they're resented, although this is changing.

Ethnic Minorities

Despite Canada's multicultural society, there are some barriers to ethnic groups in business, and recent immigrants from Africa, the Caribbean and South America have complained of discrimination. However, many Canadian businesses – at all levels – have discovered the benefit of having staff of various cultural and linguistic backgrounds.

Canada's First Nation peoples are poorly represented in the business community and workplace. Unemployment rates are high among indigenous peoples, and federal government initiatives to aid Aboriginal economic development have had little success. There are signs of improvement, however, particularly on some of the resource-rich native reserves, where those seeking to do business need to understand and develop good relations with indigenous peoples.

FINDING A JOB

Canada has a plethora of employment agencies in its major cities and towns. Most large companies engage agencies to recruit staff, particularly executives, managers, professional employees and temporary office staff (temps). Most specialise in particular trades, professions or fields, while others deal with a range of industries and positions.

Human Resource Centres of Canada (HRCC) provide free counselling and job placement in over 400 offices in towns and cities across the country. Self-help kiosks located in HRCCs provide updates on the job market, and allow you to find out which trades and professions are in demand, the skills required and the training opportunities or services available to help you find work. HRCCs also operate computerised Job Banks, containing vacancy listings in the local area and across the nation. You can select the jobs that are of interest and obtain more information from staff, who can also arrange interviews.

Language

English is by far the most important language in Canada, and you usually need to speak, read and write it well in order to succeed in a career or business. English proficiency is particularly important if you have a job requiring a lot of contact with others, speaking on the phone or dealing with other foreigners.

The ability to speak French as well as English gives you an advantage in certain industries and/or bilingual parts of Canada, and is also necessary if you work for the government. Manitoba, New Brunswick, Ontario and, of course, Quebec, have the largest numbers of bilingual workers. In Quebec, you need to speak good French in order to get just about any job, and French may also be necessary for visiting business people, although most international business is conducted in English. West of Ontario, Canada's bilingualism is rarely an issue.

Despite the efforts of the federal government to encourage everyone to learn and use both languages, barely 15 per cent of Canadians speak English and French. So if you speak good English **and** French, you have an advantage over the majority of Canada's workforce. However, if you speak French as it's understood in France, you may take a while to adjust to the Canadian dialect, although they won't have any difficulty understanding you. Canadian French (called Québécois in Quebec, where it's sometimes also known as Joual – see **Chapter 5**) is different from the French spoken in France, and can be unintelligible, even to a native of France.

Almost one in six (over 5m) Canadian residents grew up speaking a language other than English or French. West of Montreal, there are large immigrant populations from throughout the world, particularly in Toronto, Vancouver and Winnipeg. This means that Canada has many workers who speak a wide range of other languages, as well as having plenty of contacts and experience of business abroad, while the Atlantic Provinces and rural Quebec have attracted far fewer newcomers.

Skills & Qualifications

The points system on which most immigration is based depends to

> Around 60 per cent of Canadians are native English speakers and some 25 per cent French speakers.

a large extent on the skills and qualifications of applicants. Points are awarded for skills based on your current or previous employment, and whether your qualifications and occupational training are adequate. While you may be well-qualified in your own country, you may need to pass professional examinations or trade tests to satisfy Canadian standards: it isn't unusual for people regarded as highly qualified in another country to have to take a menial job to support themselves while studying for Canadian qualifications. Theoretically, qualifications recognised by professional and trade bodies overseas are recognised in Canada. However, recognition depends on the country where they were issued, and some foreign academic qualifications may be given less prominence than equivalent Canadian qualifications.

SALARY

Salaries in some companies and professions (particularly government employees) are decided by national pay agreements between unions and employers. In others, salaries vary considerably for the same job in different regions of Canada, generally being higher in the major cities such as Toronto and Montreal, and in remote areas such as the north of Canada (you need an incentive to spend most of the year buried in snow). When comparing salaries, you should bear in mind the local cost of living. For example, although salaries are much higher in Toronto and Vancouver than in Newfoundland, so is the cost of living, and the higher salary might not be adequate compensation.

EMPLOYMENT CONDITIONS

Government employees usually have considerably better job protection and legal rights than employees of private companies, although their salaries are often lower. Employees in the private sector can lose their jobs with as little as two weeks' notice, and, unless you've been working for an employer for at least three months, you won't be entitled to any redundancy (severance) pay. Even after five years' service, you're entitled only to a paltry ten days' pay. Consequently, Canadian employers are likely to lay off workers when business is bad. On the other hand, you may also quit your job at any time for any reason, although it's usual to give two weeks' notice.

Business Hours

With some variations, depending on the industry in which you're employed, the standard working day is eight hours and the standard working week 40 hours. Typical office hours are 8 or 9 am to 4 or 5 pm, with a lunch break of between 30 and 60 minutes. Many Canadian companies operate flexible working hours, which are becoming more popular because of the different time zones, particularly among office workers. It's common to start work earlier in the west, due to having to deal with businesses in an earlier, eastern time zone.

Annual Holidays

All workers in Canada must receive (and take) at least two weeks' paid holiday (invariably called vacation) per year, not including statutory (public) holidays. This miserly holiday allowance will come as a severe blow to Europeans and other foreigners who are used to receiving four to six weeks' paid annual leave (the average in Canada is 12 days per year, compared with 25 in France and 30 in Germany). After three years' consecutive employment, the official paid holiday entitlement usually rises to three weeks. Thereafter, each year of employment normally raises annual holiday entitlement by one or two days, so it can take eight years before you're entitled to four weeks'

> The average annual holiday allowance in Canada is a miserly 12 days.

paid holiday per year (although whether you have the opportunity to take all of it is another matter).

For details of statutory (public) holidays, see **Statutory & Provincial Holidays** at the end of this chapter.

Trades Unions

Trades unions are relatively strong in Canada, although economic ups and downs in recent decades have generally undermined trades union power. The country has experienced episodes of industrial strife; British Columbia, for example, has had particular problems with industrial relations. Around 4m workers in Canada are union members, most of whom are employed in government, education, manufacturing, and health and social services. Unions are strongest in traditional industries such as manufacturing and transport, but have little influence in industries such as finance, retailing and services. The two public sector unions, the Canadian Union of Public Employees and the National Union of Public and

General Employees, are the largest in Canada.

STARTING OR BUYING A BUSINESS

Entrepreneurs are respected and encouraged in Canada; little stigma is attached to business failure, which often spurs people to even greater efforts. For foreigners, one of the main attractions of buying a business in Canada is that it offers a relatively easy method of obtaining a visa, as the Canadian government is keen to encourage foreign entrepreneurs. You must demonstrate that you have sufficient funds to start a business and provide for your family for a reasonable period. In practice, this usually means investing at least $300,000.

If you're thinking of following this path, it's advisable to use a specialist business immigration lawyer to smooth the process. Always obtain a quotation in writing, and shop around a number of lawyers (check their credentials and references), as fees can run into thousands of dollars, depending on the amount of work involved. If you invest in a suitable business before you arrive in Canada, you're usually given an unconditional visa; otherwise, you receive a conditional visa that requires you to have a business in

operation (with at least one Canadian employee) within two years.

South Ontario and Vancouver are Canada's most competitive business regions, with a lot of scope for new businesses, but in much of Canada, it's more difficult for small businesses to make a mark. It may be easier to buy a business in Saskatoon or Winnipeg, for example, but harder to make a success of it.

Business Structures

There are four kinds of business structure in Canada, if you're self-employed: a sole proprietorship, partnership (general and limited), joint-venture and a corporation. Due to the ever-changing and complex tax laws, you should consult a tax expert before deciding on which one is best for you. You must also decide whether to buy an established business or a franchise, or start a new business from scratch. When buying an existing business, it's wise to employ a licensed business broker

'Business is the art of extracting money from another man's pocket without resorting to violence.'

Max Amsterdam

(buyer's broker) to advise on the purchase.

Registration & Taxation

You may need a Business Number (BN) and a Canada Revenue Agency (CRA) account when starting a new business in Canada. The BN is a unique number that simplifies and streamlines the way businesses deal with the federal government.

Most individuals and organisations engaged in commercial activities in Canada with over four consecutive calendar quarters with (worldwide) sales of over $30,000, must register for and collect Goods and Services Tax (GST) or Harmonised Sales Tax (HST). (See **SALES Tax** in **Chapter 9** for further information.) If this applies to your business you will need a BN, although not all businesses require one.

Check with the CRA (1-800-959-2221, 🖳 www.cra-arc.gc.ca/tax/business) or contact your local tax service office.

BLACK ECONOMY

There are thousands of people working illegally in Canada, most in transient occupations such as bartenders, waiters and waitresses, nannies and servants, farm workers (particularly during fruit and vegetable harvests), and workers in the fishing and construction industries, who are often paid partly or wholly in cash.

In order to secure a job in Canada legally, an employee must have a social insurance number (SIN) that's issued to Canadians and legal immigrants. It's strictly illegal

for foreigners to work in Canada without a visa or official permission. Foreigners found working illegally are fined and deported, and refused entry into Canada for five years. Illegal immigrants have no entitlement to federal or company pensions, no employment or accident insurance, and no benefits. If you work illegally with false documents, the penalties are even more severe.

The black economy is an equally risky business for employers. Harbouring or employing illegal labour, e.g. a housekeeper, isn't an offence under the criminal code of Canada, but you can be charged under the Immigration Act and face a stiff fine.

BUSINESS ETIQUETTE

Canadian business etiquette is easy to understand, and Canadians are used to working with people from around the world, and are adaptable to different types of business environment. Business relations in Canada tend to be relaxed, without the formality seen in Asia, for example. The Canadian approach is halfway between the sometimes over-familiar US way of doing things, and the more formal European approach. Most people

– usually a discreet gift with a local or regional connection (ostentatious gifts are frowned upon and may even be construed as a bribe). Christmas gift-giving is also common, when businesses often give gifts of alcohol or food, or an item featuring the company logo, to important customers. If you're invited to a Canadian business person's home – which isn't very common – you should take a gift such as flowers, chocolates or wine.

use first names with each other, which extends to many business transactions.

There are few rigid rules about how to greet people, conduct meetings, shake hands or present business cards, as there are, for example, in countries such as China and Japan. The main rules to follow are: be on time, don't lump Canada together with the US, and don't be too pushy or too laid-back.

Business Cards

Business cards are often exchanged at first meetings in Canada, but with much less formality than in Asia. In French-speaking parts of Canada, a double-sided business card is recommended, one side written in English and the other in French.

Business Gifts

No specific rules or protocol exists in Canada with regard to business gifts, which are generally warmly received and will often be reciprocated. Canadians quite often give gifts, particularly when dealing with international partners

Cultural Factors

It's difficult to generalise about the cultural aspects of doing business in Canada, because the country's population is so varied. For example, doing business with a 15th-generation French-Canadian is very different from dealing with a recently arrived Hong Kong businessman. Add the provincial/territorial variations and it's clear that there are no reliable national guidelines.

Until the mid-20th century, Canada's business approach mimicked Britain's (French-Canadians were rarely important national business players), but the growth of the US as the world's superpower has since caused Canadians to change their approach, and adopt the American rather than British style.

> 'Canada is the linchpin of the English-speaking world.'
>
> Sir Winston Churchill (politician)

Regional Differences

Canada is a mosaic of business cultures, reflecting the country's economic, ethnic and geographical diversity. Regional business environments are noticeably different; for example, Vancouver is the most Asian part of Canada, and is strongly influenced by the US, with a US West Coast mentality – relaxed, yet edgy and *avant-garde*. By way of contrast, Alberta has been called 'Dallas North', thanks to its cattle, oil and cowboys; it has a US approach to business – entrepreneurial, punchy and up-front. Manitoba and Saskatchewan, on the other hand, are more relaxed, rustic even.

Toronto has Ontario's most vibrant business culture, and one of the few things that unites most Canadians is their envy of Toronto's success. It's often portrayed as cocky and uninterested in the problems experienced in other parts of the country. However, the last few years have seen other areas begin to catch up; high oil prices helped Alberta to declare a $7bn surplus in 2006-07, and British Columbia is also prospering. As a result, some westerners have jokingly suggested that they should separate from the rest of Canada – a well-deserved payback after years of being regarded as second rate by some in the east.

Ottawa used to be a sleepy place, but is now a vibrant centre of high technology – Canada's Silicon Valley. Atlantic Canada suffers from its small population – around 3m – spread throughout four provincial governments, and Canadians joke that its people are work-shy. The far north of Canada depends heavily on federal government subsidies – even more than the Maritimes – and new businesses there often receive attractive backing and subsidies, but the region's isolation and harsh conditions restrict business opportunities.

French-Canadians

The French-Canadian business community's culture is different from that of the rest of Canada. To begin with, it's largely Francophone, although many business people also speak fluent English. Even more than France, Quebec has a strictly enforced policy of resisting English-language dominance, and Quebec's stringent language laws affect some aspects of doing business. Although most international business is conducted in English, you'll impress and please Quebecois if you try to speak at least some French.

Canada's Francophone business community is more continental European than North American in its dress, eating habits, and international experience and outlook. Business

people are very French in their approach (see *Culture Wise France*), and more passionately regional than most other Canadians (although also more international in outlook). They're also more competitive, creative and innovative than most other Canadians.

> Canada's low birth rate means that its workforce is ageing. In the decade to 2001, the age of the average Canadian worker increased from 37.1 to 39.

Dress

Business dress follows no particular rules in Canada, but it's best to err on the side of formality. A suit and tie for men and a business suit or dress for women are usual, although increasing numbers of Canadian businesses are more informal these days, particularly in the high technology sector and other creative industries, e.g. advertising, film and publishing. Casual or 'dress-down' Fridays are common and Canadians also like to dress up on special occasions – Santa hats are common at Christmas, as are jeans and cowboy boots during July's Stampede in Calgary. Halloween is another opportunity to wear ridiculous clothes, and is beginning to rival Christmas as an excuse to dress up at work.

Dress in Vancouver tends to be more casual than average, in Toronto it's similar to the British approach, while French-Canadians dress in a more relaxed continental European style. In rural areas and the north, it's advisable not to overdress, as locals can be dismissive of 'suits'. Business dress code is also sometimes dictated by the weather; in winter, you'll need a thick jacket, boots, gloves and hat, and won't impress business partners if you arrive in a thin suit and black shoes, however smart or cutting-edge they are.

Greetings

Most Canadian business people greet each other with handshakes and quickly move on to first names with new acquaintances, but don't assume this. Begin by using last names and Mr (or *Monsieur* for French-Canadians) and Ms (or *Madame*) for women. Follow the other person's lead with regards to moving to a first-name basis. People generally appreciate the correct pronunciation of their names (which isn't always easy in multicultural Canada), so don't be shy to ask.

Negotiating

Business negotiations are usually direct and succinct in Canada, and extraneous discussion is usually avoided. Canadian business people don't tend to be aggressive or overbearing, and courteous behaviour is expected. An honest, open, self-deprecating manner is appreciated, rather than too assertive or pushy. Business negotiations can be long and protracted – don't expect Canadians to sign on the dotted line after a brief business meeting – they may need some time to mull over a business proposition.

Socialising

It's common for Canadian business people to show visitors around their city or region. Indeed, many are only too happy to show you their 'patch', and are proud of the country's attractions and natural beauty. They sometimes conduct business over meals, but be careful not to drink heavily, which is not part of Canadian business practice. The person who makes the invitation invariably pays. Drinks after work are also common in the Canadian business environment, but again,

> The Canadian labour market is kept fresh by the annual addition of 250,000 new immigrants.

drinking to excess is rare. Many Canadian business people leave work relatively early (they also start early) to return home to their family, and they tend not to be late-night people.

Timekeeping

Canadians keep an eye on the time, and expect appointments and meetings to take place precisely when scheduled. You should telephone if you're going to be late, which is sometimes unavoidable due to traffic or weather-related delays, about which Canadians will be sympathetic. Socially, Canadians are also time sticklers, and often surprise immigrants by arriving at the time stated on an social invitation, rather than the 'polite' quarter of an hour late.

NATIONAL & PROVINCIAL HOLIDAYS

In Canada, the word 'holiday' means a statutory national (federal) or provincial holiday, and not an annual or school holiday, which is called a vacation. Banks, post offices, public schools, offices and most businesses are usually closed on national and provincial holidays. Shopping malls, however, tend to do their best business on holidays, and invariably close only on Christmas Day. When a holiday falls on a Saturday or Sunday, another day is usually granted as a holiday.

National Holidays	
Date	Holiday
*1st January	New Year's Day
*March/April	Good Friday
March/April	Easter Monday
*Monday before 25th May	Victoria Day – Queen Victoria's birthday (not observed in Quebec – not surprisingly!)
*1st July	Canada Day (previously Dominion Day) – the anniversary of the creation of the Dominion of Canada in 1867 (see below)
*First Monday in September	Labour Day (see below)
*Second Monday in October	Thanksgiving Day (see below)
11th November	Remembrance Day – The signing of the armistice of World War I, in which many Canadian soldiers fell in Flanders. As in the UK, people wear poppies and observe two minutes' silence at 11am. Not a full day's holiday for all Canadians.
*25th December	Christmas Day
26th December	Boxing Day

* Statutory holidays in all provences/ territories

In addition to the holidays listed, multicultural Canada celebrates a wide range of religious and ethnic holidays, such as Yom Kippur and Hindu and Muslim holidays. Those of Russian origin celebrate Christmas on January 6th, and the Lunar New Year is celebrated by the Chinese in January or February.

Statutory Holidays

The three main national holidays in Canada are Canada Day (which celebrates Canada's creation as a dominion), Labour Day (which honours Canadian workers) and Thanksgiving (which commemorates the first harvest of European settlers), each of which is described in more detail below. The holidays listed in the box (left) are observed by most Canadians, although only those marked with an asterisk are statutory holidays.

Canada Day

In Quebec, Canada Day has a particular significance – not just as a holiday – because all leases in the province expire at the end of June, therefore 1st July is often the day to move home (book a removal van months in advance, or you'll be doing it yourself!). The traditional Canadian way to celebrate Canada Day is to have a barbecue, drink beer and have a firework display. Quebec's most important holiday is Saint-Jean-Baptiste Day on 24th

June, and although the province's inhabitants celebrate Canada Day, it's more understated than in the rest of the country.

Labour Day

Labour Day in September celebrates the economic and social achievements of workers and the labour union movement, and is the equivalent of Europe's May Day. It's the last chance for families to get away before the school year begins, and many use it as an opportunity to 'winterise' their summer cabin or cottage.

Thanksgiving

Canadians celebrate Thanksgiving much like the Americans, but on the second weekend in October rather than at the end of November. Some people think that this is because the

> 'There is hardly anything in the world that some man cannot make a little worse and sell a little cheaper.'
>
> John Ruskin (English critic & author)

harvest is earlier in Canada, while others regard it as a sensible decision to put some distance between the Thanksgiving and Christmas holidays. Canada's traditional Thanksgiving fare is similar to America's: turkey, stuffing, cranberry sauce, corn, mashed potato and gravy, with pumpkin pie for dessert (pudding).

Provincial & Territorial Holidays

In addition to the national statutory holidays listed above, individual provinces designate their own holidays as shown in the box below:

Provincial & Territorial Holidays

Province	Day/Date	Holiday
Alberta	Third Monday in February	Alberta (or Family) Day
	First Monday in August	Heritage Day
British Columbia	First Monday in August	British Columbia Day
Manitoba	First Monday in August	Civic Holiday
New Brunswick	First Monday in August	New Brunswick Day
Newfoundland	Nearest Monday to 17th March	St Patrick's Day
	Nearest Monday to 23rd April	St George's Day
	Nearest Monday to 27th June	Discovery Day
	Nearest Monday to 7th July	Memorial Day
	Nearest Monday to 10th July	Orangemen's Day
Northwest Territories	First Monday in August	Civic Holiday
Nova Scotia	First Monday in August	Natal Day
Nunavut	First Monday in August	Civic Holiday
Ontario	First Monday in August	Civic Holiday
Prince Edward Island	First Monday in August	Natal Day
Quebec	24th June	Saint-Jean-Baptiste Day
Saskatchewan	First Monday in August	Civic Holiday
Yukon	Third Monday in August	Discovery Day

7.
ON THE MOVE

As in the US, the car is king in Canada and has complete hegemony over public transport, which is poor except in the major cities. If you live in a major city, it isn't always essential to own a car, although even in cities there are areas that aren't served by off-road public transport such as trains, trams (streetcars) or metro (subway); buses are subject to the same delays as other road traffic, and may be unreliable or don't operate when you need them. Crime can also be a problem when using public transport, particularly late at night. In any case, if you live in the country or a city suburb off the main rail and bus routes, it's essential to have your own transport.

> The Trans-Canada Highway is the longest main road in the world – 7,821km (4,860mi) – and joins all ten of Canada's southern provinces.

DRIVING

It's almost impossible to survive in Canada without a car, unless you live in the middle of one of the major cities and rarely leave it. Canada has more vehicles per head of population than any country in the world except the US – many families have two or more – and Canadians are keen to learn to drive as early as possible because public transport is sparse, even in the cities. In most Canadian provinces, you can learn to drive (accompanied by an adult) from as young as 14 and drive on your own from 16 (15 in Yukon). For commercial vehicles, the age limit is 18 or 19. Licensing in Canada is under a system called the graduated licensing program, run by each province. The rules vary slightly in each province, but in general, new drivers are licensed to drive in stages (whereby restrictions apply to newly-qualified drivers). Car insurance is compulsory throughout Canada and drivers must carry proof of insurance.

Canada is a huge country – in some regions you can drive for miles without seeing another vehicle – and those living in remote areas think nothing of spending several hours behind the wheel to do the weekly shopping. Unlike in most countries, responsibility for the Canadian highway system lies with provincial and municipal authorities, and not with the federal government. As a result, traffic laws often vary depending on the province and you shouldn't take it for granted that the road rules in all provinces are the same.

Canadian Drivers

Driving standards and etiquette vary across Canada. In the laid-back Maritimes, drivers tend to be considerate of others and don't speed, whereas Calgary drivers have a reputation for being impatient, even aggressive; however, drivers in Montreal are reckoned to be the worst. Torontonians are almost as bad. However, given the number of vehicles on the road and the young age at which people can start to drive, there are surprisingly few deaths from vehicle accidents in Canada. Quebec has the highest accident rate, with Montreal especially dangerous, where drivers are known for their nerves of steel, excessive confidence and devil-may-care attitude.

Canada's Roads

Canada has over 900,000km (560,000mi) of roads and a national main road (highway) system covering 24,000km (15,000mi), including the longest main road

Canada has a reality television series called *Canada's Worst Driver*, which the Canadian Safety Council has called irresponsible, pointing out that Canada has the third-lowest rate of traffic fatalities of the 30 OECD nations.

in the world – the Trans-Canada Highway, which stretches 7,821km (4,860mi) from St John's in Newfoundland to Victoria in British Columbia. Many of Canada's major thoroughfares are east-west rather than north-south, the main exception being the Alaska Highway (which runs from Dawson Creek, British Columbia to Delta Junction, Alaska via Whitehorse in the Yukon) in the west.

Streets in most cities are laid out in a grid pattern (hence the word 'gridlock' for traffic jam), all roads running either north-south or east-west; you need to know the numbering (or lettering) system so that you can find your way around. It's also useful to know which part of a town or city you want when asking for directions, e.g. uptown, downtown, eastside or westside (unhelpfully, descriptions vary with the town). Calgary is planned on a quadrant system, with numbers beginning in the centre and counting outwards, and 'avenues' running east-west and 'streets' north-south. In older cities, such as Vancouver and Victoria, the streets have 'proper' names and tend to weave and wind all over the place (in the British style).

Most major cities have multi-lane main roads, particularly Toronto, where highway 401 (one of the busiest roads in the world) has between 6 and 18 lanes. Some lanes, known as collector lanes, have exit warnings for towns several kilometres in advance. Main access routes are busy night and day, therefore, needless to say, it's best to avoid rush hours.

Direction signs are sometimes sparse, inconsistent and poorly placed (most road signs in North America are 'discreet'), and are particularly difficult to read at night in urban areas. Road signs are white (reflective) on a green background, signs for general attractions have a blue background, and for heritage attractions a brown background.

The standard of Canadian roads varies enormously, from twelve-lane freeways in urban areas to gravel or dirt tracks in remote rural areas. Suburban roads and motorways are generally well surfaced and maintained, although roads suffer frost damage in winter, which produces corrugated surfaces. On gravel roads, it's wise to keep your distance from the vehicle in front in order to avoid flying stones and dust, and you should slow down and pull over to the right when someone overtakes, or when a vehicle comes from the opposite direction. If you're likely to be doing a lot of driving on dirt roads, you're recommended to have a mesh bug and gravel screen fitted, otherwise you'll be constantly replacing your windscreen (some people also fit screens to their lights and fuel tank). Driving with your lights on during the day helps other drivers to see you through thick dust (and any time in poor visibility).

Some roads are referred to by their number, while others are referred to locally by a name, which can be confusing. Multi-lane roads are called freeways, except in Quebec, where they're called autoroutes; many freeways have just two lanes in each direction. Sometimes the number of a road is changed by adding a '4' to the number, e.g. Highway 1 (the Trans-Canada Highway) changes to '401' when it becomes four lanes around Toronto. Even this major route has some poor surfaces where it goes through unpopulated areas with little traffic. Generally, Canadian roads have fewer road markings (e.g. reflective studs and lines) than European roads. There are few toll roads in Canada, although some bridges have tolls.

'Anybody going slower than you is an idiot, and anybody going faster than you is a maniac.'

George Carlin (American comedian)

Rush Hours

As in most countries, it's wise to avoid rush hours if possible. These vary with the city, but are usually between 7 and 9.30am, and from 4 to 6.30pm (small towns usually have shorter rush hours, e.g. 7.30 to 8.30am and 4.30 to 5.30pm). In some cities, driving rules on major thoroughfares change during rush hours, when parking is prohibited.

Speed Limits

Speed limits can vary considerably with the province or town, e.g. 100kph (62mph) on primary roads, 80kph (50mph) on non-primary roads, 50kph (31mph) or 'as posted' in urban areas, 40kph (25mph) in rural school zones, and 30kph (19mph) in urban school zones. All speed limits are given in kilometres per hour.

You're more likely to be stopped for speeding in Canada than in many other countries, particularly on major holiday weekends and in rural areas, where speeding fines comprise a large proportion of local municipal revenue. In most provinces, non-freeway speed limits

are more rigorously enforced than freeway limits, and are therefore more widely observed. Speed limits are enforced by police using radar guns, fixed speed cameras, marked and unmarked cars, helicopters and light aircraft. An increasing number of authorities (particularly in Alberta and Ontario) are introducing cameras that record a speeder's number plate – the first you know about it is when you receive a ticket in the post (the owner is responsible, irrespective of who was driving, unless he can prove that the car was stolen).

On roads with a 100kph (62mph) limit, you may receive a warning if your speed is between 100 and 120kph (75mph), but at 120kph you can be fined around $100 and above 140kph (87mph) around $250.

> Canadians are generally highly competent, polite drivers, although they are becoming more aggressive as a result of increased road congestion.

Rules of the Road

The following list includes some of the most common road rules in Canada, plus some tips designed to help you adjust to Canadian driving conditions and avoid accidents. Like many things, however, some rules vary with the province.

- In Canada, traffic drives on the right-hand side of the road. It saves confusion if you do likewise! If you aren't used to driving on the right, take it easy until you are accustomed to it. Be

Parliamentary
Business
Only

Affaires
parlementaires
seulement

GOVT. OF CANADA
GOUV. DU CANADA

particularly alert when leaving lay-bys, T-junctions, one-way streets, petrol (gas) stations and car parks, as it's easy to lapse into driving on the left.

- When you want to turn left at a junction, you must pass **in front of** a car turning left coming from the opposite direction, and not behind it (as in some other countries). At major junctions in some cities there are green-arrow signals for left-hand turn lanes. Certain lanes are signposted 'RIGHT LANE MUST TURN RIGHT' or 'EXIT ONLY' and mean what they say. If you get into these lanes by mistake, you **must** turn in the direction indicated.

- There's no automatic priority to the right (or left) on any roads in Canada (as there is in many European countries), although generally, a turning vehicle must give way to one going straight ahead. STOP signs are red and octagonal; YIELD (give way) signs are an inverted triangle (yellow with black letters). You must stop completely at a stop sign before pulling out from a junction (motorists who practise the 'rolling stop' are a favourite target of traffic cops). **Not all junctions have signs.** When approaching a main road from a secondary road, you must usually stop, even where there's no stop sign. At a YIELD sign you aren't required to stop, but must give priority to other traffic.

- You must use dipped headlights (low beam) between sunset and sunrise (usually from half an hour after sunset until half an hour before sunrise) in all provinces. Dipped lights must also be used when visibility is reduced to less than 500ft (150m). Driving with dipped lights during the day is permitted in all provinces, encouraged in some and mandatory in the Yukon. Full beam (high beams) must be dipped when you're within 500ft of another vehicle.

- Headlight flashing in Canada usually means 'After you'. As in many other countries, drivers often warn oncoming traffic of potential hazards (including police speed 'traps') by flashing their headlights (which may be illegal). Hazard warning lights (both indicators operating simultaneously) are used to warn other drivers of an accident, or

DUCATI
desmodue 800

The wearing of seatbelts is compulsory for all car occupants, and adults are responsible for ensuring that anyone under 16 is wearing one. There are fines for violations and in Ontario you also 'earn' two licence penalty points.

when your car has broken down and is causing an obstruction, and shouldn't be used when merely illegally parked.

● The sequence of Canadian traffic (stop) lights is usually red, green, yellow, red. Yellow means stop at the stop line; you may proceed only if the yellow light appears after you've crossed the stop line, or when stopping may cause an accident. A green filter light may be shown in addition to the full lamp signals, which indicates that you may drive in the direction shown by the arrow, irrespective of other lights showing. Stop lights are frequently set on the far side of a junction, sometimes making it difficult to judge where to stop, and are also strung across the road rather than located on posts by the roadside. In some suburban areas, there are flashing red lights to indicate a stop light ahead. Driving through (running) red lights is a major cause of accidents in Canada, especially in winter when it's difficult to stop on the ice.

● One of the most surprising rules is that in some provinces and cities you may make a right turn at a red traffic light, unless otherwise posted. You must, however, treat a red light as a stop sign, and stop before making a right turn, and check that the road is clear. You must also give way to pedestrians crossing at traffic lights. Busy junctions often have signs indicating that turning on a red light isn't allowed (e.g. 'NO TURN ON RED') or is allowed at certain times only. If you've stopped and the motorist behind you is sounding his horn, it probably means that you can turn right. Although it appears to be a sensible rule, some people claim that it increases accidents. In some provinces, you can also make a left turn on a red light from a one-way street into another one-way street. **Never assume you can make a turn at a red light – if you do so when it's illegal, you can be fined heavily!**

● Always approach pedestrian crossings with caution, and don't park or overtake another vehicle on the approach to a crossing. Pedestrians have the right of way once they've stepped onto a pedestrian crossing without traffic lights and you must stop; motorists who don't stop are liable to heavy penalties. In some towns, a pedestrian may indicate that he intends to cross by pointing (arm fully extended), and walking in the direction he plans to go. Where a road crosses a public footpath, e.g. at the entrance to a property or a car park bordering a road, motorists must give way to pedestrians.

- Railway crossings on public roads are clearly marked, usually with a large 'X' sign (in Ontario these are white with a red border). Some crossings have

automatic gates or other barriers, and most have red lights that flash when a train is coming. On private roads, there may be no barriers or lights, so it's wise to stop and look and listen in both directions before crossing. In heavy traffic, don't attempt to cross until your exit is clear. Never attempt to cross a railway line when the barriers are down or the lights are flashing.

- Some cities have cycle lanes, indicated by double dotted lanes on the kerb side of the road, which must be avoided by motorists.

- Children getting on or off school buses (usually painted yellow and clearly marked 'SCHOOL BUS') have priority over all traffic. All motorists **must** stop at least 65ft (20m) from a school bus loading or unloading, indicated by flashing (usually red) lights or 'stop arms'. Vehicles must stop even when a school bus has halted on the opposite side of the road (children may run across the road) unless the road is divided by a barrier. Motorists must remain stopped until the bus moves off or the driver signals motorists to proceed.

  The law regarding school buses is taken seriously and motorists convicted for the first

Some provinces allow the use of radar-detectors, while in others even having a detector in your car is an offence.

time of passing a stopped bus are subject to a fine of as much as $2,000, possible imprisonment or community service, and six penalty points on their driving licence. If you're convicted a second time within five years, the fine could be many thousands of dollars and a further six penalty points, plus a possible six-month prison sentence.

- In Toronto, you must stop well away from the rear doors when a tram (streetcar) stops in front of you, so that passengers can get on and off easily and safely – unless there are safety islands in the street at tram stops, in which case it isn't necessary to stop.

- Certain provinces allow you to use studded tyres all year round, while others permit their use during the winter months only. Ontario has banned their use at any time, due to the damage they cause to road surfaces when they aren't covered with snow.

- Road rules prohibit driving in bare feet, parking on a highway, allowing passengers to ride in the back of a pick-up truck, and having an open alcoholic drink can or bottle in your car (even when it's stationary and the ignition is off).

When driving in rural areas, you need to keep a lookout for wildlife and be prepared to stop or swerve – hitting a deer or moose can do serious damage to you and your car (it won't do the deer or moose much good either).

Raccoon

- An unofficial but widely observed practice on Canadian highways is that, if you break down, you indicate this by opening the bonnet (hood) and boot (trunk) of your car, which a passing motorist will interpret as a call for help and contact the police. In some areas, emergency phones are sited along the highway, but it's usually safer to stay in the car, particularly at night and in winter. Some motorists carry a waterproof 'PLEASE CALL POLICE' sign.

- Most road signs in Quebec are only in French , except in Montreal, where motorways (autoroutes) and bridges may have dual-language signs.

All provinces publish local rules of the road, e.g. *The Official Driver's Handbook* in Ontario, available from provincial ministries of transport and bookshops.

Wildlife Hazards

In country areas (i.e. the vast majority of Canada), you should look out for wildlife on the roads; major migration routes are marked by signs depicting a black deer on a yellow background, although you should expect to encounter many types of animal at any time of the year, particularly at night. Animals often stop in the middle of the road at night and can be mesmerised by headlights, and you should try switching your lights off and on and using your horn to encourage them to move (although this may only provoke them into attacking). If confronted by a moose or elk, you shouldn't get out of your car, as they can be aggressive and can move very fast when threatened. If you meet a black, grizzly or polar bear, it's time to practise driving in reverse – fast!

Winter Driving

With the exception of some parts of southern British Columbia, Canada has long, cold, snowy winters. If your car needs to be left out of doors in unusually cold conditions, the engine can freeze solid. It's a common sight in very cold weather to see cars left, securely locked with their engines running, outside shops. Most vehicles are fitted with engine heaters that you switch on when you turn off the engine. If you need to leave your car out overnight in winter, you should be prepared to dig it out of a snow-drift in the morning (make sure that you have a shovel and a blanket in the car).

Major roads have a mixture of salt, sand and gravel spread on them to help prevent vehicles from sliding on ice. Snowploughs clear heavy falls, and it isn't uncommon to see them driving two or even three abreast on major roads. In cities, the major roads are cleared first, followed by secondary streets, although it can take a couple of days before they're all cleared. You need studded tyres in winter (where legal), plus snow chains and equipment such as a shovel, traction mats, a bag of sand and a tow-chain (plus a blanket and water) in case you get stuck. You can buy all the necessary equipment (in an 'emergency car kit') from a hardware store. If you get stuck in deep snow and cannot get yourself out, don't sit in the car with the engine running (to operate the

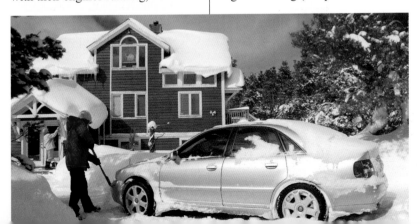

heater), as it may fill with carbon monoxide fumes and kill you. The Canadian Automobile Association (CAA) recommends that you carry matches and a candle in an open-topped tin – just one candle burning in a car keeps it reasonably warm.

When travelling in country areas in winter, the CAA recommends that you carry a warm coat and other extra clothing, sleeping bags, emergency food such as fruit, chocolate or tinned soup, a torch, warning lights or road flares, jump leads, an axe, a fire extinguisher, an ice-scraper and a brush, and some methyl-hydrate for de-icing fuel lines and windows – the sort of equipment you might assemble for an expedition to the Arctic. In spring, you should wash your car thoroughly, particularly underneath, and repair any paint chips, otherwise salt from the roads will soon cause rust patches.

Parking

Parking in Canadian towns and cities can be a problem. Streets

often have restricted parking, or parking is prohibited altogether and, if you park illegally, the authorities won't hesitate to tow your car away. Parking regulations may vary depending on the area of a city, the time of day, the day of the week and even the season. In some towns, there are different parking regulations during rush hours on major thoroughfares, where no parking is permitted on one or both sides of the street during rush hour; this may include streets with parking meters in town centres, where there's usually no parking anywhere during rush hours, e.g. between 6 and 10am and 3 to 6pm. On some streets, parking restrictions apply at certain times only (shown on signs), e.g. between 9 and 11am Mondays to Thursdays.

> Parking on some streets is prohibited during certain hours on some days for street cleaning; if you park during these periods, your car will be impounded. Be sure to read all parking signs carefully.

If you don't see a parking meter, don't assume that parking is free, as meters tend to be set well back from the kerb so that they aren't buried by ploughed snow. In winter, some streets are designated 'snow streets', meaning you mustn't park there when snowfall exceeds a certain depth (shown on a sign), in order to leave the road free for snow ploughs. A yellow or red

> 'I've just solved the parking problem. I bought a parked car.'
>
> Henny Youngman (American comedian)

kerb also indicates that parking is forbidden.

Apart from the obvious illegal parking spots, such as across entrances, at bus stops and in front of fire and ambulance stations and schools, take care not to park within 5m (15ft) of a fire hydrant, often indicated by a large gap between parked cars, or your car will be towed away. Some city centre areas are also designated tow-away zones, where all illegally parked cars are impounded. If your car is towed away, it costs from around $110 ($80 for the tow and $30 for the parking fine) to get it back. Your car may also be clamped (called a boot in Canada) if you park illegally in a major city. Payment of fines must be made within a certain period; a fine may be reduced if you pay within seven days, after which it can increase dramatically. Parking offences throughout Canada are recorded on computer and if you have a unpaid ticket when you come to renew your annual licence fee, you must pay it on the spot.

Parking on main roads in rural areas is forbidden and you must pull completely off the road if you wish to stop. Overnight off-road parking is usually prohibited or restricted when towing a trailer or driving a recreation vehicle (RV) or motor home, and you must use an official trailer or RV car park.

Petrol Stations

All petrol (gaz in Quebec, gas elsewhere) in Canada is unleaded and sold by the litre. Three grades are available: regular (87 octane), special or mid-grade (89 octane) and premium (92 octane). Some city service stations open 24 hours a day, seven days a week. When motoring in rural areas, however, it's recommended to keep your tank topped up (and check your oil and water frequently), as petrol stations are few and far between, and may be closed on Sundays and holidays (many petrol stations are also closed in the evenings and at weekends).

On major roads, truck stops have the longest opening hours. It pays to carry an emergency supply in a steel can.

PUBLIC TRANSPORT

Canadians aren't enthusiastic public transport users and, when not flying, they prefer to drive. Public transport in the major cities varies from excellent to scant, but in country areas it's invariably poor and you need your own transport. With a few exceptions, such as the luxury coach service between Calgary and Edmonton, long-distance bus services leave much to be desired, and the train service is no longer what it was in the days before the airlines dominated long-distance travel. With over half of Canada's population living in the area around the Great Lakes and in the St. Lawrence lowlands, most of whom venture beyond the urban areas only for holidays (vacations), there isn't much call for train travel other than in the tourist season.

The one area of public transport where Canada excels is air travel, and Canadians enjoy the most comprehensive and cheapest services in the world, after Americans.

Air Travel

Flying is the fastest and most convenient way of travelling in Canada and to the US, which together have the lowest air fares in the world (some are even lower than Greyhound bus fares). Canadian domestic fares vary according to the time of day, the day of the week, how far in advance you book, and the season.

There are three fare seasons: high (summer and holiday periods), shoulder (e.g. around Thanksgiving) and low or off-peak, which is most other times (particularly during school terms). The summer peak season runs from 1st June to 1st September. Christmas and New Year are peak periods for domestic flights, although not usually for international flights. The shoulder season often includes the period immediately before a public (statutory) holiday. When planning a flight during a holiday period, book **well** in advance.

The two most popular domestic routes – Montreal-Toronto and Vancouver-Toronto – each carry over a million passengers a year, and even the short route from Calgary to Edmonton (less than 320km/200mi) carries around half a million passengers a year.

Canada has excellent air links to most countries, and 100 airlines transport over 40m passengers 60bn miles a year. Canada's leading international airports are at Calgary, Edmonton, Gander (Newfoundland), Halifax, Montreal, Toronto, Vancouver and Winnipeg. These are termed gateway airports and act as hubs for domestic services to smaller airports. When taking a plane from an international airport in Canada, check in advance which terminal you require.

With few exceptions (such as Montreal Mirabel airport, which is 34mi/55km outside town and takes around an hour to reach from the city centre, and Edmonton which is 19mi/30km or 45 minutes outside town), all major airports can be reached from city centres in around 30 minutes. St John's, Winnipeg and Vancouver airports are less than 5mi (8km) outside town, and can be reached in around 15 minutes.

Trains

Canada's railways have been in decline since the '50s, and have lost much of their former business to roads, air travel and long-distance buses. Nevertheless, they've undergone something of a revival in recent years, particularly as a relaxed way to view some of the spectacular scenery in the Rockies in the west of the country. Canada's rail network is one of the largest in the world, with 31,000mi (50,000km) of track. However, in terms of passenger miles per head of population, it rates well behind other industrialised nations. The fastest and best trains carry freight, which has priority over (and subsidises) the passenger service.

> The Canadian Pacific Railway (CPR) is one of Canada's most famous icons and helped open up the country, although nowadays trains carry mostly freight.

Rail is unable to compete with the low cost and speed of air travel (e.g. it takes around five days to drive from Toronto to Vancouver, but you can fly in just five hours), and the convenience of car travel. Canadian long-distance trains are painfully slow compared with those in most European countries (but at least they give you the chance to enjoy the scenery as you crawl through the Rockies). On some routes, there's just one train a day, and trains are so often late on long-distance routes that timetables warn passengers not to book connecting transport.

If you need to buy a ticket for a long-distance train, you should get to the station at least half an hour before departure. Only the advance purchase of a ticket guarantees a seat. If you're planning to take a long-distance train during the summer or on a federal holiday, it's wise to book well in advance (you can do so up to six months ahead).

The rail system is at its best in the Montreal-Windsor corridor, which is hardly surprising because almost half the population of Canada lives there. Trains are frequent and relatively fast, particularly during commuting hours.

Long-distance Buses

Canada has an extensive network of long-distance buses (also called coaches), which are usually the cheapest form of public transport in Canada (and to the US). Although there have been cutbacks in services in recent years caused by increased competition from domestic airlines, long-distance buses continue to survive and even prosper. You can travel almost anywhere in Canada by bus, on an extensive network of scheduled routes with good connections.

You must usually buy a ticket at a bus terminal or a central office before boarding a bus, but need to allow plenty of time, as there are often long queues (lines). Always ask for the cheapest available fare, which may not be advertised. By far the cheapest long-distance company, Greyhound, offers a variety of discounts off its standard fares.

Buses stop at designated (flag) stops, where you must signal the driver if you want to get on. As with planes and trains, luggage is checked boarding a bus. Allow around 45 minutes in cities and 15 minutes in small towns. When two buses are running on the same route, make sure that your luggage is put on the right bus!

Urban Systems

Canada's major cities have good or excellent urban and suburban transit systems, operated mainly for the benefit of commuters. Fast and frequent services are available on a mixture of buses, surface and underground (metro/subway) trains, monorails and, in some cities, ferries.

Most small towns away from the major cities have some sort of bus service, but these tend to be infrequent and slow, so for convenience almost everybody has a car.

Taxis

Taxis are plentiful and relatively inexpensive in most cities, where several companies operate taxis in a variety of colours and styles. Their only common feature is a plastic 'TAXI' sign on the roof, which when illuminated means the taxi is for hire. Taxis can be hailed on the street or you can pick one up from a taxi rank. Most taxi drivers are courteous and helpful – except when they are eastern Europeans who don't speak English.

You can pay your taxi fare with a credit or debit card in most cities.

8.
THE CANADIANS AT PLAY

Becoming socially adept in a different culture is perhaps the biggest obstacle to 'fitting in' abroad. It's also the area where you're most likely to make mistakes. To help you avoid social gaffes, this chapter contains information on social customs, dress code, dining, and social and leisure activities.

APPEARANCE & DRESS

Your appearance and, most of all, how others see you is generally of less importance in Canada than in many other countries, although much depends on the circles you move in and whether you're trying to make a good impression, e.g. on a prospective boss or a member of the opposite sex. Canadians (at least in the cities) have become more fashion conscious in recent years, particularly young people. Nevertheless, most people will 'take you as they find you' and expect you to do likewise.

Smart casual wear is the order of the day in most situations, shoes, long trousers (slacks) and a shirt with a collar is an acceptable outfit almost anywhere for men, and a dress or skirt and blouse for women. However, if you're invited to a formal social occasion, you should inquire about the appropriate dress beforehand. As ever in Canada, there are regional differences, with less (US-style) formality in the west and a more European attitude in Quebec.

'When I'm in Canada, I feel this is what the world should be like.'

Jane Fonda
(American actress)

DRINKING

Canada has an ambivalent attitude towards alcohol. Some Canadians don't drink it and Puritanism stills holds sway in certain rural areas, particularly in parts of the Prairie Provinces, which are sometimes called the Canadian 'Bible Belt'. In Quebec, on the other hand, **not** drinking is sometimes viewed suspiciously, and in Canada generally, drinking beer is integral to the lives of many people. Generally, however, there's a much stricter attitude towards drunkenness than in many other countries and, if

'I saw a notice which said 'Drink Canada Dry' and I've just started.'

Brendan Behan (Irish playwright and writer)

Beer marketing has been cleverly tailored to the Canadian climate: the handles on Canadian beer cases are big enough to fit hands wearing mittens.

you look as if you've had one too many in a bar, you're likely to be refused service and may even be asked to leave. Business drinking is modest and disciplined, and drunken behaviour is socially unacceptable and regarded with contempt. When in groups, Canadians tend to buy their own drinks rather than rounds.

Beer

Even though beer wasn't invented in Canada and Canadians aren't in the top ten of consuming nations, beer has a central place in the lives of many Canadians and is integral to the national self-image. It's the favoured tipple of most Canadian drinkers, accounting for over 80 per cent of all alcohol sold in Canada.

Canada has a long tradition of beer brewing dating back to its pioneer days, although the major producers have been swallowed up by foreign companies. Most people consider Canadian beer to be better than American beer – it's darker and tangier than most American brews – it's generally fairly weak and rarely more than 5 per cent alcohol by volume. Exceptions are ice beer, and a few extra-strong beers such as Molson's XXX, which packs 7.3 per cent alcohol by volume (Canadians say the XXX means 'three beers and you're outta here'). All beer, not just ice beer, is usually served ice cold – much colder than most foreigners (except Americans and Australians) are used to. Many households, especially in rural areas, have an old refrigerator kept on the porch or utility room, which is used for keeping beer supplies cold, and known, not surprisingly, as the 'beer fridge'.

The best-known Canadian brewers are Alexander Keith's, Carling-O'Keefe, Kokanee, Labatt, Molson (North America's oldest beer maker, founded in 1786), Moosehead and Schooner. However, the tastiest beers often come from small, local breweries ('microbreweries') and 'brewpubs', where beer is brewed on the premises. Among the most popular beers are Molson's Canadian, Golden, Oktoberfest, Export, Dry and Ice; and Labatt's Blue, Extra and Dry. In Quebec and the Atlantic provinces, locals also

---

Drinking Terminology

Mickey: A pint liquor bottle.

40-pounder: A liquor bottle larger than a pint.

Six-pack: A package of six cans or bottles of beer.

Stubby: A short-necked beer bottle, which used to be standard but is now, sadly, rare.

Two-four: 24 beers, also referred to as a 'two-fer', a 'flat' or 'four times the fun' (as a six-pack).

Bloody Caesar: A Bloody Mary (vodka, Worcestershire sauce, 'clamato' juice – clams and tomato – and celery salt), which is an interesting blend of drink, pick-me-up and meal. A Virgin Caesar is the same, minus the vodka.

Calgary Red Eye: A mixture of Canadian beer and tomato juice, sometimes with the addition of an egg. It's also called the 'breakfast of champions' as it's reputed to cure a hangover.

---

province, but most bars, pubs and lounges open at noon and close at 1 or 2am. Laws in Quebec are more liberal, allowing bars to stay open until 3 or 4am. Large cities usually have after-hours bars that stay open for music and dancing after regular bars close (but they stop serving alcohol).

The minimum age for drinking alcohol in Alberta, Manitoba and Quebec is 18, while in the rest of Canada it's 19. The bartender is supposed to ask your age and may ask for identification (ID), but in practice this rarely happens if you look old enough. Acceptable identification usually consists of a driving licence or a provincial identification card, which you can obtain from your local motor licence office. Some city bars run 'designated driver' schemes, whereby the appointed driver of a group gets free non-alcoholic drinks all night (drinking and driving is a serious offence throughout Canada).

drink non-alcoholic spruce beer, although the taste takes some getting used to.

Whisky

Canadians are also fond of whisky, which is often referred to as rye. It's a blend of whiskies (usually barley and rye corn) distilled only in Canada. Popular brands include Canadian Club, Crown Royal and Seagram.

Licensing Hours

Like many laws in Canada, licensing hours vary depending on the

EATING

There's a widespread perception that Canadians toss all their food into a deep fat fryer or drown it in sugar or perhaps both. This is thought to explain the popularity (indeed ubiquity) of the Tim Horton's chain, which sells doughnuts (and is famous for its coffee). However, it's an outdated view of Canada's relationship with food. The country actually has a huge range of interesting cuisines, in part thanks to its many ethnic groups. Most regions have a dish or dishes with which they're identified, e.g. Pacific salmon in the west, beef and Taber corn in Alberta, bannock with First Nation peoples, fruit in the Okanagan region of British Columbia, cod in Newfoundland, sourdough bread in the Yukon and potatoes on Prince Edward Island.

Canada has also been responsible for some 'creative' foods, including prairie oysters (claimed by western Canada), which are fried young bull's testicles. Aboriginal Canadians

have contributed pemmican, which is made from pounded buffalo meat, cranberries and fat, dried to a leathery texture and convenient for carrying on long journeys. Tougher pieces of pemmican can take ages to chew properly – several weeks if your teeth are dodgy.

The above notwithstanding, a lot of Canada's favourite foods **are** sweet (to cheer people up during the long winters?), including butter tart (similar to pecan pie, but with raisins), maple fudge and the Nanaimo bar (a layered confection of cracker crust with a sugar-cream filling and a chocolate topping, named after a town on Vancouver Island).

The Food Court is a popular phenomenon in Canada's shopping malls, consisting of fast-food versions of a range of the world's cuisines, including American, Chinese, Greek, Italian, Japanese, Mexican and Vietnamese.

Meals

Meal times in Canada are, to some extent, dictated by working hours. Because Canadians begin work earlier than Europeans, meals are

---

Potatoes

A lot of Canadian meals involve potatoes in some form or other: fried, mashed, boiled, diced, hashed, cubed, scalloped, sliced or whipped or made into dumplings. Norwegian immigrants even use them to make a seasonal dessert, *lefse* – pastries consisting of thinly sliced potatoes flavoured with sugar and cinnamon.

also taken earlier. The lunch break begins at 12 and is usually a light, quickly eaten affair – sandwiches and 'wraps' are popular. The day's main meal is eaten at 6pm, sometimes at 5 in farming regions. Few Canadians linger over meals and many eat in front of the television. Fast food and frozen dinners are popular, but sales of organic food are also increasing.

Invitations

When you receive a written invitation to dinner, it's always necessary to respond, although not always in writing. An invitation will usually have RSVP (*Répondez s'il vous plaît* – literally 'please reply') written on it, and possibly a date by which you should reply. With both formal and informal invitations, if you need to cancel you should always ring and apologise for not being able to attend – and have a good excuse if you want to be invited again. It's also usual to ring friends and tell them if you're going to be more than 15 minutes late. On formal occasions you should **never** be more than a few minutes late and it's considered very bad manners to arrive after the main guest or speaker (when it's better not to arrive at all).

If you're invited to a French-Canadian's home, bear in mind that homes are divided into private and public rooms, and the kitchen is usually a private room where you may enter only upon invitation.

Most Canadian homes have two doors – outer and inner – to help retain the heat. The area between (the mud room) is where layers of clothing and footwear are put on or removed. It's normal to remove your footwear on entering a home, whether or not there's snow outside.

If you have medical, dietary or religious reasons for not eating certain foods, you should explain this to your host when accepting an invitation, although you may have no choice with a formal meal and may just have to refuse or leave anything you cannot eat.

Table Manners

If you're invited to dine in a Canadian home, dinner occasionally begins with grace (which is more usual when guests are present than when they aren't). It's important to wait for the host or hostess to be seated before beginning to eat, and you're expected to ask for items such as a butter dish or bowl of peas to be passed to you, rather than reach for them yourself. Relaxed, American-style table manners hold sway in most of Canada, with a little more European formality in Quebec.

Wine is invariably served with meals. In Quebec, it's considered bad form to ask for a martini or whisky before dinner, as French-Canadians (unlike the French) regard them as palate-numbing. Instead, champagne, kir (white wine with a dash of blackcurrant liqueur), pastis and vermouth are usual pre-dinner drinks. French-Canadians usually serve liqueurs after dinner.

Maple Syrup

Canada is famous for its maple syrup and produces over 80 per cent of the world's output. Most of the country's sugar maples are grown in eastern Canada (mainly in Quebec), where the syrup is a major export; the new season's produce is eagerly awaited every spring. It's a popular topping, particularly on pancakes/flapjacks, ice cream, rice pudding and toast. It's especially loved in Quebec, where people have a particularly sweet tooth, and features in or on *tarte au sucre* (sugar pie) and *trempette* (bread soaked in maple sugar).

> Maple syrup is made from maple tree sap; Canada's eastern forests are filled with 'sugar shacks' (also used for social gatherings), where the sap is collected from pipes which lead from taps in the trees.

Quebec's Cuisine

It's a common misconception that the same food is served in Quebec as in France. In fact, the province isn't always a paradise for lovers of fine food: *steamés* (steamed hot dogs) are the national food of the province, and Québécois are more likely to fill their stomachs with the usual range of fast foods than with foie-gras and snails. They're as fond of tomato ketchup as other North Americans and the legendary *poutine* (a fast-food dish of French fries covered in cheese curds and gravy, sometimes with another sauce too!) hails from Quebec; when made badly, it congeals in the stomach like ready-mixed concrete.

The well-to-do Québécois tend to have a French or Italian attitude to food, however, and consider cooking a fine art. Montreal has more fine dining establishments than most Canadian cities, and even small communities in Quebec often boast eateries with excellent chefs. This is partly explained by immigration in the '60s and '70s from Belgium, France and Switzerland, which brought many chefs and waiters to Canada.

Historically, Quebec cuisine dates from the fur trade period, and many dishes have a high fat content to provide energy for surviving long, cold winters, and for getting out and about to trap animals and relieve them of their skins. Traditional dishes include *cretons* (a meat paste, made from ground pork, onions and spices), pea soup and *tourtière* (a minced meat pie). Contemporary Quebec inventions include the above-mentioned *poutine*, *La Riopelle de l'Isle* (a triple-cream cheese) and whippet cookies (a biscuit base, topped with marshmallow and covered in chocolate – nothing to do with racing dogs you'll be pleased to learn).

CAFES & RESTAURANTS

Canada's ethnic diversity is most evident in the range and variety of its eating establishments, the most common of which are Chinese (most regional styles), Italian (plus pizza parlours), Japanese (particularly sushi bars), Jewish, Korean, Mexican (or 'Tex-Mex'), Thai and Vietnamese, and (in Quebec) French. Vancouver and Toronto have many Chinese and other Asian restaurants, although in Vancouver and Victoria the trend is to follow the fads from California – whether for Italian, Korean or 'fusion' cooking (a mix of cuisines). Ethnic restaurants are one of the joys of eating out in Canada.

Canada's most unusual dining experiences are found in the Atlantic provinces, where some Newfoundland eateries pride themselves on such bizarre dishes as cod cheeks, capelin (tiny fish which have been pickled and smoked before being pinned to fences to dry), brewis (soaked hard-tack biscuit boiled with cod), seal flipper pie, seal soup, and moose and rabbit pie. However, the Atlantic Provinces also offer some of the best seafood in North America, including superb lobster in New Brunswick, scallops in Nova Scotia and mussels on Prince Edward Island. British Columbia is famous for its salmon, where the annual barbecues of Pacific sockeye salmon, hot-smoked over alder wood, shouldn't be missed.

Coffee Culture

Coffee culture is most associated with British Columbia but is found throughout Canada. Coffee is served in a mind-boggling variety of ways in a plethora of coffee shops and cafes. If you want a regular white coffee, it's best to stick with an 'Americano'. If you like your coffee with cream and sweet, ask for a 'double-double' – that's double cream, double sugar! Coffee also comes in various sizes including short (small) and long (large) and may be served in a cup (usually) or a glass. You can also order decaf coffee (made with decaffeinated coffee beans), low-fat milk (skinny) or soya milk (soy).

Vancouver waterfront

CLUBS

There are numerous social clubs, societies and associations in Canada, and all Canadian cities and towns have a wide range of clubs. Joining a club or society is an excellent way to meet people, make business contacts and be accepted into the local community. In smaller towns, social life revolves around the church and social clubs, and if you aren't a member your life may be dull. In the major cities, there are exclusive private clubs where the 'old boy' network thrives, such as the Chelsea club in Ottawa, and there are also posh country clubs, although these are usually golf or tennis clubs rather than strictly social clubs.

Popular and widespread clubs and organisations include the Royal Canadian Legion, Masons, Shriners, YWCA/YMCA, Kiwanis (who hold an annual charity fundraising duck race on Ottawa's Rideau Canal), Lion and Lioness, Toastmasters, Oddfellows, and the Canadian Federation of University Women and Big Brothers/Sisters (a charitable organisation that pairs adults with young children whose parents have died or are divorced). There are a number of fraternal associations and professional organisations, many of which have an ethnic, political or labour orientation, with large memberships and extensive facilities.

Canada has a variety of children's groups and clubs such as the Girl Guides (including the Sparks, Brownies and Pathfinders) and the Boy Scouts (including the Beavers and Cubs).

> '**I had no idea Canada could be so much fun.'**
> Bruce Willis (actor)

NIGHTLIFE

Canadian nightlife includes nightclubs, dance clubs (which may have various levels or rooms, each with a different kind of music), karaoke clubs, comedy clubs, cabaret bars, theatre restaurants, gay clubs, pool halls, ex-servicemen's clubs and casinos. There are nightclubs (where you can dance to live and/or recorded music) in all major Canadian towns and cities.

- **Opening hours** – Nightclubs may open as early as 7 or 8pm, particularly if they have a restaurant, but many don't liven up until 10pm or later and they may not close until dawn.

- **Age limit** – Nightclubs and dance clubs are usually restricted to those over 18 or 19, and the doorman may ask for proof of your age (in the form of a drivers' licence, provincial ID card or passport). Some nightclubs are for members only and have high prices, which tend to attract an older, more well-to-do clientele.

- **Dress code** – The dress code is usually smart-casual, which normally excludes jeans, leathers, T-shirts and trainers, although in some establishments these may be *de rigueur* (fashion usually dictates, depending on the venue). Dress may also be at the whim of the doorman (bouncer) and if he doesn't like the look of you, you're out. Some nightclubs have strict dress codes (and high prices – see above).

- **Bouncers** – Nightclub bouncers (doormen) are sometimes security guards earning extra cash in their time off, and some like to throw their weight around (literally). If a bouncer refuses you entry, it's best not to argue (particularly if you're a man) but go elsewhere.

- **Entrance fees** – Admission fees to nightclubs vary, but there's usually a $10 to $25 cover charge, which may include a drink. Some provide free entry to women on certain days (e.g. Wednesdays), and half-price drinks before 9pm (before the real 'action' starts) on some days.

- **Drinks** – Clubs serve all types of alcoholic and non-alcoholic drinks, with the exception of hot drinks, which are usually expensive, for example from $10 for a beer and even $2.50 to $5 per glass for water. Venues with live music may charge as much as $20 for entry and $6 to $12 per drink.

- **Paying** – In most clubs you order at the bar and pay when

Visitors to nightclubs, particularly women, should be wary of leaving their drinks unattended as they can be spiked with drugs (in order to rob or rape victims).

your drinks are served. In venues where there's waiter service, you pay when the waiter brings the round of drinks rather than ask for a bill later. As in bars, it isn't usual to buy rounds.

FAMILY OCCASIONS

As elsewhere, 'traditional' family life is under threat in Canada. Nearly half of marriages end in divorce and increasing numbers of Canadians cohabit; the law recognises cohabitation and the same rights and obligations as marriage apply. A third of children born in Canada are born to unmarried parents and less than half of Canadian families conform to the traditional nuclear family model.

The former importance of the family to the average Canadian used to be reflected in their homes – spacious, with plenty of bedrooms – which were retained after the children had left home to provide them with somewhere to stay when they returned to visit. However, nowadays Canadians tend to downsize and buy an apartment when their children leave home.

> 'The best way to remember your wife's birthday is to forget it once.'
>
> Joseph Cossman (American entrepreneur)

Birthdays & Anniversaries

Birthdays (and anniversaries, such as wedding anniversaries) can be low-key or elaborate occasions, depending on the age attained and the family background. 'Landmark' birthdays, e.g. 21, 40 or 50, are usually celebrated with a big bash, and in some families all birthdays are cause for a huge celebration. It's usual to send close friends a card on their birthday, although you aren't usually expected to buy a present. Small children often have huge birthday parties, which may be held at McDonald's or a similar venue, and can be costly events.

Christenings

Christenings aren't usually a big occasion in Canada, although this depends very much on the family and their background. Immigrant Catholic families (and those in Quebec, where Catholicism is the dominant religion) often have a huge celebration, while those from the UK may make little fuss and just have a small family celebration. Dress at a christening party is smart-casual and you should take a gift for the child.

If you're asked to be a godparent, you should consider it a great honour and privilege. Duties include helping with the child's upbringing, giving generous presents at birthdays

and Christmas, and taking over guardianship should the parents die.

First Communions

Although increasing numbers of Canadian Catholics are ambivalent about religion and don't attend mass regularly, the vast majority of Catholic children take their First Holy Communion between the ages of 8 and 10; the accompanying celebrations are a major social event in the family's life, and can be expensive. Dress is smart-casual, although the parents usually dress very smartly. You're expected to take a gift for the child.

Engagement Parties

When a couple have announced their intention to marry, some families have an engagement party, although this practice is dying out. An engagement party may be anything from a small, private affair, with only the couple's immediate family members present, to a huge bash with all the couple's friends and family invited.

Weddings

Weddings are a major social event for many Canadians and a chance for women to dress up in all their finery. Weddings can cost a fortune, and it isn't unusual for families (the bride's father traditionally pays, although it's common nowadays for the bridegroom's parents to contribute)

'No matter who you marry, you wake up married to someone else.'

Marlon Brando (American actor)

to spend $25,000 or more on the occasion. There are often as many as 100 guests, with celebrations lasting well into the morning. On the other hand, a simple garden civil ceremony with a minister or a civil celebrant costs around $250.

Not surprisingly, given the predominantly secular nature of the country, around half of all marriages take place outside church.

Gifts

It's usual to buy a gift when someone gets married. Many couples have a wedding gift list – you choose something and inform the keeper of the list so that he can cross it off – so that the couple don't receive dozens of similar gifts. The list may also tell you where an item can be purchased and the price (suggested gifts usually cover a wide range of prices). Some people prefer to choose something themselves and take it to the wedding. It isn't customary in Canada to give a couple cash as a wedding present, although some couples prefer this, particularly if they already own a fully-equipped home. If you know the couple reasonably well and cannot go to the wedding, you're still expected to buy a gift.

Dress

A wedding is an opportunity for people to dress up, and you'll certainly be expected to make an effort. If you're invited to a formal wedding, men may be expected to wear a suit and tie, and some weddings request that men wear morning suits with top hats (usually hired), which will be indicated on the invitation. However, it's usually expected only of the key players and family members. Women usually wear cocktail dresses, with sumptuous matching accessories (including hats).

Christmas

Christmas is an important family occasion, when the whole family usually gets together for lunch or dinner on Christmas day. There's no standard fare, although many people eat the traditional meal of turkey (or other poultry) and all the

'trimmings'. Most people decorate their homes with a Christmas tree and some go overboard, with garish decorations, including myriad flashing lights outside their homes – there are even competitions in some towns. It's traditional to pull crackers before the meal.

Family and friends exchange gifts on Christmas day, although young children traditionally receive theirs first thing in the morning from a stocking at the end of their bed (supposedly brought by Santa Claus during the night).

If you're invited to Christmas lunch or dinner, it's usual to bring a present for your hosts, which could be a good bottle of wine or champagne.

Funerals

Funerals may be huge, lavish celebrations (of the deceased's life, not the fact that he or she is dead) at a church or cathedral, or a low-key, simple affair (conducted by a celebrant), depending on the status of the deceased and their background. Families from countries where funerals are elaborate affairs usually continue the tradition in Canada.

Dress for a funeral is traditionally black or a dark colour, with a black tie for men, although it's no longer necessary to wear black or for men to wear a suit. There's a social gathering before or after a burial or cremation (often one of the few times that a whole family will get together), when drinks and snacks are served. It's traditional to send flowers or a wreath to the family, church or funeral directors (as

> For English-speaking Canadians, high culture tends to be associated with anything that comes from Europe, whereas popular culture is anything that comes from the US.

requested), although some families ask for donations to be made to a charity instead.

POPULAR CULTURE

Amusement Parks

Canada is a great country for the young (and young at heart) and many leisure facilities are geared to children. Among the most popular amusement parks are the rollercoaster parks, which have a cult following in Canada. One of the country's largest amusement parks is Paramount's 'Canada's Wonderland', which is a 30-minute drive from the centre of Toronto on Highway 400. In addition to the obligatory rollercoaster that lands in a pool of water, it has a climbing wall (harness mandatory), a James Bond simulator and over 200 other attractions.

Camping

Canada has over 4,000 caravan (trailer) and chalet parks and campsites (campgrounds), both public and private. Camping in Canada ranges from backpackers sleeping rough or with a 'pup' tent, to retirees or townies touring in a luxury mobile home or recreational vehicle (RV). For older Canadians, camping means using an RV or motor home or a caravan, rather

than a tent, which rather belies their image as outdoor pioneers.

Facilities at privately owned campsites range from non-existent (sometimes not even water) to cabins and cottages with all mod cons. All provinces with a shoreline have seafront campsites, ranging from bare stretches of beach to luxury developments. Tent campers are advised to avoid RV-oriented campsites, which may offer superior facilities but are plagued by noise and vehicle fumes. (Few RV 'campers' stray further than a few hundred feet from their vehicles.)

Campsites have strict rules regarding noise (e.g. none between 11pm and 7am), alcohol (only on your site) and dogs (which must be on leads and must not foul the site).

You're usually prohibited from parking a motorhome or caravan overnight on a public road, but most national and provincial parks permit camping. Canada has 41 national parks (and is in the process of creating more) and numerous provincial parks, with around 550 in British Columbia alone.

Bush Parties

Bush parties, also known as field parties, are a Friday night ritual for some young Canadians, involving lighting a bonfire (often a large hay bale) in the countryside, large enough to attract people – although hopefully not the police.

Some sites display a 'No Vacancy' sign all summer, therefore if possible you should book well in advance, especially for bank holidays. If you cannot book in advance, you should try to arrive by 5pm, as queuing all night for a space isn't unheard of at the most popular parks, and many parks close their gates at 11pm and don't reopen until 6am. The peak season runs from mid-May to the end of September, and the most popular parks have a one- or two-week limit on stays during the summer.

Festivals

Canadians don't let the long, harsh winters put a stop to their fun, and most cities stage winter festivals, which may include dog-sled races, events celebrating the early fur trappers and explorers, ice-skating, ice-sculpture, and almost anything else you can think of connected with snow and ice (including a wide range of winter sports).

The Winter Carnival in Quebec City has been described as 'New

Orleans' Mardi Gras on ice', with sculptures, parades, a canoe race across the frozen St. Lawrence river, an ice hotel and copious quantities of a local drink called Caribou (a mixture of whisky and red wine!).

Other major events include a Winterlude festival in Ottawa, held over several weekends in February; a Festival of Lights in Niagara, Montreal and Vancouver; a First Nations Storytelling Festival in mid-January in Saskatchewan; and events celebrating the return of the sun in January in the Northwest Territories, after a month of uninterrupted darkness.

Open-air events at other times of the year include a Tulip Festival held in May in Quebec, with concerts, parades and a flotilla on the canal, floral sculptures, floral tapestries and garden displays. Vancouver hosts a four-day (or rather four-night) firework festival, the Symphony

> 'The urge to gamble is so universal and its practice so pleasurable, that I assume it must be evil.'
>
> Heywood Broun (American journalist)

of Fire, at the end of July; there's a similar event in Toronto in August.

Gambling

The kill-joy attitude introduced to Canada by Presbyterian Scottish immigrants has taken a long time to die out, and it's only since the early '90s that gambling of any sort has become acceptable – which isn't to say that it didn't exist before then. Now Canadians and visitors can legally visit casinos without having to cross the border to the US, but some of the old attitudes still linger, particularly when it comes to dress codes. Some casinos merely suggest that appropriate dress is 'smart-casual', while others explicitly prohibit blue jeans, jogging outfits, cut-offs, shorts and beachwear – one even proclaims 'no bustiers or clothing associated with organisations known to be violent' – whatever that means!

The most popular forms of gambling are the games red dog, roulette, stud poker, baccarat and blackjack, and the ubiquitous slot machines. All of Canada's provinces and territories run their own lotteries (there's no national lottery) each week called 'Lotto 649' – so called because you need to select six numbers out of 49 – and Lotto Super 7 (Fridays). To participate, you simply complete an entry form at a lottery kiosk in a shopping mall or convenience store. Tickets are $1 each and must be purchased by 5pm on the day of the draw (which, cleverly, is at 6.49pm on Wednesdays and Saturdays in each province). You can also choose a 'quick pick' option, whereby a computer selects the numbers for you. Prizes vary, depending on the number of tickets sold, but jackpots of $5m to $20m aren't uncommon. Instant lotteries are also popular, where you buy a 'scratch' card costing $1, $2 or $5 and can win prizes of $10,000 to $50,000.

Another popular form of gambling is the Video Lottery Terminal (VLT), a machine similar to a 'one-armed bandit' but more lucrative (but usually not for players), as it's possible to pump as much as five to ten thousand dollars into a VLT in just half an hour! They're located at racetracks, in public halls, bars, Legion clubs and convenience stores (making losing your money all the easier). The proceeds of VLT machines go directly to the provincial government (otherwise they would be banned).

> In many provinces, the First Nations peoples are granted licences to operate casinos as a means of improving the economic conditions in their communities. These are subject to the same gaming and liquor laws that apply elsewhere in a province.

Canada offers racing fans a choice between trotting (saddle and harness horse racing) and ordinary horse racing, and most cities have at least one track, although very few are open in winter as it's difficult to see the horses in ten-foot snowdrifts. All legal horse race betting is based on the totaliser (tote) system, where the total amount bet on a race is divided among the winners (after the organisers and Canada Revenue Agency have taken their cuts). Bets of between $1 and $1,000 can be made.

Generally, bets are the same as in other countries, although the terminology may be different. Bets can be made for a win (or 'on the nose'), a place (to come second) and to show (to come third). An 'across the board' bet is a bet on a horse to win or be placed second or third. The different kinds of bet are explained in the official programme, as is the form of the horses and riders. In the major cities, illegal bookies who take bets on horses and many other things (particularly professional sports) are commonplace.

SPORT

Sport is popular in Canada, where people take it very seriously, both as participants and as spectators. Over half of all Canadians participate regularly in some form of physical activity, and those who don't play are usually keen spectators – if only when watching TV. The top spectator sports (including TV audiences) are ice hockey, baseball, football and basketball, while the most popular participant sports include swimming, hiking, cycling and running. Other popular sports are lacrosse, skiing, flying (in various forms), boxing, golf, fishing, motor racing, softball, tennis, bowling, athletics and watersports (particularly boating). Working out is popular in Canada, where many people go to gyms or have equipment at home, as exercising outdoors in the winter can be unpleasant and/or dangerous.

The big sporting occasions of the year are the Grey Cup for the Canadian Football League (CFL), at around the same time as Canadian Thanksgiving (mid-October), the Stanley Cup for the National Hockey League (NHL) at the end of May or early June (when Canada grinds to a halt), and baseball's World Series, which Canadians are proud to tell you was won in 1992 and

1993 by the Toronto Blue Jays. The NHL Super Bowl is also a big deal in Canada, being celebrated with almost as much fervour as in the US.

The major TV networks compete vigorously for the TV rights to top sporting events – professional sport is dominated by TV – although the frequency of commercial breaks makes watching most TV sport a frustrating experience.

Canadian Football

Canadian football is Canada's version of American Football (or Gridiron) and is virtually the same. The main differences are that the field is slightly larger, there are 12 instead of 11 players, and only three 'downs' (the Americans have four). Other minor differences make for a faster, higher-scoring game, but Canadian football has failed to garner the international audience that American football has, and struggles to gain media and spectator support. That said, the climax of the Canadian Football League (CFL) season – the Grey Cup Final – is the single most-popular televised sporting event in Canada.

Hockey

With such long, cold winters, Canada produces lots of athletes who are at their happiest sliding about on ice. Ice hockey (usually referred to simply as hockey) is by far the

> 'Hockey is a sport in which millionaires on skates are paid to assault each other.'
>
> Anon.

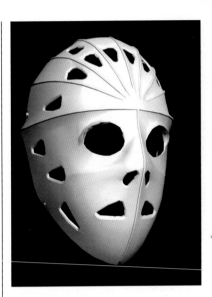

most important sport in Canada (there's even a hockey scene on the back of the Canadian $5 bill). It's the country's official national winter sport, while lacrosse (see below) is Canada's official national summer sport; even the smallest settlement has an ice rink, where girls tend to learn figure skating, and boys learn to skate in order to play hockey.

Hockey is so popular and the gear such a common sight, that you could get on a bus wearing a goalie's pads and helmet, and hardly anyone would give you a second look (but don't go into a bank with a face mask on, as they may think you're planning to rob it). Canada produces around 65 per cent of North America's ice hockey players, most of the rest coming from Europe.

Hockey Night in Canada is a weekly TV programme and a Canadian institution – some people claiming that its theme tune is

Canada's unofficial national anthem. Professional hockey players in the NHL are superstars in Canada, and visitors to the country will find it easier to strike up conversations if they're on at least surname terms with the top hockey players, past and present. There are fewer Canadian teams than there used to be (only six), and the NHL is expanding elsewhere, but not in Canada. (If you mention this to a Canadian, you might well be subjected to an earnest discourse about the game's perilous future.)

In view of the importance of hockey in the lives of so many Canadians, you should become at least vaguely acquainted with the rules. The NHL (🖥 www.nhl.com) was formed in 1917, and in 2006 consisted of 30 teams, only six of which were Canadian: the Calgary Flames, Edmonton Oilers, Montréal Canadiens, Ottawa Senators, Toronto Maple Leafs (*sic*) and Vancouver Canucks. Teams are divided into two 'conferences', western and eastern, each of which has two divisions. For example, the Montréal Canadiens and the Ottawa Senators play American teams from Buffalo, Boston, Carolina and Pittsburgh, while the Toronto Maple Leafs play Chicago, Dallas, Detroit, St Louis and Phoenix.

The NHL season starts in October and finishes in May, during which teams play over 90 games, culminating in the play-offs for the Stanley Cup (played over a seven-game series). The Stanley Cup was an all Canadian affair from 1893 to 1917, when it was strictly an amateur competition. Over the 90 years of the Cup from 1918 to 2006 (there was no 2005 winner because of the NHL lockout), Canadian teams have won the cup 50 times.

Six players from each side are permitted on the ice at any time, but substitutions are allowed throughout a game, so players are constantly changing. The centre is free to roam all over the ice and is the team's most important player and goal scorer, and there are two wingmen, two defence men and a goalie (who's well padded to protect him from injury, the puck being struck at up to 130 mph/210 kph). The referees

> 'Our team lives hockey, it dreams hockey, it eats hockey. Now if it could only play hockey.'
>
> Milton Berle (American TV host)

(there are two) call the two centres to 'centre ice' where the puck is dropped and the game begins.

Although games are meant to consist of three 20-minute periods, the clock is stopped each time there's a pause in play and games usually last around three hours. Hockey is often a violent sport, with frequent body checking (especially against the side walls), and players striking each other with their sticks almost as often as they hit the puck – hence the old joke, 'I went to a fight and a hockey game broke out'. Punch-ups are an integral part of the game, although there can be severe penalties for the guilty parties.

Lacrosse

Lacrosse is North America's oldest organised sport and Canada's official national summer sport, although it doesn't begin to compare with hockey in popularity. It was invented by the Algonquin Indians of the St. Lawrence valley, who called it *baggataway* or *tewaarathon* and played it as part of a religious rite, starting each game with rituals and dances. Lacrosse is more popular on the west coast, although there are some enthusiasts in parts of Ontario.

It's played with a stick like a broom handle, with a long thin net made from woven leather at one end, in which the hard rubber ball is carried and passed between players. The original sticks were thought to look like a bishop's crozier, hence the French name '*la crosse*', from which lacrosse derived.

As no physical contact is permitted, players wear no protective headgear, facemasks or padded gloves, with the exception of the goalie. As in ice hockey, the object is to get the ball into the opposing team's net. A men's lacrosse team consists of ten players: three attack (offence), three midfield, three defence and a goalkeeper. Women's lacrosse teams have 12 players, who, apart from the goalkeeper, can play anywhere on the field.

Motor Sports

Motor sports have a large following in Canada and attract more spectators than any other sport. Among the most important events are the Indy races in Toronto (June) and Vancouver (September), which are part of the CART Indycar World Series, the North American equivalent of the Formula One Grand Prix series. The most popular form of motor racing is, however, stock car racing, which is a professional sport and attracts many of Canada's and America's best drivers.

Snow Sports

Canadians have made full use of their excess of ice and snow by inventing or perfecting every

> 'We'll explain the appeal of curling to you if you explain the appeal of the National Rifle Association to us.'
>
> Andy Barrie (Canadian radio presenter)

conceivable sport that can be practised on or in it. Canadians play snow golf (using coloured balls on hard-packed snow), ice fishing (by making holes in it), ice sailing and ice motor racing (with spiked tyres).

Curling: Curling (a cross between chess, bowls and competitive sweeping) is also very popular: over 90 per cent of the world's players live in Canada. It's a democratic sport because anybody can take part, however unfit. Indeed, for many curlers, the main challenge is to see how much beer they can drink and still play.

Skiing: Skiing is one of the biggest participant sports in Canada, which boasts the most reliable skiing conditions in the world and is one of the top destinations for experienced skiers. The Rockies have excellent 'powder' and are regarded as the best place for downhill skiing; eastern Canada, with its wetter, heavier snow, is good for cross-country skiing. The Canadian skiing season lasts from October or mid-November until May or even June in some areas, and most resorts are extremely busy over Christmas, New Year and Easter. During these periods, it's usually necessary to book well in advance (or better still, avoid them altogether).

Queues (line-ups), although practically unknown in some resorts, are orderly; and staff everywhere are usually friendly and helpful (a pleasant change from many European resorts). Skiing in Canadian resorts is generally much more regulated than in Europe, and to avoid crowding, some resorts restrict the number of passes sold. Stewards armed with walkie-talkies are posted everywhere, and, if you ski recklessly, you're given a warning, and repeat offenders have their ski lift passes confiscated.

Snowmobiling: Invented in Canada in 1922, snowmobiles are motorbikes without wheels, driven across the snow by a spinning rubber track, and steered by metal skis connected to handlebars. They're a standard way of getting around in winter for people who live in the great white north, although many Canadians own one just for fun. Modern snowmobiles are capable of speeds of up to 100mph (160kph), but if you're planning to do that sort of speed, it's wise to stick to the marked tracks; it isn't unknown for landowners to discourage trespassers by stringing wires across their land at neck height! Avoid frozen lakes

people even swim in the winter – the Polar Bear Club is a group of masochists who enjoy swimming in waters that are frozen over (which again entails cutting a hole in the ice).

> 'When they said Canada, I thought it was up in the mountains somewhere.'
>
> Marilyn Monroe (American actress)

because fatal accidents occasionally occur when snowmobiles crash through the ice. Even at lower speeds, you need to wrap up well to protect yourself from the constant blast of icy air.

Snowmobile clubs stage competitions and other events throughout the winter, such as the North American Snowmobile Festival in Thetford Mines, or the Provincial Snowmobile Festival in Saint-Gabriel (both in Quebec, which has a vast linked network of snowmobile trails). A snowmobile Grand Prix is held in Valcourt, which has a snowmobile museum. New Brunswick has 6,000km (3,728mi) of groomed trails, and Newfoundland has an annual snowmobile endurance race, the Viking 1,000, covering over 1,250km (777mi) of untracked wilderness and lasting four days – or much longer if you get lost!

Watersports

Canada makes good use of its vast number of lakes. Many Canadians are keen watersports enthusiasts and many families have a small cabin or cottage close to a lake. Ice fishing is popular in the winter, and involves cutting a hole in the ice after setting up a small heated shack. Some

Summer Camp

Summer camp is a notable feature in the life of many Canadian adolescents, although they don't tend to go away for the whole summer, as in the US. Summer camps usually run for a week, and allow children to experience a range of sporting and other leisure activities. Parents sometimes take the opportunity to holiday without their children.

The Great Outdoors

Many Canadians love the Great Outdoors, which is fortunate because much of the country is undeveloped parkland or wilderness. Getting out and about in the countryside includes hunting (see below), which many Canadians enjoy, but Canada also has a healthy animal rights movement, which protests against shooting and trapping animals. Only First Nation peoples have the right to hunt year-round, which is to compensate for the loss of their traditional lifestyle.

Canada takes steps to protect its environment: the forestry industry is required by law to reforest the

The biggest and most dangerous of all bears are the majestic polar bears, which may look cuddly in a zoo but are the mightiest predators on earth; males can weigh 1,500kg/3,300lb.

crown lands that it logs, and the rate of replanting currently exceeds that of logging. However, this isn't to say that Canada has impeccable green credentials, as there's still logging of old-growth forest in some areas.

Wildlife

Canada has a rich wildlife that includes various species of bear, beaver and buffalo (bison), over 500 species of birds, a plethora of fish, including the famous Atlantic and Pacific salmon, whales, wolves, coyote, deer, moose, elk, caribou, rocky mountain goats, lynx, cougars, skunks, porcupines, raccoons and chipmunks. Some of Canada's animals are dangerous, including the seemingly cute raccoon, which sometimes carries rabies; the normally placid moose, which charges at humans when scared; and, of course, bears.

Bears: Although there are few bear attacks in Canada, they're widely reported, and, if you're a victim, you're likely to be seriously injured and may even be killed. Canada has four types of bear: black, brown, grizzly and polar. All are very large, and dangerous when provoked. They aren't, as many people think, slow and lumbering, although they take a while to get up speed, and are expert (and fast) tree climbers (apart from grizzlies).

Bears don't just inhabit remote regions (one fatal attack took place in a car park in Banff) and, if you're likely to be visiting an area inhabited by bears, you should take precautions and heed the warnings. When camping, you should keep your food (and rubbish) in an airtight container and store it a good distance from your camp, preferably up a tree to deter other animals such as raccoons. Some campsites have bear-proof wooden cupboards where campers can store their food.

Bear- & Whale-watching

Polar bears live in the Arctic and sub-Arctic regions and, if you want to see them in the wild, one of the best places is Churchill (Manitoba) on the edge of Hudson Bay. Here, bear-watching from huge tundra buggies is a popular pastime, and the bears come right up to the buggies to inspect their occupants. The bears migrate past Churchill twice a year:

in October/November and from June to August, when white beluga whales feed in the Bay (they're a favourite prey of polar bears).

You can join a whale-watching boat trip from many places along the Canadian coast. The sights off the Atlantic coast include blue, finback, humpback, beluga and sometimes minke and right whales. In the Pacific, Californian grey whales reach Vancouver Island on their annual migration north in March and April, returning south in September and October. Orcas (or killer whales) can be seen in the Inside Passage between Vancouver Island and the mainland. The cheapest way to see them (and other whales) is to take a whale-watching tourist boat from Victoria. Another option is the regular ferry from Vancouver to South Alaska (a 15-hour trip), which costs around $100, compared with thousands of dollars for a whale-watching cruise.

'Undiscovered' Wildlife

Canada has a number of creatures whose existence is attested by cryptozoologists, who search for undiscovered animals which aren't recognised by mainstream scientists. The two most famous are the Sasquatch and Ogopogo. The former is also known as Bigfoot, and is a large, upright, ape-like creature. Although many people associate it with the US, it's just as much a Canadian phenomenon. Ogopogo is Canada's answer to the Loch Ness Monster (Scotland), and reputedly lives in British Columbia's Lake Okanagan.

Fishing

Given its bewildering number of lakes (some of them the size of small seas), large rivers and long coastline on three oceans, it isn't unsurprising that fishing is popular in Canada. The fishing season is usually from mid-April until October, and there's a range of regulations designed to preserve fish stocks. Ice fishing is also popular, and consists of fishing through a hole in the ice from inside a fish-house (a wooden hut on the ice, usually with a wood-burning stove). The most popular ice-fishing lakes turn into little villages in winter, with anything up to 2,000 fish-houses.

Hiking

Hiking is popular in Canada – probably because it has some of the most dramatic and unspoiled countryside in the world. Every province and territory boasts vast areas of natural beauty, but perhaps the most popular region is the

Rockies. Summer and early autumn are the best times to hike, as spring comes late, and trails in mountainous areas are often snowbound until June or July. If you're hiking in national or provincial parks and camping or sleeping rough, you may require a permit, and should obtain information about weather conditions and your intended route.

Hunting

Hunting is popular in Canada, where it isn't the preserve of the wealthy or upper classes as in some countries. The game available includes bear, caribou, moose, elk, deer, wild hog, bighorn sheep, rabbit, raccoon, opossum, coyote, nutria, skunk, beaver, squirrel and game birds (e.g. partridge, pheasant, grouse, wild turkey, waterfowl, quail, goose and duck). Some animals and birds, such as Canada Geese, are protected, and there's a huge fine for killing them.

Hunting is prohibited in Canada's national and provincial parks, game reserves and adjacent areas, and guns are strictly forbidden in these areas. Elsewhere, you can hunt big game during certain seasons only, which may be limited to a month (e.g. for moose) and varies for grizzlies according to their numbers.

You must generally be aged 16 or over to hunt big game, although younger people are often permitted to hunt small game. You must pass a three-day hunter's safety course costing $100, and obtain a hunting licence from the authorities in the province or territory where you plan to hunt. Fees vary with the location and the prey. You should expect to pay $40 for a licence to hunt moose, $33 for a bear/deer licence and $17.50 for small game and birds. With your licence, you receive a tag that must be attached to the carcass, and there are fines of up to $100,000 and jail sentences of up to two years for shooting an animal you don't have a licence to kill. You're usually restricted to only one deer or moose.

> 'Hunting is not a sport. In a sport, both sides should know they're in the game.'
>
> Paul Rodriguez (Mexican comedian)

THE ARTS

Don't make the mistake of assuming that Canadians care for nothing but beer, hockey, wrestling bears

Vancouver is often referred to as 'Hollywood North', as many major films and TV series are filmed there because of its smog-free air and competitive costs; while Calgary was the setting for *Superman III* and the television series *Viper*. Toronto hosts an annual film festival in September that some (not all Canadians) claim is better than Cannes; each year over 250 films from more than 50 countries are screened in around 20 cinemas. Toronto has also become a popular film location, and now competes with Vancouver for the 'Hollywood North' title.

and messing around outside in temperatures below freezing: 'high' culture also has a healthy following. Thanks to Canada's multicultural population from all corners of the globe, it has a diverse and vibrant arts scene.

Cinema

Canada has an important and successful film industry, although, not surprisingly, it's much smaller than Hollywood. Universal Studios is Canadian-owned, but Canadian films have tended to receive more critical than commercial success – Cannes recognition rather than big box-office takings. Exceptions to this are the films of Canadian directors James Cameron and David Cronenburg. Among the many world-famous Canadian film stars (past and present) are Dan Ayckroyd, John Candy, Jim Carrey, Michael J. Fox, Lorne Greene, Mike Myers, Mary Pickford, Christopher Plummer, William Shatner and Donald Sutherland.

Canadian-made films account for just 5 per cent of the fare in Canadian cinemas, most of which show the latest American blockbusters. Every large city, however, has a review theatre, where classic films, foreign (subtitled) and obscure releases are screened. In Ottawa, the Bytown and Mayfair theatres publish a monthly newsletter available from news-stands. In cities such as Toronto and Vancouver, where there

Film Classification	
Classification	**Restrictions**
G (general)	None
PG (parental guidance)	Some material may be inappropriate for children
PG-13	Some material may be inappropriate for children under 13
R (restricted)	Children under 18 require an accompanying parent or adult guardian

are large ethnic populations, some cinemas specialise in Chinese and Indian films. Outside the major cities, however, it's difficult to find a cinema showing serious, classic, art (avant-garde), experimental or foreign-language films, or anything other than the latest smash hits, and many cinemas are under threat of closure.

> 'Canadian girls are so pretty it's a relief now and then to see a plain one.'
>
> Mark Twain (American writer)

All films on general release in Canada are given a rating under the Motion Picture Code of Self-Regulation, as follows:

Children (or adults) who look younger than their years, may be asked for proof of their age, e.g. a school or student card, social insurance card or driving licence, for admittance to restricted films.

Literature

As might be expected, given the country's pioneer background and harsh climate, themes of survival (often against the elements) loom large in Canadian literature. Robert Service's poems, about the Yukon and life in the far north, have been influential and reinforced the idea of Canadians as tough pioneers, battling against inhospitable conditions. French-Canadian literature also deals with survival against the odds, and political struggle.

Canada has a range of successful novelists including Margaret Atwood, Robertson Davies, W. O. Mitchell and Michael Ondaatje, but the most famous and enduringly popular Canadian novel is Lucy Maude Montgomery's *Anne of Green Gables*, published in 1908.

Museums & Art Galleries

Canada has some 2,500 museums, art galleries and related institutions. The capital region of Ottawa alone is home to 29 museums, including 12 national museums and institutions, most of which appeal to all interests and age groups. The National Gallery of Canada in Ottawa is one of the world's great museums, housed in a beautiful, purpose-built building – and entry is free!

Many galleries and museums contain works by a number of excellent Canadian artists. The so-called 'Group of Seven' artists (though it wasn't limited to the seven founding members) led by Tom Thompson, and including Franklin Carmichael, A. J. Casson, Lawren Harris, A. Y. Jackson, Arthur Lismer, J. E. H. Macdonald and Frederick Varley, are famous for their paintings

Canadian War Museum, Ottawa

of the eastern Canadian lakelands. Over 2,000 of their works, as well as many by Inuit and north-west coast Native artists, can be seen at the McMichael Canadian Collection at Kleinburg near Toronto. Other famous Canadian artists include Emily Carr, who painted the west coast (particularly the villages of the Haida Indians with their totems and the surrounding forest) and Paul Kane.

Native Indian art includes some paintings and prints, but the majority (and the best) consist of carvings of animals, birds, fish and native figures. Inuit carvers use bone, ivory (often from walruses), antlers and soapstone. A group of soapstone musk oxen standing in a defensive circle with the calves in the middle, displayed at Calgary airport, is in the 'once seen, never forgotten' category. The Winnipeg Art Gallery houses the world's largest collection of Inuit art, and the Inuit Gallery of Eskimo Art in Toronto also has an extensive collection.

Somewhat more mainstream are the commercial (contemporary)

Inuit sculpture

galleries in many cities (and shopping malls), which are often well worth a visit even if you have no intention of buying. Many rural museums are operated by local historical societies and private interests, and they often commemorate local history or long-defunct local industries.

The opening hours of museums and galleries vary considerably. Many close on Mondays and open in the early evening one day a week, e.g. until 9pm, when admission may be free or cheaper. Entrance to some galleries and museums is free at all times.

Museums

Canada has many unusual or bizarre museums, including a shoes museum, a theatre museum of 'the unusual, the absurd and the ridiculous' and the History of Contraception Museum, which houses such fascinating exhibits as a recipe for an oral contraceptive consisting of dried beaver's testicle brewed in strong alcohol.

Music

Pop

Canada has a dynamic and varied music scene. Although they're often assumed to be American, Bryan Adams, Paul Anka, Leonard Cohen, Céline Dion, Diana Krall, K. D. Lang, Avril Lavigne, Gordon Lightfoot, Sarah McLachlan, Joni Mitchell, Alanis Morrissette, Anne Murray, Robbie Robertson (most famous as a member of The Band, who worked with Bob Dylan), Shania Twain (the world's best-selling country music artist) and Neil Young (one of the world's great songwriters and performers, playing everything from folk and country to grunge and hard rock) are all Canadian – and just a few of the country's singers who enjoy worldwide fame. Canadian bands include recent independent (indie) favourites Arcade Fire, Bachman-Turner Overdrive, Barenaked Ladies, Rush and Tragically Hip. A record label called First Nations specialises in native Canadian music.

Jazz & Street Music

Jazz is popular in Canada, where Montreal hosts a world-famous jazz festival in summer, when many musicians perform in the streets and plazas for free. In fact, some of the best musical entertainment in Canada is provided free by street musicians (buskers), and free concerts are staged in the major cities. Street music caters for all tastes, including jazz, rock, folk, blues, country and classical. In the Atlantic Provinces, there's a tradition of Celtic-based music, top bands including the Barra MacNeils, the Rankin Family and the Irish Descendants. The club and bar music scene thrives in Canadian cities, where most clubs have a cover charge, but few are restricted to members only.

> 'The secret of my piano playing is that I always make sure that the lid over the keyboard is open before I start to play.'
>
> Artur Schnabel (Austrian classical pianist)

Classical

Classical music concerts and opera and ballet performances are major social events in Canada, and are regularly staged by the cream of Canadian and international performers. Concerts have a strong following and performances are of a high (often international) standard. The leading Canadian orchestras are the internationally renowned Montreal Symphony Orchestra, the National Arts Centre Orchestra, based in Ottawa, and the Symphony Orchestras of Ottawa, Toronto and Vancouver. Many smaller towns and cities also have orchestras, including Kanata and Nepean.

Opera & Ballet

The leading opera companies are the Canadian Opera Company (based at the O'Keefe Centre in Toronto), the Vancouver Opera Association and *L'Opéra de Montréal*.

Canada has three internationally renowned ballet companies: the Royal Winnipeg Ballet, *Les Grand Ballets Canadiens* and the National Ballet of Canada (also based at the O'Keefe Centre in Toronto), plus the *Ballet Classique de Montréal*.

Theatre & Circus

Canada has a healthy theatre scene, with thriving professional and amateur theatre companies in the major cities and many smaller towns. Toronto is the world's third-largest centre for English-language theatre (after New York and London). Stratford (Ontario) is home to a world-renowned Shakespeare company and hosts an annual summer festival, most of which consists, not surprisingly, of performances of works by Shakespeare. Amateur dramatic companies thrive throughout the country. As would be expected, most of the theatre in Quebec, particularly in Montreal, is in French.

There's also an abundance of free street theatre in the major cities, including a ten-day International Busker Festival in Halifax (Nova Scotia) in August, which attracts

> '*Hamlet* is a terrific play, but there are way too many quotations in it.'
> Hugh Leonard (Irish dramatist & journalist)

street performers from around the world. 'Fringe' theatre festivals are new to Canada and are typically held in smaller communities (suburbs or smaller towns), where 'new' performers aim to attract attention from show business bosses. These often run alongside a town's annual commemorative events.

Quebec has become internationally renowned for its 'circus arts', most famously the *Cirque du Soleil* (French for 'circus of the sun'), which is an entertainment empire based in Montreal. It was founded in 1984 by two former street performers, and has been called 'modern circus', using only human performers (with none of the animals found in traditional circuses). *Cirque du Soleil* combines elements of ballet, busking, circus, gymnastics, opera and rock music. In many performances, the accompanying music is played live, and the spoken parts are in 'Cirquish', an imaginary language invented by the company.

9.

RETAIL THERAPY

Canada is a great place to shop, and offers a diverse and exciting shopping experience and a wide range of goods at competitive prices, although perhaps not quite as keen as they are south of the border. All major cities offer a wealth of department, chain and international stores, plus a wide range of boutiques and specialist stores. Toronto's Yonge Street, Montreal's underground city and the West Edmonton Mall are considered Canada's best shopping areas, although all the major cities offer plenty of opportunities to part with your money.

> 'I always say shopping is cheaper than a psychiatrist.'
>
> Tammy Faye Bakker (ex-wife of televangelist Jim Bakker)

CUSTOMER SERVICE

If you're carrying open food or drink containers, smoking, have bare feet or aren't wearing a shirt, you'll be refused entry to most shops in Canada. In the major cities, you may encounter shop assistants (store clerks) who are brusque and rude, but in general they're friendly and helpful. Canada has a retailing philosophy that the customer is always right, and most shops exchange goods and give refunds without question. On the rare occasion when there's a problem, a complaint to the local consumer protection agency or Better Business Bureau usually resolves the matter.

> You can find shops in a particular city or territory online via websites such as Shop in Canada (🖳 www.shopincanada.com).

OPENING HOURS

Canada's cities and large towns have long shopping hours. Many drugstores, petrol stations and convenience stores are open 24 hours a day, seven days a week (24/7) in most areas, so that you can shop at 3am if you want to. On major roads, 24-hour service stations sell food. Other shops, particularly supermarkets and drugstores, are generally open from 7.30am to 9pm. In almost all major cities, at least one chemist is open until midnight or even 24/7.

In town centre (downtown) shopping areas, major shops may open from 9.30am to 6pm from Mondays to Wednesdays, 9.30am to 9pm on Thursdays and Fridays, and from 9.30am to 7pm on Saturdays,

PAYMENT

Most shops accept major credit cards, although American Express is becoming unpopular with smaller shops and many won't accept it (due to the high charges). Unlike American shops, where the offer of cash may cause panic, Canadian shops are usually happy to accept it (there are ATMs in most malls, large stores and supermarkets). Most transactions, however, are made by debit card, of which Canada has the world's highest rate of use.

> 'Is there anything more humiliating than shopping in a store you feel is beneath you, and one of the customers mistakes you for an employee?'
>
> Dennis Miller (American comedian)

BARGAINS

The best bargains in Canada (apart from shopping online) are found at discount malls and centres, factory outlets and warehouse clubs. There are also chains of discount stores in ordinary shopping malls, such as Winners (fashion), Homesense (furniture and homewares) and Loonie Stores (after the colloquial name for a dollar coin), where everything in the store originally cost under $5.

Factory outlets are common in Canada. They specialise in obsolete, overstocked and out-of-season goods, rather than poor quality goods or 'seconds' (flawed or damaged goods). Some are owned and operated by manufacturers,

while malls open at around 10am and close at 9pm. In smaller towns, shops usually open between 9 and 10am and close at 6pm, Mondays to Saturdays. It's wise to avoid shopping at lunchtimes and on Saturdays, when shops are usually packed.

Sunday opening was banned nationwide under the 'Lord's Day Act', but is now subject to provincial and/or municipal laws. It's rare in New Brunswick, Newfoundland, Nova Scotia and Prince Edward Island, although in most other provinces some shops open from noon to 5pm on Sundays. Business hours on statutory holidays are usually at the discretion of individual shopkeepers, although you'll rarely find a shop open on Christmas Day. Shops usually post their holiday business hours a week or so before a holiday.

although there are also special outlet malls dedicated to them. Canada One Outlet Mall (💻 www. canadaoneoutlets.com) in Niagara Falls is the top brand name outlet mall, with 40 brand name stores with prices up to 75 per cent below recommended retail prices.

In most cities there are also huge warehouse stores specialising in selling remainders, leftover stock, overruns and cancelled orders at reduced prices, which can be as little as 10 per cent of the normal retail price. Since the mid-1980s, 'warehouse clubs' such as Costco have become the fastest-growing retail sector in Canada. They charge an annual membership fee of $50 ($100 for business membership), which can often be recouped in one visit, and offer huge discounts on branded goods, particularly food, with prices for bulk quantities typically 20 per cent below supermarket prices. The hackneyed slogan 'the more you spend, the more you save' is true, although discerning shoppers profit most.

SALES

Many Canadians delay making major purchases until the seasonal

> Sales tax not only applies to new goods and goods sold by businesses, but also to the sale of certain used items such as cars, motor homes, boats and aircraft.

sales, which offer attractive bargains. Most shops hold sales at various times of the year, the largest of which are in January, July and October. Sales are also common on statutory holidays such as Labour Day and Canada Day weekends, although the biggest sales traditionally start on Boxing Day (26th December).

SALES TAX

There are two types of sales tax in Canada: federal goods and services tax (GST – known to Canadians as the 'gouge and screw tax'), which is levied at 6 per cent on most things you buy. (GST is known as *taux produits et services*/TPS in Quebec.) A provincial sales tax (PST) – *taux des ventes et services Québec* (TVQ) in Quebec – is also levied in six provinces/territories at various rates (see box). In Nova Scotia, New Brunswick, and Newfoundland & Labrador, PST is combined with GST, resulting in a Harmonised Sales Tax (HST) of 14 percent.

The prices of goods and services in Canada are shown exclusive of sales taxes (as in the US) and tax must be added to the price shown. This means that, if you have only $10 in your pocket, you won't usually be able to buy something

priced at $10, which will cost at least $10.60 and as much as $11.67 (in Prince Edward Island).

Sales tax is levied at the following rates on most goods:

SECOND-HAND GOODS

Canada has a huge market for second-hand goods. As well as auctions and charity shops, there are frequent private yard and garage (tag) sales. Families moving house or clearing out their cupboards sell unwanted possessions in their garage or drive or on the front lawn. Most garage sales take place on spring or summer Saturdays. Prices are usually negotiable and items can be bought for next to nothing, as Canadians don't expect to get much for second-hand goods.

In Victoria, unwanted goods are placed on a kerbside with a sign saying 'Free', which is an

	Sales Tax		
Province/Territory	**GST/HST Rate**	**PST Rate**	**Combined Rate**
Alberta	6%	n/a	6%
British Columbia	6%	7%	13%
Manitoba	6%	7%	13%
New Brunswick	14%	n/a	14%
Newfoundland	14%	n/a	14%
Northwest Territories	6%	n/a	6%
Nova Scotia	14%	n/a	14%
Nunavut	6%	n/a	6%
Ontario	6%	8%	14%
Prince Edward Island	6%	10%	16.7%*
Quebec	6%	7.5%	13.95%*
Saskatchewan	6%	7%	13%
Yukon	6%	n/a	6%

* In Quebec and Prince Edward Island, GST is included in the PST base, and you're therefore also charged PST on GST, hence the higher than expected combined rate.

easy way to dispose of everything from kitchen cupboards to skis. Consignment stores have become popular in Canada over the last 15 years, where you can dispose of unwanted clothes and receive a few dollars in return.

TYPES OF SHOP

Many Canadians work long hours, which leaves little time for shopping, so they prefer one-stop shopping in department and chain stores, suburban malls and supermarkets.

Department & Chain Stores

Canada is served by excellent department and chain stores, many of which specialise in clothing. In Canadian department stores, the floor at street level is designated the first floor (not the ground floor), the floor below the ground floor is usually called the basement (often containing a bargain department), and the floor above may be called the mezzanine. Some stores, such as Army & Navy, operate basement stores famous for their cut-price branded clothes and unbeatable prices.

The best Canadian department stores include The Bay (run by the Hudson's Bay Company, established by Royal Charter in 1670 – see entry under **Icons** in **Chapter 2**) and Sears Canada (formerly Sears Roebuck, which invented the shopping catalogue in the 19th century). The largest nationwide discount department stores, sometimes called mass merchandisers, include Wal-Mart and Zellers (owned by The Bay), which have branches in a number of cities, along with Fields and Saan. Most department stores have mail order catalogues and operate a home delivery service (many will deliver goods anywhere in the world).

There are dozens of chain stores in Canada, selling everything from electrical items to food, books and clothes. Some are countrywide, while others are regional. For example, Canadian Superstore (which is owned by Loblaws), IGA, Safeway and Save-on-Foods are dominant in the west, while in Ontario, you're more likely to find Independent Grocers, Loblaws and Loeb. Saan is a typical chain store, which started business in 1947 (in Winnipeg) and now has some 140 stores throughout Canada (it used to have 350, but downsized after filing for court protection due to financial problems).

Malls

As a result of its often harsh climate, Canada has been obliged to perfect indoor shopping, and is noted for its 'reinvention' of the mall (pronounced 'mawl'), a concept which spread through North America and is now found throughout the world. The mall is much more than a retail facility; it's also a meeting place, often with many forms of entertainment, including cinemas (movie theatres) and bowling alleys. Not only are individual malls completely under cover, but many buildings in Canadian cities are connected by underground tunnels or skywalks, allowing you to visit many different retail buildings without ever having to face the elements.

West Edmonton Mall (Edmonton) is one of the largest in the world, the size of 48 city blocks, housing over 800 stores and services, over 100 eating places and many attractions. These include an amusement park, bars, a bowling alley, bungee jumping, casinos, 30 cinema screens, a hotel, nightclubs, a skating rink, an indoor water park and a life-

Canada boasts the dubious distinction of having popularised the shopping mall, which was invented by the Romans.

size reproduction of Christopher Columbus' ship *Santa Maria* (an essential feature of any self-respecting shopping mall). The West Edmonton Mall attracts so many visitors that it has had a noticeable effect on airline passenger numbers to the area.

Markets

Many Canadian cities have markets selling good quality fresh food, although they don't compare with markets in Europe. Flea (junk) markets are also common in major cities, specialising in antiques, bric-a-brac, clothing and jewellery. In the provinces and territories with severe winters (i.e. almost all of them), outdoor markets are held between spring and autumn only. Second-hand markets are common in cities and towns across Canada and are generally held in vacant buildings, in malls or (in the summer) in car parks (parking lots). Markets on the west coast tend to specialise in arts, crafts and organic produce.

BUYING FOOD

Most Canadians buy their food in supermarkets. The quality and variety of produce (fruit and vegetables) in Canadian supermarkets is excellent and sometimes bewildering. Stores are huge and packed year-round

with mountains of meat, dairy products, and convenience foods by the truckload, including imported produce. Canadian supermarkets invariably carry larger stocks, and offer a wider variety of merchandise than their counterparts in Europe.

Most Canadian supermarkets sell own brand (private label) foods and also have a 'generic' section, where tins and packets bear only the name of the product, statutory information (e.g. weight, ingredients, etc.) and a bar code. These sometimes sell for as little as half (average three-quarters) the price of their name-brand counterparts (it's estimated that a family of four can save at

Metric/Imperial Conversion

Weight

Avoirdupois	Metric	Metric	Avoirdupois
1oz	28.35g	1g	0.035oz
1lb	454g	100g	3.5oz
1cwt	50.8kg	250g	9oz
1 ton	1,016kg	500g	18oz
2,205lb	1 tonne	1kg	2.2lb

Length

British/US	Metric	Metric	British/US
1in	2.54cm	1cm	0.39in
1ft	30.48cm	1m	3ft 3.25in
1yd	91.44cm	1km	0.62mi
1mi	1.6km	8km	5mi

Capacity

Imperial	Metric	Metric	Imperial
1 UK pint	0.57 litre	1 litre	1.75 UK pints
1 US pint	0.47 litre	1 litre	2.13 US pints
1 UK gallon	4.54 litres	1 litre	0.22 UK gallon
1 US gallon	3.78 litres	1 litre	0.26 US gallon

Note: An American 'cup' = around 250ml or 0.25 litre.

least $2,000 a year by buying generic items) and in some cases are virtually identical to equivalent branded items. When comparing different brands, ensure that the quality (grade) and quantity are the same.

There are numerous specialist food shops, gourmet food shops, markets and delicatessens in the major cities, selling every luxury food imaginable, although they're generally too expensive for basic foodstuffs.

BUYING ALCOHOL & TOBACCO

Licensing laws are set by provinces and municipalities, and the sale of alcohol (liquor) in Canada is strictly controlled in most areas. The minimum legal age for buying alcohol is 18 in Alberta, Manitoba and Quebec, and 19 in the rest of Canada. (This is also the minimum drinking age in bars.) A retailer is supposed to ask your age and may ask for identification, although in practice this rarely happens if you look old enough. Acceptable identification usually consists of a driving licence or a Provincial Identification Card issued by the provincial Liquor Control Board (where there is one).

You can buy spirits only at shops operated by the provincial Liquor Control Board (LCB), but wine and beer are sold in supermarkets. Shops selling alcohol cannot open before 10am and must close no later than local bars. LCB stores close any time between 6pm and 11pm

The Beer Store

on weekdays and Saturdays, while beer and wine shops usually close at 11pm. All shops selling alcohol are closed on Sundays. When shops are closed, you can buy beer or wine from some local bars or hotels (called off sales, for drinking off the premises).

Prices vary little (if at all) in LCB stores, although in some cities, prices are lower and people may travel from out of town to stock up. Sales tax (PST) on alcohol varies from province to province, so people who live near the border of a province with lower PST often drive over the border to buy it. It's illegal to import large quantities of alcohol from the US (where

An 'open container' law forbids the consumption of any alcoholic drink in public, and it's illegal to have an open container in a vehicle, even in the boot (trunk).

it's cheaper), which is classed as smuggling.

Canada produces some good wine (particularly ice wine, although it's **very** expensive), although not as good as most Californian and imported wines. There are high import duties on foreign wine to protect the Canadian wine industry, although you can still find reasonably priced French and Californian wines. When buying Canadian wine, look for the Vintner's Quality Assurance (VQA) sign on the labels, the Canadian equivalent of the French *appellation contrôlée* system.

Beer is sold in 341ml and 355ml sizes, usually in packs of six (a 'six-pack' or 'half-sack') or cases of 12 ('twelve-pack') or 24 (a 'two-four'); 'supercans' are also available in 473ml or 950ml sizes. In Quebec and the Atlantic provinces, a non-alcoholic spruce beer is made (from the sap of spruce trees), and in the fruit-growing areas of British Columbia, Ontario and Quebec you can find apple and cherry 'ciders'.

Like alcohol, the purchase and use of tobacco and tobacco products is restricted to those aged 18 in Alberta, Manitoba and Quebec, and 19 elsewhere. Canadian cigarettes are generally milder than American; major brands include Player's, Craven A, DuMaurier, Matinee and Export A. You can also buy Cuban cigars, which are banned in the US.

BUYING CLOTHES

Most Canadians are conservative in their dress, especially those in the eastern provinces; in the western provinces, people dress more casually. Whatever the style of dress, people tend to dress in layers, and take them off and put them on again as they go from centrally heated home to the cold outdoors to a car that takes a while to warm up to an overheated shop, etc. If you arrive in winter from a country that doesn't have cold winters, you'll need to buy warm clothing as soon as you arrive. For outdoor winter sports, you may need thermal underwear (ideally made of fabric such as polypropylene, which draws perspiration away from the body), woollen or thermal socks, mittens and hats, and a pair of waterproof fur-lined boots. Most Canadians in the north wear jackets and under-vests filled with duck or goose down that keep out the wind as well as the cold.

Apart from the Puffa down-filled jacket, Canada's favourite garment is the humble blue jean – good value at around $40 to $50 for top brands such as Levi's and Wrangler. Canada's national 'uniform' is the checked (plaid) shirt and jeans, and for many years, it provided Canadians with a sense of national identity, while Canadian rock musician Neil Young's adoption of the outfit promoted it globally. Since the 'grunge' revolution, however, the uniform isn't the Canadian identifier it once was.

As in many countries, large department stores are the showcases for new fashions, and stage fashion shows to which they invite clients with platinum credit cards (i.e. those who spend lots of money). Trendy boutiques, where the emphasis is on designer labels and chic accessories, are everywhere.

Among the most famous Canadian men's stores is Henry Singer, which has a reputation for selling high quality, classic men's clothing; Holt Renfrew is the equivalent for women. The most popular mainstream clothes stores are Banana Republic, Benetton, Esprit, Gap (and GapKids), Roots Canada and Zara. The best-value clothing chains include Below the Belt, Bootlegger, Off the Wall, Old Navy, Stitches and Thrifty's. A popular chain of sports shops is Play It Again Sports, with over 475 outlets in the US and Canada, selling second-hand as well as new clothing and equipment.

One of the most surprising things about shopping for quality clothes in Canada is the number of shops selling quality branded clothes at much lower prices than in other countries. However, in smaller

Continental to UK/US Size Comparison

Women's Clothes

Continental	34	36	38	40	42	44	46	48	50	52
UK	8	10	12	14	16	18	20	22	24	26
US	6	8	10	12	14	16	18	20	22	24

Men's Shirts

Continental	36	37	38	39	40	41	42	43	44	46
UK/US	14	14	15	15	16	16	17	17	18	-

Shoes (Women's and Men's)

Continental	35	36	37	37	38	39	40	41	42	42	43	44
UK	2	3	3	4	4	5	6	7	7	8	9	9
US	4	5	5	6	6	7	8	9	9	10	10	11

towns the reverse may be true. Some successful clothing companies, particularly those that sell clothing for outdoor activities, sell almost entirely by mail order, a tradition dating from the pioneer days. Some of the best outlets for bargain-priced clothes are chains such as Winners and Hangers, which buy factory overruns and clothes that department stores cannot sell (although there may be no refunds or exchanges). Department stores also have their own bargain stores such as Sears Clearance Centre and The Bay Clearance Centre.

The average North American is larger than the average person in most other countries, and therefore Canadian and American clothes are often cut generously. Men's shirts come in different sleeve lengths (as well as collar sizes), which is fine as long as you know the size you need. Whenever possible, try clothes on before buying, and don't be afraid to return them if they don't fit.

HOME SHOPPING

Home shopping by post, phone or via the internet is extremely popular in Canada, particularly in rural areas. In addition to dedicated mail-order companies, major department stores produce mail-order catalogues. TV shopping is also increasingly popular

> 'They should put expiry dates on clothes so we would know when they go out of style.'
>
> Garry Shandling (American comedian)

and there are a number of 24-hour shopping channels in Canada.

Internet shopping has proliferated in recent years and now accounts for an increasing percentage of purchases. With internet shopping, the world is literally your oyster and savings can be made on a wide range of goods and services, including holidays and travel. Small, high-price, high-tech items (e.g. cameras, watches, and portable computers and software) can usually be bought more cheaply in the US or even further afield, with delivery in just a few days by courier. However, you need to bear in mind that you may have to pay GST/PST on goods purchased abroad.

RETURNING GOODS

Returning goods is stress-free in Canada, but you need to keep your receipt as proof of payment (which is also useful if an automatic alarm is activated as you're leaving a store). It may be difficult or impossible to return or exchange goods without a receipt, and you may also need it to return an item for repair or replacement under a warranty. It's

Price Comparisons

To find the best deals on the web, you can use price comparison websites such as the Price Network (💻 www.pricenetwork.ca) and Shop Bot (💻 www.shopbot.ca).

wise to check receipts immediately on paying (particularly in supermarkets); if you're overcharged you cannot obtain redress later.

Although the law doesn't require it, most shops will give a cash refund or credit on a charge account or credit card within a certain period, e.g. one to two weeks (although you may be offered only a shop credit or exchange on discounted goods). Some discount and outlet stores don't allow any returns. Shops display their refund policy on a sign or print it on your receipt.

Warranties

All goods sold in Canada carry an implied warranty of merchantability, meaning that they must perform the function for which they were

designed. If they don't, you can return them to the shop where you purchased them and demand a replacement or your money back. In addition to the implied warranty, some goods carry written warranties, which although voluntary, must be written in clear, everyday language; the precise terms and duration must be specified at the top of the warranty document.

The period of a warranty varies considerably, e.g. from one to five years, which may be an important consideration when making a purchase. Warranties can also be full or limited – a full warranty provides you with maximum protection, although usually for a limited period. You may be offered the chance to purchase an extended warranty when you buy certain goods. These aren't usually worth the cost, as they rarely extend beyond the natural working life of a product, during which few products malfunction.

Warranties may be transferable when goods are sold or given away during the warranty period. You're often asked to complete and post a warranty card confirming the date of purchase, although under a full warranty this isn't necessary. Most warranties are with the manufacturer or importer, to whom goods must usually be returned. A local or provincial consumer protection agency, Better Business Bureau (see below) or consumer association can usually advise you of your rights.

No, I Don't Want the F****** Extended Warranty. Slogan on T-shirt

CONSUMER COMPLAINTS

There are a number of consumer organisations in Canada, including the Consumers Association of Canada (436 Gilmour Street, 3rd Floor, Ottawa, ON K2P 0R8, ☎ 613-238 2533, 🖥 www. consumer.ca), which promotes and explains consumer rights, and helps individuals to resolve disputes with retailers.

The Canadian Council of Better Business Bureaus (2 St Clair Avenue East, Suite 800, Toronto, ON M4T 2T5, ☎ 416-644 4936, 🖥 www. canadiancouncilbbb.ca) promotes high ethical standards of business practice, and provides a platform for the discussion of retailer-consumer relations, as well as helping to resolve disputes.

10.

ODDS & ENDS

A country's culture is influenced by various factors and reflected in myriad ways. Among the principal influences are its climate, geography and religion, which are considered here along with various cultural manifestations, including crime, the national flag and anthem, government and international relations, pets, tipping and toilets.

> 'In Canada, there are two seasons: six months of winter and six months of poor snowmobile weather.'
>
> Anon.

CLIMATE

Life in Canada is heavily influenced by the climate, which is nothing less than daunting in much of the country. It doesn't just get very cold, but very hot too: while it can be -40°C in the winter, it can be 40°C in the summer – and as humid as the tropics. Having to put up with such extremes has made Canadians impressively adaptable, able to tolerate anything that Mother Nature throws at them. It also means that they spend a lot of time indoors (to keep warm in the winter and cool in the summer), which probably explains why they invented the board game Trivial Pursuit.

The long, severe winters in much of Canada have a significant effect on how people live their lives. You have to be patient in winter and take things at a leisurely pace, because it can take a long time to get anywhere, to have things delivered or to get anything done. Temperatures of -20°C are common and -40°C is often exceeded in the east and north, sometimes for weeks on end. This type of weather can be wearing and depressing: many institutional buildings such as schools, especially in the coldest areas, have few or no windows (for reasons of insulation), and people can spend only a minimal amount of time outdoors in the winter, leading to seasonal affective disorder (SAD – which is depression and lethargy caused by a lack of natural light). The population in the bleakest northern areas of Canada is very sparse – too low for there to be a variety of activities – which has an obvious effect on people's state of mind. This is best illustrated by the fact that Inuit suicide rates are six times the national average, although this is the result of cultural alienation as well as climate.

Apart from Vancouver and Victoria, Canada's cities also have harsh winters. Montreal has more snow than any other major city in the world, and major blizzards regularly strike Toronto and other east Canadian cities, especially between December and March. The Maritimes (New Brunswick, Nova Scotia and Prince Edward Island) have less snow than much of the country, but are still colder than the west coast. Alberta has relatively little snow because it's dry, and some Canadians maintain that Calgary has the perfect winter, due to its blue skies and warming Chinook winds. In comparison with the rest of Canada, winter on the west coast is very mild, similar to winters in Western Europe.

However, having to put up with severe cold has its benefits: it has meant that many Canadians are resilient and good at smiling in the face of hardship. Indeed, they tend to be dismissive of people who say they can't handle the cold. With

Temperature Conversion Chart		
Temperature	**World Effect**	**In Canada**
50°F (10°C)	New Yorkers turn on the heat	Canadians plant gardens
40°F (4.4°C)	Californians shiver uncontrollably	Canadians sunbathe
35°F (1.6°C)	Italian cars won't start	Canadians drive with the windows down
32°F (0°C)	Distilled water freezes	Canadian water get thicker
0°F (-17.9°C)	New York City landlords finally turn on the heat	Canadians have the last cookout of the season
-40°F (-40°C)	Hollywood disintegrates	Canadians rent some videos
-60°F (-51°C)	Mt St. Helens freezes	Canadian Girl Guides sell cookies door-to-door
-100°F (-73°C)	Santa Claus abandons the North Pole	Canadians pull down their ear flaps
-173°F (-114°C)	Ethyl alcohol freezes	Canadians get frustrated because they can't thaw the keg
-460°F (-273°C)	Absolute zero; all atomic motion stops	Canadians start saying, "Cold, eh?"
-500°F (-295°C)	Hell freezes over	the Toronto Maple Leafs win the Stanley Cup

a pioneer background, enduring loneliness, harsh conditions and long winters, Canadians have developed a positive attitude towards most things, including the weather, and they frequently counter a negative remark with a positive one. They've also turned the weather to their advantage, love the outdoor life and have a thriving winter sports industry. Nevertheless, many Canadians become 'snowbirds': comfortably-off, elderly Canadians who migrate south in the winter – usually to Florida, Arizona or Hawaii.

Snow

Eastern Canada receives enormous amounts of the white stuff every winter. Unlike many places, however, the country isn't incapacitated by snow. In fact, it's a positive force, strengthening the sense of community: people need to stick together in inclement weather and are used to helping each other out. They often do so unasked, and if strangers see you digging your car out of a snowdrift, they're likely to pitch in to help. Each household is required to keep the pavement (sidewalk) in front of their house clear of snow, and it's common for neighbours to do this for each other.

Snow clearance is well organised in eastern Canada, and you need to check the local schedule: if you don't move your car when the streets are due to be ploughed, it may be buried. Indeed, so much snow has to be shifted that people are at risk too, and in Sault St. Marie, parents are required by law to ensure that their children are off the streets when the snowploughs are operating. Canadian trains have snowplough cars (units) to clear the line through the Rockies – a vital communications link. The usually snow-free west coast, on the other hand, is much like the UK: if there's a bit of snow, life grinds to a halt and everyone complains.

CRIME

Unlike its neighbour to the south, Canada experiences relatively little crime. In fact, its low crime rate is cited as one of the reasons why Canada is one of the most desirable places in the world to live. That isn't to say that you should leave

> 'I don't trust any country that looks around a continent and says, "Hey, I'll take the frozen part."'
>
> Jon Stewart (comedian and television presenter)

your valuables in an unlocked car or walk the city streets on your own late at night. Crime is naturally more common in the major cities and popular tourist areas, where petty thieves haunt bus and train stations, car parks and camping areas.

Guns

Canada has strict laws regarding firearms, and since 1st January 2001, all guns have had to be licensed (a licence is valid for five years), and since 31st December 2002 they have also had to be registered. A licence allows you to own a gun, while registration is required to inform the government who owns guns and where they're kept. However, in 2006, it was estimated that as many as 70 per cent of guns presently owned were unregistered. The minimum age to register and own a gun is 18.

There's a long list of guns that are illegal to own or import, including various automatic shotguns, automatic and semi-automatic rifles and carbines, submachine guns, stun guns and assault pistols – not to mention other prohibited weapons, including tear gas, spiked wristbands and brass knuckles. Even sporting guns must be registered, licensed

> 'I'm Canadian. That's like American but without the guns.'
>
> Dave Foley (Canadian actor)

and declared when taking them into Canada. You cannot import anything except a regular sporting rifle or shotgun with a barrel at least 18.5in (470mm) long and an overall length of 26in (660mm), manufactured for sporting, hunting or competition use.

FLAG & ANTHEM

Flag

The Maple Leaf Flag (*l'Unifolié* in French, meaning 'the one-leaved') has only been Canada's flag since 1965, but has quickly become one of the country's most important and ubiquitous symbols (few nations 'fly the flag' as much as Canadians). It's a red and white striped flag with a stylized, 11-pointed, red maple leaf in the central white band (which is as wide as the two outer red bands put together). Before adopting this flag, Canada used variants of the British red ensign, with the Union Flag in the top left corner and the shield of the royal arms of Canada in the right half.

Anthem

The national anthem of Canada is 'O Canada', which was officially endorsed in 1980, although it was composed a century earlier. The music was composed by Calixa Lavallée in 1880 as a patriotic song for that year's St. Jean-Baptiste Day ceremony, and the first lyrics were

O Canada

English	French
O Canada! Our home and native land!	Ô Canada! Terre de nos aïeux,
True patriot love in all thy sons command.	Ton front est ceint de fleurons glorieux !
With glowing hearts we see thee rise,	Car ton bras sait porter l'épée,
The true North strong and free.	Il sait porter la croix !
From far and wide,	Ton histoire est une épopée
O Canada, we stand on guard for thee.	Des plus brillants exploits.
God keep our land glorious and free!	Et ta valeur, de foi trempée,
O Canada, we stand on guard for thee.	Protégera nos foyers et nos droits;
O Canada, we stand on guard for thee.	Protégera nos foyers et nos droits.

written in French by Sir Adolphe Basile Routhier (in 1880) for the same ceremony. An English version (only a loose translation), made by Robert Stanley Weir in 1908, was altered in 1968 to its present form (see box).

GEOGRAPHY

Canada is a federation of ten provinces – Alberta, British Columbia, Manitoba, New Brunswick, Newfoundland, Nova Scotia, Ontario, Prince Edward Island, Quebec and Saskatchewan – and three territories: the Northwest Territories, Nunavut and the Yukon. It's the world's second-largest country (only Russia is larger), although it's best not to mention to Canadians that much of the country is a frozen wasteland. Canada is slightly larger than the US but only two-thirds the size of Russia.

Canada's name supposedly derives from an ironic misunderstanding: one of the first European explorers, Jacques Cartier, is alleged to have asked natives the name of the area, and they replied 'kanata'. As a result, the term was used for the entire northern portion of the North American continent, and it was only later realised that it means 'a settlement or village' in the language of the Huron.

It's easy to be blasé about Canada's vastness, but it really is

Canada's motto is: *A Mari Usque Ad Mare* (From Sea to Sea).

huge: many other countries could fit several times into just one of Canada's provinces or territories, let alone into the whole country. Its largest island – Baffin Island – is twice the size of the UK, yet has only 30 settlements. Some of Canada's national parks are bigger than Switzerland, and some of its lakes are larger than the world's smaller seas. Canada also has more coastline than any other country and borders three oceans.

Statistics

Area: 3.85m mi² (9.97m km²)

Width (west to east): 4,800mi (7,700km)

Height (north to south): 3,000mi (4,800km)

Length of coastline: 125,567mi (202,080km)

Highest point: Mount Logan (19,550ft/ 5,959m)

Longest river: Mackenzie River (2,635mi/4,241km)

It has been said that Canada's geography belies its people: while the former is often bleak and harsh, the latter are invariably gentle and kind; and while the former is on a vast scale, most places are sparsely populated. Former Prime Minister William Lyon Mackenzie Smith famously said, 'If some countries have too much history, Canada has too much geography.'

'I don't even know what street Canada is on.'

Al Capone (American gangster)

Parliament building, Ottawa

The country's geography has certainly affected the people's character. Its prairies in particular are thought to have had a role in moulding the Canadian character: they're vast and remarkably flat – so much so that it's said you can watch your dog running away for three days. This sense of space produces very different responses in people, e.g. a feeling of insignificance or of power in being able to live amid such emptiness. It makes people feel weak and strong at the same time, and is said to explain Canadians' general lack of pretentiousness.

GOVERNMENT

Canada is a constitutional monarchy, which means that it pays lip service to the British Crown, but the government does what it wants. Canada's balance of power is illustrated by the fact that the Queen's head is on its coins, but local heroes are depicted on most notes (the Queen is shown on the $20 note).

Canada has only had its own constitution since 1982, prior to which changes to its laws had to be 'approved' by the British House of Lords, and signed by the Queen. Its new-found authority should have made life easier for Canada, but it actually made it more difficult, as the constitution had to be ratified by the ten provinces. Not surprisingly, Quebec refused, sparking a constitutional crisis that has yet to be resolved; Quebec still isn't legally within the country's constitutional framework, despite several concerted efforts to resolve the matter.

> 'I am a Canadian, free to speak without fear, free to worship in my own way, free to stand for what I think is right, free to oppose what I believe wrong, or free to choose those who shall govern my country. This heritage of freedom I pledge to uphold for myself and all mankind.'
>
> John Diefenbaker (Canadian Prime Minister, 1957-1963)

Levels of Government

Canada's administration is split into three levels: federal, provincial and municipal. Consequently, a bewildering number of elections are held, with at least one a year. With a federal government in Ottawa, ten provincial governments, three territorial governments and 4,200 local municipal governments, 20 per cent of Canada's workforce works directly or indirectly for the government. This system gives Canada an impressive culture of bureaucracy, bettered only by the now-defunct Communist Eastern Europe and France. Increasing Canada's burden of bureaucracy is the fact that everything has to be done in two languages – English and French – thereby creating vast amounts of paper.

> 'In Pierre Elliott Trudeau, Canada has at last produced a political leader worthy of assassination.'
>
> Irving Layton (Canadian poet)

Political Parties

Canadian politics have been dominated for many years by the rivalry between the country's liberal and conservative extremes, the government tending to alternate between the Liberals and the Progressive Conservatives. The former are slippery and hard to pin down on just about every issue (which probably explains why they

City Hall, Toronto

keep winning), while the latter have had to rebuild their party after a disastrous term in office ending in 1993, and only recently managed to convince voters that they were a viable alternative to the Liberals again. Other parties include the Canadian Alliance, a right-wing party that actually believes in something (they have religious leanings, are anti-abortion and pro-capital punishment); the NDP, Canada's socialist party, which provides the country's conscience; and the Bloc Québécois, which is a 'federalist separatist' party (a startling contradiction in terms).

The organisation of elections is affected by the fact that the country is spread across six time zones: it's dark in the east long before the last of the west's votes have been gathered in. As a result, information used to be withheld until all polling stations had

> **'I'm a Quebecker; I was born alienated.'**
> Laurier LaPierre (Canadian politician & author)

closed, the results only released late that night. This is no longer the case, however, and easterners can now find out how westerners have voted before they cast their own ballot.

The Quebec Question

Among Canada's major problems is the acrimonious debate over the future of Quebec. A long-standing animosity between French-Canadians and English speakers dates back to the beginning of the 17th century, when France and Britain were competing to gain a toehold in North America. The running war between them culminated in the defeat of the French forces at Quebec City in 1759 and the ceding of 'New France' to Britain in 1763. Despite its defeat, the province of Quebec remained a stronghold of French nationalism and 200 years later, in the early '60s, French-Canadians, dismayed by their almost second-class citizen status in a country dominated by Anglo-Saxons, formed a separatist movement.

The campaign forced referenda on the question of Quebec separation in 1980 and 1995, both of which were only narrowly defeated (in 1995, just 52 per cent of Québécois voted to stay Canadian), although a recent poll showed that over 75 per cent want Quebec to remain part of Canada.

In an effort to appease French-Canadians, the French language was

made the first language of Quebec, and Canada became officially bilingual. To the intense irritation of the rest of Canada, all official documents and much other printed matter must be dual-language, most of the civil service speaks only French, and the dreaded 'language police' have garnered the sort of power that enables them to force Chinese businesses in Chinatown to remove their Chinese signs. The average English-speaking Canadian has a jaundiced view of the Québécois and the French language, which many believe has more influence and government funding than it merits.

INTERNATIONAL RELATIONS

Relations with the US

Canada has a predictably close relationship with the UK and France, the countries of origin of most of Canada's founders (if you exclude native peoples). But despite the fact that the majority of Canadians are misplaced Britons and other Europeans, modern Canada's closest relationship is, not surprisingly, with the US, although it's very much a love-hate relationship. Many Canadians have close connections with the US, being married to Americans or having lived or worked in the US; and 90 per cent

of Canada's population lives within 175mi (300km) of the US border.

Canadians routinely cross the border to the US – to shop, sightsee and, most importantly, to do business: the US supplies 70 per cent of Canada's imports and receives 80 per cent of Canada's exports. In a much-quoted speech in 1969, the then Canadian Prime Minister, Pierre Trudeau, remarked that 'living next to the US is like sleeping with an elephant. No matter how friendly and even-tempered the beast, one is affected by every twitch and grunt.'

Canadians understandably worry about being swamped or swallowed by the US, culturally if not literally. The proximity of the world's only superpower has left Canadians in the position of being a distant cousin: the US invariably gets all the attention, leaving Canadians feeling ignored and unloved. (New Zealanders feel the same way about the Australians.)

Canadians are perpetually concerned that anything they do successfully will be appropriated or claimed by the Americans. A good example is McDonald's, which was started by two Canadians before an American, Ray Kroc, bought it and turned it into a global phenomenon.

> 'I want to thank all the Canadians who came out today to wave at me – with all five fingers!'
>
> George W. Bush (during a visit to Ottawa)

> 'The US is our trading partner, our neighbour, our ally and our friend ... and sometimes we'd like to give them such a smack!'
>
> Rick Mercer (comedian & TV personality)

Other examples include the fact that shopping malls were pioneered by Canadians, basketball was invented by a Canadian and Warner Brothers was founded by two Canadians.

To make things worse, many Canadian celebrities (past and present) are mistaken for Americans by foreigners. These include jazz maestro Oscar Peterson and singers Bryan Adams, Leonard Cohen, Céline Dion, Joni Mitchell, K. D. Lang, Shania Twain and Neil Young. A host of television and film stars assumed to be American are Canadian, including Pamela Anderson, Dan Aykroyd, Raymond Burr, Neve Campbell, John Candy, Jim Carrey, Hayden Christensen, Michael J. Fox, Brendan Fraser, Monty Hall, Howie Mandel, Mike Myers, Leslie Nielsen, Christopher Plummer, Jason Priestly, Keanu Reeves, Devon Sawa, Donald Sutherland, Alex Trebek, and the actors who played Captain Kirk (William Shatner) and Scottie (James Doohan) in *Star Trek*.

American cultural incursions into Canada have made Canadians so nervous that they've taken steps to control the phenomenon, e.g. the Canadian content laws, which control the Canadian media: television and radio must have a minimum of 30 per cent Canadian content in their programming.

Not surprisingly, Canadians are keen to emphasise the differences between themselves and their neighbours and they **really** don't like being mistaken for Americans, whom they regard as arrogant, brash and vulgar. To avoid confusion when travelling, Canadians often wear a maple leaf badge on their jacket or backpack, and/or put a Canadian flag sticker on their suitcase. (Even the Québécois are known to do this, although they wouldn't dream of parading the Canadian flag in Quebec.) But there's another reason for this: travellers are treated much better as Canadians than Americans, who themselves have been known to use the Canadian flag as a disguise!

International Relations

Canada has been an active and committed participant in the United Nations since its founding in 1945 in San Francisco, where Canada played a key role in the

Canadians are sensitive about being confused with Yanks, so if in doubt ask 'Are you Canadian?' rather than 'Are you American?'. You should avoid referring to the US as 'America', as this (or at least North America) is the name of the continent of which Canada is by far the larger country.

drafting of the Charter. Individual Canadians have played vital roles in the United Nations, and many of the organisation's great accomplishments have had a Canadian dimension. For example, 50 years ago John Humphrey was the principal author of the Universal Declaration of Human Rights; Lester Pearson helped to invent the concept of peacekeeping, winning the Nobel Peace Prize for his efforts to resolve the Suez Crisis of 1956; and Maurice Strong chaired both the 1972 United Nations Conference on the Human Environment (Stockholm) and the 1992 United Nations Conference on Environment and Development (Rio de Janeiro), and also served as the founding Executive Director of the United Nations Environment Programme.

Canadians have occupied key positions in the United Nations, including the Presidency of the General Assembly (Lester Pearson, in 1952-53), and Canada served on the Security Council in 1948-49, 1958-59, 1967-68, 1977-78 and 1989-90. In January 1998, a Canadian, Louise Fréchette, was appointed the first-ever UN Deputy Secretary-General.

THE LEGAL SYSTEM

The Canadian legal system is based on federal law, augmented by provincial laws and local by-laws. Canada's huge bureaucracy extends to the law, of which there are some 40,000 different laws, excluding municipal by-laws. Most rights and freedoms enjoyed by Canadians are enshrined in the Canadian Charter of Rights and Freedoms, which became part of the constitution in 1982. Canadian law and the constitution apply to everyone in Canada, irrespective of citizenship or immigration status, and even illegal immigrants have the same basic legal rights as a Canadian citizen.

Under the Canadian constitution, each province has the right to make its own laws in certain areas, and you shouldn't assume that the law is the same in different provinces. In most of Canada (Quebec being, as usual, the exception), laws are a mixture of statute and common laws. Common law is particularly valid in the case of civil law, which is based on precedent and deals with private matters between individuals, such as property disputes or business transactions.

In Quebec, a written *Code Civil* (based on the French Napoleonic Code) contains principles and rules for different cases. Unlike common law, the judge looks at the written code for guidance before considering any precedents set by earlier judgements.

Canada differs considerably from the US in the matter of private litigation. Obviously, people and companies go to court to settle their differences, but suing a large corporation in the hope that a sympathetic jury will award you millions of dollars for burning your mouth with hot coffee is rare in Canada.

MILITARY SERVICE

Canada doesn't have a draft (conscription) and all members of the armed forces are volunteers, although they are struggling to maintain their strength. The country has a relatively small number of military personnel,

> 'The Canadian military is like Switzerland's – without the knife.'
>
> John Wing (Canadian comedian)

which has fallen from 112,000 in 1986 to 63,000 regulars and 23,000 reservists in 2006. Women are allowed to serve in combat roles in the military, although prejudice is rife, as has been evidenced by the number of high-profile lawsuits for sexual harassment and other abuses in recent years.

Canada has more land to defend than anywhere except Russia and with its limited armed forces, the task would be impossible in the event of an invasion. Some people argue that Canada's defence strategy is to rely on the Americans, although if they decided to invade Canada there's little the Canadians could do. The country's ultimate weapon is probably the climate: as Napoleon's retreat from Moscow in 1812 proved, winter can defeat the most powerful armies.

PETS

Canada is a nation of animal lovers and there are severe penalties for cruelty to animals (there are plans to increase the maximum penalty to five years in jail), which help to ensure that pets are properly looked after. In most Canadian municipalities, dogs must have licences, and some also require cats to be licensed. Some communities levy a higher licence fee for un-neutered animals, and may require

Not recommended as a pet!

you to hold a breeder's licence if an animal isn't neutered. In some municipalities, animals must be tattooed or have a microchip inserted under their skin so that they can be traced when lost. Proof of vaccination against rabies may also be required to obtain a licence.

Most communities require dogs to be kept on leads in public and for owners to clear up after them. This is taken seriously and there are large fines for those who don't comply, which accounts for the lack of canine waste on Canada's streets, although some parks are 'off-leash', to allow dogs to run around. With the exception of seeing-eye and hearing guide dogs, which can travel on buses and trains free of charge, dogs aren't allowed on public transport or in most restaurants and shopping malls. Many apartments and rented accommodation have regulations forbidding the keeping of dogs and other animals (cats are sometimes allowed), and finding accommodation that accepts dogs is difficult in most cities.

RELIGION

Canada has no official religion, which doesn't play a large part in Canadian life; however, the country has long had a policy of religious freedom, which is included in its Charter of Human Rights and Freedoms. The majority of Canadians are Christian, fairly evenly divided between Roman Catholics (of French descent) and Protestants (of British descent); but for most a religious affiliation is nominal and they limit church

attendance (if they go at all) to Christmas, weddings and funerals. Many younger people describe themselves as agnostic or atheist. On the other hand, many towns and even villages have a wide variety of churches of various denominations, although there's less variety in Quebec, where the Catholic Church is dominant. In smaller towns and communities, churches are often the main centres of social and community life, and most organise a wide range of social activities; there are concentrations of devout Christians in some of the Prairie Provinces (sometimes called Canada's 'Bible Belt').

Church attendance has steadily declined since the '50s, and a general lack of interest in religion by the children of immigrant families has led to some domestic strife. Most of the First Nations population describe themselves as Catholic, thanks to Jesuit missionaries. A revival of ancient customs and beliefs has occurred in recent years, with many Aboriginals (and immigrants) turning to belief systems based on the natural world, and the legends of their ancestors (as evidenced by the huge popularity of the fantasy books written by the Canadian author Charles de Lint). There are also pockets of traditional sects such as Mennonites, Hutterites and Doukhobors in rural areas.

There are Jewish sizeable communities in Montreal, Toronto and Winnipeg, while Vancouver has the highest concentration of Sikhs outside the Punjab. In recent years, immigration has brought Buddhists, Hindus and Muslims to Canada, as well as followers of a range of obscure faiths; the large Chinese population in Toronto is mainly Buddhist.

Time Zones	
Zone	**Time**
Pacific Standard Time (PST)	noon
Mountain Standard Time (MST)	1pm
Central Standard Time (CST)	2pm
Eastern Standard Time (EST)	3pm
Atlantic Standard Time (AST)	4pm
Newfoundland Standard Time	4.30pm

TIME DIFFERENCE

Canada has six time zones – see map and the table below, which shows e time in each zone when it's noon in Vancouver.

Canada operates a 'daylight saving' scheme, whereby each province except Saskatchewan moves its clocks forward one hour on the last Sunday in April, and back to standard time on the last Sunday in October. When telling the time,

Canadians say 'twenty to three' and 'twenty after three'. Times are commonly written with a colon, e.g. 2:40 or 3:20, and Canadians don't generally use the 24-hour clock.

TIPPING

Many Canadians don't tip (or tip very little) and don't mind being thought cheap – they like to think they're being thrifty. In Canada, tips are given only to people in service jobs such as bartenders, restaurant staff and cab drivers. Many restaurant owners and other employers exploit the practice of tipping by paying 'starvation' wages in the knowledge that employees can supplement their wages with tips.

If you don't tip a waiter, he may not starve, but he will certainly struggle to survive on his meagre salary. In general, a service charge isn't included in the bill in restaurants, and you're expected to tip the waiter, waitress and bartenders around 15 per cent, depending on the class of establishment.

Don't be bashful about asking whether service is included, although it should be shown on the menu. Restaurant tips can be included in credit card payments or given as cash. The total on credit card counterfoils is often left blank (even when service is included in the price) to encourage you to leave a tip. Some bills include separate boxes for gratuities, but don't forget

'What's the difference between a canoe and a Canadian? A canoe tips!'

to fill in the total before signing it. Most restaurant staff prefer you to leave a cash tip, as tips included in credit card payments aren't always given to staff.

Most people give the doorman or superintendent of their apartment block a tip (or 'sweetener') for extra services, usually ranging from a few dollars to $20, depending on the services provided. Christmas is generally a time for giving tips to all and sundry, e.g. your doorman, newspaper boy, parking attendant, hairdresser, laundryman, handyman, etc. Generally, tips range from a few dollars up to $50 or more for the superintendent of your apartment block (it pays to be nice to him), which is usually placed inside a Christmas card. If you're unsure who or how much to tip, ask your neighbours, friends or colleagues for advice (they will all tell you something different!).

TOILETS

Some Canadians find the word 'toilet' distasteful, and they use a myriad of 'genteel' euphemisms instead, such as bathroom, restroom, ladies' or men's room (the most commonly used terms), powder room, washroom, and even 'comfort station' (but never 'water closet').

Public toilets can be found in most public buildings, restaurants and other public places. Separate toilets are usually provided for men and women. Take care when using public toilets, as it isn't always easy to tell from the sign on the door whether it's the ladies' or gents'. There's

usually no charge for using them, but bars and restaurants may try to deter non-customers with intimidating signs such as 'Restrooms for Patrons Only', although you can usually get away with using the toilet in a busy bar, and many people use the facilities in large hotels. Some toilets in large hotels and restaurants have an attendant, when it's customary to 'tip' around 50¢.

Some toilets provide nappy (diaper) changing facilities or facilities for nursing mothers (nursing isn't usually performed in public in Canada). Many shopping centres (malls) have toilets for the disabled, as do airports and major railway stations, although most public toilets for motorists aren't accessible to disabled drivers.

Anything dropped in the bathroom falls in the toilet.

APPENDICES

APPENDIX A – EMBASSIES & HIGH COMMISSIONS

In Canada

Listed below are the contact details for the embassies and high commissions (Commonwealth countries) of the main English-speaking countries in Ottawa. A full list of embassies and consulates in Ottawa is available from the website of the Foreign Affairs and International Trade Canada (🖳 http://w01.international.gc.ca/Protocol/main-en.asp)

Australia: Australian High Commission, 50 O'Connor Street, Suite 710, Ottawa, Ontario K1P 6L2 (☎ 613-236 0841, 🖳 www.ahc-ottawa.org).

Ireland: Irish Embassy, 130 Albert Street, Suite 1105, Ottawa, Ontario K1P 5G4 (☎ 613-233 6281).

New Zealand: New Zealand High Commission, Clarica Centre, 99 Bank Street, Suite 727, Ottawa, Ontario K1P 6G3 (☎ 613-238 5991, 🖳 www.nzembassy.com/canada).

South Africa: South African High Commission, 15 Sussex Drive, Ottawa, Ontario K1M 1M8 (☎ 613-744 0330, 🖳 www.southafrica-canada.ca).

UK: British High Commission, 80 Elgin Street, Ottawa, Ontario K1P 5K7 (☎ 613-237 1530, 🖳 www.britishhighcommission.gov.uk).

USA: American Embassy, 490 Sussex Drive, PO Box 866, Station 'B', Ottawa, Ontario K1P 5T1 (☎ 613-238 5335, 🖳 http://ottawa.usembassy.gov).

Abroad

A full list of Canadian diplomatic missions abroad is available from the website of the Foreign Affairs and International Trade Canada (🖥 www.dfait-maeci.gc.ca/world/embassies/cra-en.asp).

Australia: The High Commission of Canada, Commonwealth Avenue, Canberra, ACT, Australia 2600 (☎ +61-2-6270 4000, 🖥 www.canada.org.au).

Ireland: Canadian Embassy, 7-8 Wilton Terrace, Dublin 2, Ireland (☎ +353-1-234 4000, 🖥 www.canada.ie).

New Zealand: The High Commission of Canada, Level 11, 125 The Terrace, Wellington 6011, New Zealand (☎ +64-4-473 9577, 🖥 www.wellington.gc.ca).

South Africa: The High Commission of Canada, 1103 Arcadia Street, Hatfield, Pretoria, South Africa (☎ +27-12-422 3000, 🖥 www.canada.co.za).

UK: The High Commission of Canada, MacDonald House, London W1K 4AB, United Kingdom (☎ +44-20-7256 6600, 🖥 www.london.gc.ca).

USA: Canadian Embassy, 501 Pennsylvania Avenue NW, Washington DC, USA 20001 (☎ +1-202-682 1740, 🖥 www.canadianembassy.org).

> The business hours of embassies vary and they close on their own country's national holidays as well as on Australian public holidays. Always telephone to confirm opening hours before visiting.

APPENDIX B – FURTHER READING

Culture

Blame Canada!: 'South Park' and Contemporary Culture, Toni Johnson-Woods (Continuum)

Canada and the British World: Culture, Migration, and Identity, Phillip A. Buckner & R. Douglas Francis (UBC)

Canada – The Culture: Bobby D. Kalman (Crabtree)

How to be a Canadian: Will & Ian Ferguson (Douglas & McIntyre)

The Indians of Canada: Their Manners and Customs, John McLean (Asian Educational Services)

Language, Culture and Values in Canada at the Dawn of the 21st Century: André LaPierre (Carleton University Press)

So you want to be Canadian?: Kerry Colburn & Rob Sorensen (Chronicle)

Why We Act Like Canadians: Pierre Berton (McClelland & Stewart)

History

A Brief History of Canada: Roger Riendeau (Fitzhenry & Whiteside)

Canadian History for Dummies: Will Ferguson (John Wiley)

A History of the Peoples of Canada: J. M. Bumstead (OUP)

An Illustrated History of Canada: Craig Brown (Key Porter)

Maclean's Canada's Century: An Illustrated History of the People and Events That Shaped Our Identity: Carl Mollins (Key Porter)

The Penguin History of Canada: Kenneth McNaught (Penguin)

A Social History of Canada: George Woodcock (Penguin)

A Traveller's History of Canada: Robert Bothwell (Cassell)

Literature

Anne of Green Gables: Lucy Maud Montgomery (Puffin Books)

Canadian Literature in English! 1 and 2: W. J. Keith (Porcupine's Quill)

The Colony of Unrequited Dreams: Wayne Johnston (Vintage Canada)

The Diviners: Margaret Laurence (McClelland & Stewart)

A History of Canadian Literature: W. H. New ((McGill-Queen's University Press)

Jade Peony: Wayson Choy (Douglas & McIntyre)

Joshua Then and Now: Mordechai Richler (McClelland & Stewart)

Of Girls and Women: Alice Munro (Penguin)

The Shipping News: E. Annie Proulx (Fourth Estate/Collier MacMillan)

Surfacing: Margaret Atwood (Virago/Fawcett)

White Fang: Jack London (Penguin)

Living & Working

How to Move to Canada: A Primer for Americans: Terese Loeb Kreuzer & Carol Bennett (St Martin's Griffin)

How to Start a Small Business in Canada: Tariq Nadeem (Self-Help)

Living and Working in Canada: Graeme Chesters (Survival Books)

Start Your Own Business in Canada: James Stephenson & Rieva Levonsky (Entrepreneurs Press)

People

The Big Picture: What Canadians Think about almost Anything: Allan R. Gregg (Macfarlane, Walter & Ross)

Canada: A People's History Volume 2: Pierre Turgeon & Don Gillmor (McClelland & Stewart)

Canada – The People: Bobby D. Kalman (Crabtree)

The Canadian Atlas: Our Nation, Environment, and People: (Reader's Digest)

The Canadians: George Woodcock (Fitzhenry & Whiteside)

Native People Native Lands: Canadian Indians, Inuit and Metis: B.A. Cox (McGill-Queen's University Press)

The People of New France (Themes in Canadian Social History): Alan Greer (UTP)

A People's Dream: Aboriginal Self-government in Canada?: Daniel Russell (UBC)

Xenophobe's Guide to the Canadians: Vaughn Roste (Oval)

Tourist Guides

Baedeker Canada: (AA/Baedeker)

Birnbaum's Canada: Alexandra Mayes Birnbaum (Harper-Perennial)

Blue Guide Canada: (A & C Black)

Canada (Eyewitness Travel Guides): Hugh Thompson (DK Publishing)

Canada: 25 Ultimate Experiences: (Rough Guides)

Fodor's Canada: (Fodor's)

Frommer's Canada: Hilary Davidson & Others (Frommers)

Insight Guide: Canada (APA Publications)

Lonely Planet Canada: Andrea Schulte-Peevers & Others (Lonely Planet)

Michelin Green Guide Canada: (Michelin)

The Rough Guide to Canada: Phil Lee, Tim Jepson & Others (Rough Guides)

Miscellaneous

Brain Quest Canada; 1,000 Questions & Answers: Linda Granfield (Workman)

Canada – A Portrait: (Statistics Canada)

Canadian Wine for Dummies: Tony Apier & Barbara Leslie (John Wiley)

The Complete Guide to Walking in Canada: Elliot Katz (Firefly)

Cooking Collections: Canadian Feasts from Land & Sea: (Centax)

A Day in the Life of Canada: Rick Smolen (Collins)

The Definitive Canadian Wine and Cheese Cookbook: Gurth Pretty & Tony Aspler (Whitecap)

Flavours of Canada: Anita Stewart & Robert Wigington (Raincoast)

The Good Life: Up the Yukon Without a Paddle: Dorian Amos (Eye)

Hiking Canada's Great Divide: Dustin Lynx (Rocky Mountain)

Nothing More Comforting: Canada's Heritage Food: D. Duncan (Dundurn Group)

In Search of Canada: Desmond Morton (McClelland & Stewart)

Trans Canada Rail Guide: Melissa Graham (Trailblazer)

APPENDIX C – USEFUL WEBSITES

Below is a list of websites for anyone wishing to learn more about Canada and Canadians.

Business

Canada Business (💻 www.cbsc.org): The government website covering all aspects of business in Canada.

Canadian Business (💻 www.canadianbusiness.com): Everything you need to know about Canadian business.

Canada Business Directory (💻 www.cdnbusinessdirectory.com)

Doing Business with Canada (💻 www.canadainternational.gc.ca/dbc/DoingBusinessWithCanada-en.aspx): Government website for those planning to do business in Canada.

Culture

Bella Online (💻 www.bellaonline.com/ site/canadianculture): Canadian culture site.

Canadians.ca (💻 www.canadians.ca): Famous Canadians and more.

Canadian Culture (💻 www.canadianculture.com): Canada's networking resource directory.

Canadian Cultural Web Directory (💻 www.artscanadian.com)

Civilization.ca (💻 www.civilization.ca): Information about the archaeology and history of Canada's Aboriginal peoples.

Council of Canadians (💻 www.canadians.org): Canada's largest citizens' organization with members and chapters across the country.

Culture-Canada (💻 www.culture-canada.ca): A multicultural website.

Culture, Heritage and Recreation (💻 www.culturecanada.gc.ca/index_e.cfm): Government programs and services.

Culture Online: Made in Canada (🖥 www.culture.ca/english.jsp): Website of the Department of Canadian Heritage.

Culturescope.ca (🖥 www.culturescope.ca): Canadian cultural observatory, which disseminates cultural policy and research information in Canada and abroad.

The Greatest Canadian (🖥 www.cbc.ca/greatest): Great Canadians, as chosen by Canadians in a CBC poll.

Memorable Canadians (🖥 www.collections.ca): An index of Canadian biographies from the National Library of Canada.

Shaw (🖥 http://members.shaw.ca/kcic1/index.html): Miscellaneous information about Canada and the Canadians.

Wikipedia (🖥 http://en.wikipedia.org/wiki/Canada): The Canada pages of the free online encyclopaedia.

Education

Association of Universities and Colleges of Canada (🖥 www.aucc.ca): The voice of Canada's universities.

Canlearn (🖥 www.canlearn.ca): Source of interactive and comprehensive information and services designed to help individuals save, plan and pay for lifelong learning opportunities.

Canada Education Association (🖥 www.cea-ace.ca): An organisation dedicated to improving education in Canada.

Education Canada (🖥 www.educationcanada.com): Online source for teaching and other education jobs.

Education@Canada (🖥 www.educationcanada.cmec.ca): International gateway to education in Canada.

Government

Government of Canada (🖥 www.gc.ca/main_e.html): Comprehensive information about the Canadian government and the services it provides to Canadians, non-Canadians and businesses.

Government of Canada – Prime Minister (🖥 www.pm.gc.ca): The website of Canada's Prime Minister.

Statistics Canada (🖳 http://statcan.ca): Canada's national statistical agency.

Living & Working

Citizenship and Immigration Canada (🖳 www.cic.gc.ca): Government website devoted to immigration and citizenship information.

Immigration.ca (🖳 www.immigration.ca): The website of the extravagantly named Canadian Citizenship and Immigration Resource Center, a legal firm specialising in immigration.

Living in Canada (🖳 www.livingin-canada.com): Information about emigration to Canada.

Media

Canadian Broadcasting Corporation (🖳 www.cbc.ca): Information about CBC's radio and television output as well as coverage of the arts, business, news, sports and much else.

Canadian Newspaper Association (🖳 www.cna-acj.ca)

Canadian Newspapers (🖳 www.onlinenewspapers.com/canada. htm): Links to all Canadian newspapers.

Radio-locator (🖳 www.radio-locator.com): Find online radio stations throughout Canada.

Miscellaneous

About Canada (🖳 www.canada.gc.ca/acanada/ViewCategory. htm?lang=eng): General information from the Government of Canada.

Atlas of Canada (🖳 http://atlas.nrcan.gc.ca/site/index.html): An atlas from Natural Resources Canada.

Blogs Canada (🖳 www.blogscanada.ca): Canada's blog site.

Canada411 (🖳 www.canada411.ca): Online yellow pages.

Canada.com (🖳 www.canada.com): A comprehensive network, with news and information about everything Canadian, from careers to shopping.

Canada Online (🖥 canadaonline.about.com): General information from About.com.

Canada Post (🖥 www.canadapost.ca)

Canadian Atlas (🖥 www.canadiangeographic.ca/atlas): Canadian Geographic's atlas of Canada.

Canadian Beer Index (🖥 www.realbeer.com/canada): Site dedicated to Canada's favourite tipple.

The Canadian Council for the Arts (🖥 www.canadacouncil.ca): Information about dance, music, theatre, the visual arts and writing.

The Canadian Encyclopedia (🖥 www.thecanadianencyclopedia. com): The most comprehensive and authoritative source of information on all things Canadian.

Canadian Favourites (🖥 http://canadianfavourites.com): A website dealing with Canadian food.

Canadian Wildlife Federation (🖥 www.cwf-fcf.org)

FactsCanada.ca (🖥 www.factscanada.ca): Information and news about Canada.

Inuit Art of Canada (🖥 www.inuitartofcanada.com): Authorised by the Canadian government to promote and distribute Inuit art.

The National Hockey League (🖥 www.nhl.com): Information about all aspects of ice hockey.

Neil's Garage (🖥 www.neilyoung.com): The website of Canada's most respected and influential musician, Neil Young.

Parks Canada (🖥 www.pc.gc.ca): Official website of the Parks Canada Agency.

Statistics Canada (🖥 www.statcan.ca): Government statistics on all aspects of Canada and Canadian life.

Wayne Gretsky (🖥 www.gretsky.com): The official website of Canada's greatest hockey player.

The Weather Office (🖥 www.weatheroffice.ec.gc.ca): Environment Canada's weather information website.

Wines of Canada (🖥 www.winesofcanada.com): A website about Canada's wine industry, which encompasses over 400 wineries.

Travel & Tourism

Canada Travel (🖥 www.canadatravel.ca): Good general travel information.

Canada.Travel (🖥 www.canada.travel): The official travel guide to Canada.

Canadian Tourism Commission (🖥 www.canadatourism.com): Comprehensive information and links about all aspects of life in Canada.

Trail Canada (🖥 www.trailcanada.com): All you need to know about travel and holidays in Canada.

Transport Canada (🖥 www.tc.gc.ca): The government website about everything to do with travel in Canada.

Trail Canada (🖥 www.trailcanada.com): Comprehensive travel guide.

Train Travel in Canada (🖥 www.seat61.com/Canada.htm)

Via Rail (🖥 www.viarail.ca): Canada's railway company.

Wikitravel Canada (🖥 http://wikitravel.org/en/Canada): Canada travel guide from Wikitravel (part of Wikipedia).

APPENDIX D – GLOSSARY OF CANADIAN WORDS & PHRASES

A

Allophone: Somebody whose first language is neither English nor French.

Anglophone: Somebody whose first language is English.

B

The Basketweave: Highway 401 across Toronto.

BC Bud or BC Hydro: Marijuana grown in British Columbia, often in 'grow-ops' (hidden hydroponic growing operations). It's reputedly very strong and sought-after, especially in the US. Marijuana is thought to be British Columbia's largest cash crop and a significant contributor to the province's economy.

Beaver Tail: A dessert food in the sahpe of a beaver's tail consisting of a pastry usually covered with lemon juice and cinnamon sugar.

Blah Blahs: Loblaws grocery chain.

Blochead: A derogatory term for an Anglophone (English speaker) in Quebec. It's the equivalent of an Anglo-Canadian calling a French-Canadian a 'frog'.

Bloody Caesar: Vodka & Clamato juice (Clam & tomato).

Blue Neck, Blueneck: Canadian version of the stereotypical American redneck.

Bluenoser: Somebody from Nova Scotia.

Bogan: A derogatory term for a First Nation person.

Break-up: Spring thaw of ice on lakes & rivers.

Brutal: To be bad at something.

Buckle Bunny: A female rodeo groupie who chases and tries to date rodeo riders; generally used in western Canada, particularly Alberta.

Bunny Hug: A Saskatchewan term for a hooded sweatshirt, with or without a zip, with a pocket in the front. It's known as a 'hoodie' in most other provinces.

The Bush: Forested areas.

Bytown: The name of Ottawa before it was the national capital and sometimes still used (as are 'Hogtown' for Toronto and 'Cowtown' for Calgary).

C

Caisse Populaire: A type of co-op bank, found mainly in Quebec. Often abbreviated to caisse pop.

CanCon: Short for Canadian Content. Refers to the requisite number of Canadian songs, films, programs, etc., that Canadian broadcasters must air.

Canuck: A slang term for a Canadian, used in Canada and the US. It sometimes means French-Canadian in particular, especially when used in Canada and the northeast US. The name has been adopted by Vancouver's NHL team.

Canucklehead: A derogative term for a vancouver Canucks hockey team.

Caper: Somebody originally born on Cape Breton Island, Nova Scotia, and who probably left there to look for work.

CBC: The acronym for the Canadian Broadcasting Corporation, used to refer to somebody who's ethnically Chinese but born and brought up in Canada (Canadian-born Chinese).

Centre of the Universe: A derogatory term for Toronto and its inhabitants, who're widely thought to regard the city and themselves as just that.

Chinook: A warm wind experienced along the eastern side of the Rocky Mountains in Canada and the US.

Chips, Pop and a Bar: A term to describe a tasty, nutritious snack ensemble comprising a bag of crisps (potato chips), a soda drink (usually a cola) and a chocolate bar.

Choad: So bad, it's good.

Chucklehead: A stupid person.

The City That Fun Forgot: Ottawa.

Cougar: An older woman trying to attract a younger man. Also a mountain lion.

Cowtown: The nickname for Calgary, Alberta.

D

Deadmonton: A nickname for Edmonton, derived from its supposed lack of interesting things to do and/or its worryingly high murder rate.

Dead Rear: A local term for Red Deer, Alberta, which is a play on its proper name and meant to indicate the Albertans' supposed lack of culture and of anything interesting to do.

Dec: Slang derived from a shortening of the word 'decent' (and hence pronounced 'deess'). It's popularly used in reference to decent marijuana, to describe its quality.

Deke: A hockey term to describe a fake or feint intended to deceive a defensive player and draw him out of position. It comes from 'decoy'.

Dekey: Fashionable or cool.

Dépanneur: A corner shop, often open seven days a week and selling life's essentials: beer, cigarettes, lottery tickets and snack foods. It's a French loanword.

Double-double: A coffee with double cream and double sugar.

Double Sawbuck: A twenty-dollar bill.

Down South: In most of Canada, this means the US, but in the Northwest Territories, it usually means Edmonton.

E

Eavestroughs: What the British and Americans call 'gutters', i.e. the things that catch water on the eaves of buildings.

Edmonchuk: A name for Edmonton, Alberta, due to its large Ukrainian population.

Eh: An interjection intended to gauge the agreement, comprehension or continued interest of the person or people you're talking to, e.g. 'that was a great meal last night, eh?' It might derive from the French hein, which is used in a similar way.

F

Farmer Tan: A suntanned lower left arm, gained by driving with the window open while wearing a short-sleeved shirt. It can also mean a suntan on both arms, from the mid-bicep and lower.

Fire Hall: Fire station.

First Nations: Anyone of direct descent from the original inhabitants.

Fish Police: A derogatory term for Federal or Provincial Fisheries or Wildlife Officers.

Flat: An Atlantic Canadian term for a box containing 24 bottles of beer. In central and western Canada, the term 'case' is used for 24 bottles, with 'flat' referring to 48. 'Flat' can also mean a tray of small flowerpots.

FOB: An acronym for 'Fresh off the Boat'. In British Columbia, it's a derogatory term for somebody of Asian descent. In Ontario, it's a derogatory term for someone who's (visually) obviously an immigrant and ill-adjusted to the Canadian way of life.

Forty Pounder: A 40oz bottle of alcohol.

Francophone: Somebody whose first language is French.

Frog: A derogatory term for French-Canadians. It's rarely used in Quebec, where 'pepper' is the preferred slur.

From Away: A term used by the inhabitants of Prince Edward Island to describe those who are from other Canadian provinces.

G

Garburator: A garbage disposal unit located under the drain of a kitchen sink.

Gastown: The name of a district in the northeast corner of Vancouver, considered the birthplace of the city. It's a contraction of 'Gassy's town', after steamboat captain and bartender 'Gassy' Jack Deighton.

Gino: A name for somebody of Italian descent, especially young men who display stereotypical Italian behaviour, dress sense and driving habits.

Givin' 'er: Descriptive of an act which is carried out with some gusto and exuberance, often used with regard to heavy drinking and partying. It's short for 'giving her hell'.

Goal Suck: Somebody who stays around the opposing teams goalie and does not play defence.

Gorby: Tourist.

Gouge and Screw Tax: Goods and Services Tax.

Grit: A member of the Liberal Party of Canada.

Grocery Police: A Canadian Customs and Revenue Border Agent.

GTA: A frequently used acronym, standing for the Greater Toronto Area.

H

Had the Biscuit: Broken or dead, e.g. 'Our old TV has had the biscuit'.

Half-sack: A six-pack of beer.

Haligonian: A resident of Halifax.

The Hammer: Hamilton, Ontario.

Here Before Christ: The Hudson's Bay Company (which was founded in 1670 – ancient history by Canadian standards).

Hitting the Rhubarb: Losing control of a vehicle and leaving the road.

Hogtown: A nickname for Toronto.

Hollywood North: A term used to describe Toronto or Vancouver, both of which are popular, inexpensive film locations, often used to represent US cities in films and television programmes.

Homo Milk: Short for homogenised milk (nothing to do with marketing dairy products to gay people).

Hongcouver: A vaguely insulting name for Vancouver, referring to that city's large number of immigrants from Hong Kong. The term was apparently invented by immigrant Chinese youths, but when it appeared in the press, it was denounced by Chinese community leaders and blamed on white Canadians.

Horny Tim's: Tim Horton's doughnut chain.

Hosed: Broken, not working.

Hoser or Hosehead: A slacker or an idiot.

Humidex: A meteorological

measure to reflect the combined effect of heat and humidity (which is a problem in the summer in eastern Canada).

I

The Interior: A term used by British Columbians to describe the entire province other than Greater Vancouver and the Islands.

Inuit: Native peoples of the far north of Canada.

J

Jacked: To have something stolen or be ripped off.

Jigger: Term used instead of ATV, or 4-Wheeler.

Joe Job: An inferior, low-paying job.

Jono: Feeling embarrassed for someone else; a painfully awkward situation

K

Keener: Brown-noser.

Kentucky Fried Pigeon, Kentucky Fried Rabbit and Dead Bird in a Box: Disparaging terms for Kentucky Fried Chicken.

Kokanee: A British Columbian term for a species of land-locked salmon (pronounced with the accent on the first syllable). It's also the name of a popular beer (also known as 'Blue Cocaine').

Kraft Dinner: The Canadian brand name for Kraft Macaroni Cheese (also charmingly known as a 'Krap Dinner' or KD).

L

Language Police: A Quebec provincial government body charged with imposing a controversial language law passed in the '70s decreeing that Quebec businesses must use the French language on menus, signs, etc.

Lard Tunderin: A form of 'Lord Thundering', used on the east coast, e.g. 'Lard Tunderin it's cold today'.

Leafs: The Toronto Maple Leafs (hockey team).

Left Coast: A term for British Columbia (in the US it's used for California), referring to its geographical location and the liberal, left-wing views of its inhabitants in comparison with the rest of the country.

Line-up: Queue.

Liquor Store: A government-operated liquor store.

Logey: Tired or sluggish.

London, England: To distinguish it from London, Ontario.

Loon: A water bird with a distinctive call.

Loonie: A Canadian one-dollar coin. The nickname comes from the image of a loon (a bird) on one side.

Lord Stanley or Lord Stanley's Mug: Slang terms for the Stanley Cup, awarded to the winner of the National Hockey League.

Lot: A house's plot of land.

Lumber Jacket: A thick flannel jacket (either red/black or green/ black plaid), favoured by blue-collar workers and hard rock and grunge fans. It's often called a 'Mackinac' or 'Mackinaw'.

M

Mainlander: A derogative term used by Cape Bretoners, Newfoundlanders and Prince Edward Islanders for a person from mainland Canada. It's also used by Vancouver Islanders to refer to residents of the Greater Vancouver/Lower Mainland area.

Mall Crawlers: Young people who hang around in shopping malls.

Manisnowba: A nickname for Manitoba, due to the large volume of snow that falls in winter.

Maritimer: A resident of the Maritime provinces of Canada's east coast, i.e. New Brunswick, Nova Scotia and Prince Edward Island.

Masi: Thank you, derived

from the French merci by way of Chinook Jargon. It's used mainly in northern British Columbia, the Northwest Territories and the Yukon.

Meat-head: An idiot.

Mickey: A small (13 oz) bottle of alcoholic beverage, shaped to fit into a pocket. Winos favour them.

Mukluks: Knee-high moccasins.

Muskeg: Swamp.

N

Nanaimo Bar: A sweet concoction of egg custard with a Graham-cracker base and a thin layer of chocolate on top. The name comes from the town of Nanaimo, British Columbia.

Nate: An offensive term for a First Nation person, derived from 'native'.

Newfie: The name (often used derisively) for an inhabitant of Newfoundland. It's also used for the Newfoundland breed of dog.

North of Sixty: The area north of the 60th degree of northern latitude. It's also the name of a popular television programme about Aboriginal life in northern Canada.

O

O Town: A nickname for Ottawa.

Oilpatch or The Patch: A local term for Calgary's oil company head offices.

Oil Town: A nickname for Edmonton, from the oil refining done in the region.

Outlet: An electric plug or a shop/store.

P

Paris, France: To distinguish it from Paris, Ontario.

Peg, Peg City or The Peg: Winnipeg, Manitoba.

Pemmican: Dried smoked meat.

Pepper or Pepsi: Derogatory terms for Francophone inhabitants of Quebec.

Pogie or Pogey: Mildly sneering Atlantic Canadian terms for Welfare Assistance, especially Employment Insurance.

Pop: Soft drinks or soda pop.

Poutine: French fries covered in cheese curds and gravy (and sometimes also another sauce).

Poverty Pack: A six-pack of beer. The term comes from New Brunswick.

Prairie Nigger: Offensive and derogatory term for Aboriginal people living in the prairies.

Prairie Oysters: A bovine bull's castrated testicles.

Puck Bunny or Puck Slut: Disparaging terms for a female who pursues hockey players.

R

Regular: A coffee with one cream and one sugar. It also means 'small', rather than a large or extra large coffee.

Rigpig: An oilrig drilling employee.

Rink Rat: A person who works at a hockey rink and maintains the ice and the building.

The Roc: An acronym for The Rest of Canada, used in Quebec and Ontario.

Rocks: Money.

Rotten Ronnies: Nickname for McDonalds.

Runners: Running shoes, sneakers, trainers.

Rye: Canadian whisky.

S

Sasquatch: An 'undiscovered' tall, hairy, primate-like creature, similar to Bigfoot and the Yeti. The name is derived from the Halkemelem word sesqac.

Sawbuck: A ten-dollar bill.

Scare Canada: A derogatory nickname for the national airline, Air Canada.

Screech: A potent, rum-like, alcoholic drink from Newfoundland.

Skidoo: Motorised sled or snowmobile.

Skookum: Big, powerful or strong, derived from Chinook

Jargon, used in British Columbia, Alberta and the Yukon.

Skull Cramp: Headache.

Smogtown: A nickname for Toronto.

Snocked or Snokked: Very drunk indeed.

Snowbirds: Senior citizens who leave Canada during the freezing winter to live in the warm southern US (usually Florida). Also the name of the Canadian military's aerobatics team.

Soother: A baby's dummy.

Spudhead: A person from Prince Edward Island, derived from the importance of potato farming to the province.

Street dog: A hotdog or sausage in a bun, sold from a street vendor (ubiquitous in Toronto).

Stubble Jumper: Somebody from the prairies. It comes from the fact that when the Prairie Provinces' vast fields of wheat are harvested, stubble is left.

Suitcase: A case of 24 cans of beer, derived from the fact that the handle is placed so that the case carries like a suitcase.

Swack: A large amount, e.g. 'I seen a swack of TV last night'.

T

Take Off: Expression of disagreement or command to leave, similar to 'get lost'.

Takitish: Slang for 'Take it easy', especially in central Canada.

Timbit: A round, bite-sized treat made from what's cut from the middle of a doughnut to make the hole. The term derives from the Tim Horton's doughnut chain, but it's now widely used in various doughnut outlets.

Timmie or Timmie's: Affectionate name for a cup of coffee or an outlet of Tim Horton's coffee shop chain.

Thongs: Flip-flops.

TML: The Toronto Maple Leafs (hockey team).

Toonie: A Canadian two-dollar coin. The name comes from 'loonie' (see above).

Tory: A member of the Progressive Conservative party.

Tuque: A knitted winter hat, often sporting a pompom on the crown. It's pronounced 'toook'.

Turkeytown: Derogatory East Coast term for Toronto.

Two-four or Twofer: A case of 24 cans of beer.

U

Ukrainian Tire: A racial slur against Canadian Tire and Canadians of Ukrainian Descent.

W

Washroom: The lavatory, toilet, etc. The word 'bathroom' is a room in a house with a bath and/or shower.

Way too: Superlative, e.g. 'That was way too funny'.

Wenis: A stupid or intolerable person.

Wet Coast: The west coast of British Columbia, where it rains a lot.

Whack or Whackload: A large amount, often used in conjunction with 'whole', e.g. 'I made a whole whack of money when I sold the house'.

What's-his-nuts: A term for somebody whose name is unknown.

Whiteout: Heavy snowstorm with almost no visibility.

Winterpeg: Winnipeg, from that city's frigid winters.

INDEX

Survival Books

Essential reading for anyone planning to live, work, retire or buy a home abroad

Survival Books was established in 1987 and by the mid-'90s was the leading publisher of books for people planning to live, work, buy property or retire abroad.

From the outset, our philosophy has been to provide the most comprehensive and up-to-date information available. Our titles routinely contain up to twice as much information as other books and are updated frequently. All our books contain colour photographs and some are printed in two colours or full colour throughout. They also contain original cartoons, illustrations and maps.

Survival Books are written by people with first-hand experience of the countries and the people they describe, and therefore provide invaluable insights that cannot be obtained from official publications or websites, and information that is more reliable and objective than that provided by the majority of unofficial sites.

Survival Books are designed to be easy – and interesting – to read. They contain a comprehensive list of contents and index, and extensive appendices, including useful addresses, further reading, useful websites and glossaries to help you obtain additional information as well as metric conversion tables and other useful reference material.

Our primary goal is to provide you with the essential information necessary for a trouble-free life or property purchase and to save you time, trouble and money.

We believe our books are the best – they are certainly the best-selling. But don't take our word for it – read what reviewers and readers have said about Survival Books at the front of this book.

Order your copies today by phone, fax, post or email from:
Survival Books, PO Box 3780, Yeovil, BA21 5WX, United Kingdom.
Tel: +44 (0)1935-700060, email: sales@survivalbooks.net,
Website: www.survivalbooks.net

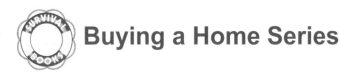

Buying a Home Series

Buying a home abroad is not only a major financial transaction but also a potentially life-changing experience; it's therefore essential to get it right. Our Buying a Home guides are required reading for anyone planning to purchase property abroad and are packed with vital information to guide you through the property jungle and help you avoid disasters that can turn a dream home into a nightmare.

The purpose of our Buying a Home guides is to enable you to choose the most favourable location and the most appropriate property for your requirements, and to reduce your risk of making an expensive mistake by making informed decisions and calculated judgements rather than uneducated and hopeful guesses. Most importantly, they will help you save money and will repay your investment many times over.

Buying a Home guides are the most comprehensive and up-to-date source of information available about buying property abroad – whether you're seeking a detached house or an apartment, a holiday or a permanent home (or an investment property), these books will prove invaluable.

For a full list of our current titles, visit our website at
www.survivalbooks.net

Living and Working Series

Our Living and Working guides are essential reading for anyone planning to spend a period abroad – whether it's an extended holiday or permanent migration – and are packed with priceless information designed to help you avoid costly mistakes and save both time and money.

Living and Working guides are the most comprehensive and up-to-date source of practical information available about everyday life abroad. They aren't, however, simply a catalogue of dry facts and figures, but are written in a highly readable style – entertaining, practical and occasionally humorous.

Our aim is to provide you with the comprehensive practical information necessary for a trouble-free life. You may have visited a country as a tourist, but living and working there is a different matter altogether; adjusting to a new environment and culture and making a home in any foreign country can be a traumatic and stressful experience. You need to adapt to new customs and traditions, discover the local way of doing things (such as finding a home, paying bills and obtaining insurance) and learn all over again how to overcome the everyday obstacles of life.

All these subjects and many, many more are covered in depth in our Living and Working guides – don't leave home without them.

The Survival Handbooks!

Culture Wise Series

Our *Culture Wise* series of guides is essential reading for anyone who wants to understand how a country really 'works'. Whether you're planning to stay for a few days or a lifetime, these guides will help you quickly find your feet and settle into your new surroundings.

Culture Wise guides:
• Reduce the anxiety factor in adapting to a foreign culture
• Explain how to behave in everyday situations in order to avoid cultural and social gaffes
• Help you get along with your neighbours, make friends and establish lasting business relationships
• Enhance your understanding of a country and its people.

People often underestimate the extent of cultural isolation they can face abroad, particularly in a country with a different language. At first glance, many countries seem an 'easy' option, often with millions of visitors from all corners of the globe and well-established expatriate communities. But, sooner or later, newcomers find that most countries are indeed 'foreign' – and many come unstuck as a result.

Culture Wise guides will enable you to quickly adapt to the local way of life and feel at home, and – just as importantly – avoid the worst effects of culture shock.

The essential guides to Culture, Customs & Business Etiquette

Other Survival Books

Investing in Property Abroad: Essential reading for anyone planning to buy property abroad, containing surveys of over 30 countries.

The Best Places to Buy a Home in France/Spain: Unique guides to where to buy property in France and Spain, containing detailed regional profiles and market reports.

Buying, Selling and Letting Property: The best source of information about buying, selling and letting property in the UK.

Earning Money From Your Home: Income from property in France and Spain, including short- and long-term letting.

Foreigners in France/Spain: Triumphs & Disasters: Real-life experiences of people who have emigrated to France and Spain, recounted in their own words.

Making a Living: Comprehensive guides to self-employment and starting a business in France and Spain.

Renovating & Maintaining Your French Home: The ultimate guide to renovating and maintaining your dream home in France.

Retiring in France/Spain: Everything a prospective retiree needs to know about the two most popular international retirement destinations.

Running Gîtes and B&Bs in France: An essential book for anyone planning to invest in a gîte or bed & breakfast business in France.

Rural Living in France: An invaluable book for anyone seeking the 'good life', containing a wealth of practical information about all aspects of French country life.

Shooting Caterpillars in Spain: The hilarious and compelling story of two innocents abroad in the depths of Andalusia in the late '80s.

Wild Thyme in Ibiza: A fragrant account of how a three-month visit to the enchanted island of Ibiza in the mid-'60s turned into a 20-year sojourn.

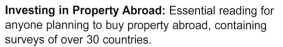

For a full list of our current titles, visit our website at
www.survivalbooks.net

 # Photo Credits